CH00546964

LONDON RECORD SOCIETY
PUBLICATIONS

VOLUME XLI
2006

Kathleen Tipper in 1937.

A WOMAN IN WARTIME LONDON:

THE DIARY OF KATHLEEN TIPPER 1941–1945

EDITED BY

PATRICIA AND ROBERT MALCOLMSON

Queen's University, Kingston, Ontario

LONDON RECORD SOCIETY
2006

Typeset and printed by
Q3 Print Project Management, Loughborough, Leicestershire

CONTENTS

ILLUSTRATIONS AND MAPS

ABBREVIATIONS

All abbreviations in the diary are, on their first appearance, fully identified in the text. Those that appear only once are not included in this list.

AA	Anti-Aircraft (also known as Ack-Ack)
AFS	Auxiliary Fire Service
ARP	Air Raid Precautions
ATC	Air Training Corps
ATS	Auxiliary Territorial Service
CBS	Columbia Broadcasting System
d	penny, pence
DFC	Distinguished Flying Cross
DFM	Distinguished Flying Medal
FAP	First Aid Post
MOI	Ministry of Information
NFS	National Fire Service
OCTU	Officer Cadet Training Unit
RAAF	Royal Australian Air Force
RAF	Royal Air Force
RAOC	Royal Army Ordnance Corps
s	shilling, shillings
Speeches	*Winston S. Churchill: His Complete Speeches 1897–1963* (8 vols., 1974), ed. Robert Rhodes James
STC	Senior Training Corps
WAAF	Women's Auxiliary Air Force
WRNS	Women's Royal Naval Service
YMCA	Young Men's Christian Association

ACKNOWLEDGEMENTS

In preparing this text, easily our most important debts are to Kathleen Tipper and her sister, Joyce Tipper. We met with them on five occasions between August 2004 and May 2006, talked on the phone from time to time, and had numerous written communications from Kathleen during these months. Kathleen and Joyce have been exceptionally helpful and informative, in a variety of ways. Both answered dozens of questions we raised, usually about factual matters concerning their family, their neighbourhood, their jobs, and their wartime conditions of life. Kathleen wrote for us a three-page account of her recollections of the year 1943, when she did almost no diary-writing. She and Joyce also helped to clarify several passages in the diary that we were struggling to understand, and they lent us some of their family photographs, several of which have been reproduced in this volume. Their cooperative participation in this project has, we are sure, significantly strengthened and enhanced our editorial efforts, and we are deeply grateful for their generous assistance.

Several people have given academic support of various sorts, and we would like to mention in particular Jenna Bailey, John Coulter, Heather Creaton, Fiona Courage, Cathy Dickison, Marjorie Hodgson, Jennifer Grek Martin, Jenny O'Keefe, and Llinos Thomas. Approximately one page of the Introduction, concerning Mass-Observation, is reproduced with minor changes from the Appendix to *Love and War in London: A Woman's Diary 1939–1942*, by Olivia Cockett, edited by Robert Malcolmson (Waterloo, Ontario: Wilfred Laurier University Press, 2005) and we are grateful to the editors of this Press for allowing us to reprint these words. The Mass-Observation Archive at the University of Sussex, where Kathleen's diary is held, is headed by Dorothy Sheridan, and we are pleased to record, not only her help as we undertook this edition, but also the impressive leadership that she has exercised during her years in charge of the M-O Archive. The excellence of this archive, in its services to researchers as well as in the quality of its holdings, is now well established, and Dorothy Sheridan has undoubtedly done more than any other person to foster this excellence and ensure that M-O's rich resources are available for study.

Finally, we wish to thank Vanessa Harding, one of the Hon. General Editors of the London Record Society, for her supportive encouragement, for her pertinent comments on and questions about Kathleen's diary, and for her sound advice on the presentation of this (relatively) modern historical source.

Cobourg, Ontario
June 2006

INTRODUCTION

Mass-Observation and Wartime Diaries

Mass-Observation, the organization for which Kathleen Tipper wrote her wartime diary, was founded in 1937. It was created to meet a need; and that need, in the eyes of its founders, was to overcome Britons' ignorance about themselves in their everyday lives. Mass-Observation (it is often spoken of simply as M-O) aimed to lay the foundation for a social anthropology of contemporary Britain. Given that so many basic facts of social life were then unknown – 'then' being initially the late 1930s, and later the early 1940s – how could the nation's citizens, whatever their class or status, adequately understand themselves? This ignorance was thought to be especially pronounced with regard to the beliefs and behaviour of the majority of Britons: that is, those who lacked social prominence, and who had little polit-ical or intellectual influence. It was vital, according to M-O, to study the 'normal and everyday behaviour problems of our own lives, as actually lived in the houses and factories, pubs and chapels and shops in this sort of civilisa-tion'.[1] The goal was to help establish a 'science of ourselves', rooted in closely-observed facts, for a proper science, it was assumed, had to be based on evidence, methodically and laboriously collected. As M-O's two leading figures wrote early in World War Two, 'our first job is to record and publish factual data to enable other students, in other countries and other times, to get from our work a fair objective picture of what was happening, and to use these data to fit in their own ideas and re-interpretations'.[2]

In order to pursue this science of society, M-O recruited hundreds of volun-teer 'Observers'. These Observers were asked to collect facts; to describe; sometimes to count; to listen – indeed, even, in a way, to eavesdrop – and perhaps to ask questions. Their efforts at social recording were thought to be akin to those of an anthropologist working in the field. Mass-Observation, with hundreds of data-collectors working in different parts of the country, aspired to make a major contribution to social science; and from the start it was espe-cially interested in casting light on matters of social life that had been previously largely ignored, such as jokes, superstitions, pub-going, ways of

1. Charles Madge and Tom Harrisson, *Britain, by Mass-Observation* (Harmondsworth; Middlesex: Penguin Books, 1939), p. 231. This was a Penguin Special, published a half-year before the outbreak of war.
2. Tom Harrisson and Charles Madge, *War Begins at Home, by Mass-Observation* (London: Chatto and Windus, 1940), p. 24. An interpretation of Mass-Observation as an intellectual project rooted, in particular, in the 1930s, is presented in Nick Hubble, *Mass-Observation and Everyday Life: Culture, History, Theory* (Basingstoke, Hampshire: Palgrave Macmillan, 2006).

saving money, betting on football-pools, 'smoking as a social habit', and 'Doing the Lambeth Walk' (a new and very popular dance). While a persistent objective of M-O was to describe events in detail, there were other and larger goals. One of these aims, as the preface to M-O's first book declared, 'is to see how, and how far, the individual is linked up with society and its institutions'.[3]

Volunteers were vital to Mass-Observation. Without them, it would not have been possible to acquire most of the facts on which a 'science of ourselves' was to be based. The volunteer Observers were likened to 'cameras with which we are trying to photograph contemporary life.... Mass-Observation has always assumed that its untrained Observers would be subjective cameras, each with his or her own individual distortion. They tell us not what society is like, but what it looks like to them.'[4] This acceptance of the legitimacy of subjectivity in social observation was of signal importance, and it must have been one major reason why diary-keeping came to be promoted by M-O as a promising tool of both social and self-observation. A diary was another form of recording; and it was a form that inevitably tapped into the personalities, peculiarities, and inner lives of the individual diarists. The pursuit of science, then – a science in which the mass was being observed (and occasionally, perhaps, observing itself) – facilitated the production of a particularly personal form of writing, and, from August of 1939, many people responded to M-O's invitation to people to keep diaries and send them to M-O's headquarters. This was, we might say, an invitation to speak out – to give voice, perhaps, to one's own thoughts and feelings; to report on one's own experiences and contacts with others; to put into words one's own perspective on 'life', whatever that might mean for each diarist.

There are some 480 wartime diaries in the Mass-Observation Archive at the University of Sussex, and they are impressively varied. Many diaries did not last for long. Indeed, the majority of diarists abandoned their writing within a year of starting it; no doubt the demands of regular journalling were too heavy for most people to sustain, given all the daily pressures and even emergencies in their lives. Keeping a daily journal, month after month, year after year, sometimes during times of intense busyness, was not for the irresolute or ill-disciplined. Only a minority of diarists stuck with their writing for long enough to produce a text that might, theoretically, be made into a book. These fairly substantial diaries are of many different characters. Because M-O's invitation to write was open-ended and non-directive, each diarist had to find his or her own way of writing, and to create a voice with which he or she was comfortable. Some diaries mainly itemize the day's activities or respond to the news of the day; others are ruminative and opinionated, and often unpredictable. Some diaries are sketchy while others are richly elaborated (at least on occasions) and attentive to all sorts of minutiae. Some diaries are impersonal in tone and reveal little of the writer's emotional life or intimate relations. A few diaries offer passages that are candid and self-disclosing –

3. *May the Twelfth: Mass-Observation's Day-Surveys 1937*, edited by Humphrey Jennings and Charles Madge (London: Faber and Faber, 1937), p. v.
4. Charles Madge and Tom Harrisson, ed., *First Year's Work, 1937–38, by Mass-Observation* (London: Lindsay Drummond, 1938), p. 66.

and shed light on that person's pain and unhappiness that may well have been conveyed nowhere else.

At their most revealing, diaries encompass a broad spectrum of reality, from the deeply personal to the formidably public. A diary can bring together, in intense and unexpected ways, self and society. A compelling diary is a sort of letter addressed to the world, even if that world may be only one other person – for the teenage Anne Frank, holed up in wartime Amsterdam, it was a fictional person. A diary permits a distinctive angle of vision on the human experience: an angle that tends to highlight the uncertainties, the confusions, and the messiness of day-to-day life. A diary testifies to the power of the moment. It is ideally suited to seizing the mood of the often chaotic present. World War Two brought, of course, an avalanche of chaos, which each individual had to respond to in his or her own way. Diaries – and Kathleen Tipper's is one of these – are among the most vivid recordings of these responses, disclosing fear and hope, consternation and confidence, irritation and patience, and revealing, with minimal artifice, how fragile human natures struggled to contend with the savagery of total war.

Only a few Mass-Observation diaries have been (up to 2006) edited for publication. The first two to be published appeared in the 1980s: *Nella Last's War: A Mother's Diary 1939–1945*, edited by Richard Broad and Suzie Fleming (Bristol: Falling Wall Press, 1981), and *Among You Taking Notes ...: The Wartime Diary of Naomi Mitchison 1939–1945*, edited by Dorothy Sheridan (London: Victor Gollancz, 1985). The first was written by a previously unknown middle-aged mother of two adult sons who lived with her husband in Barrow-in-Furness, the second by a slightly younger and well-known intellectual and literary figure who was living in Scotland. Both original diaries are massive, and while these published volumes cover the whole period of the war, each presents only a small fraction (less than 20 per cent) of the original text. One M-O diary has been published in unabridged form for a period of slightly less than a year-and-a-half, *Wartime Norfolk: The Diary of Rachel Dhonau 1941–1942*, edited by Robert Malcolmson and Peter Searby (Norfolk Record Society, vol. 68, 2004), and one London diary from the M-O Archive has now appeared in print, *Love and War in London: A Woman's Diary 1939–1942*, by Olivia Cockett, edited by Robert Malcolmson (Waterloo, Ontario: Wilfred Laurier University Press, 2005). While a few London diaries not from Mass-Observation have been turned into books – one example is *Civilians at War: Journals 1938–1946*, by George Beardmore (London: John Murray, 1984) – most remain unpublished. A valuable finding aid lists almost 200 diaries that were rooted in the Greater London of World War Two,[5] and no doubt other manuscript diaries will be uncovered in due course, as personal and family papers find their way into public libraries and archives.

Any diary offers a view of time and place as experienced, for the most part, by just one individual, and the value of a particular diary will be determined by

---

5. Heather Creaton, *Unpublished London Diaries: A Checklist of unpublished diaries by Londoners and visitors with a Select Bibliography of published diaries* (London Record Society, vol. 37, 2003), pp. 78–92. Diaries in the M-O Archive comprise 115 of these almost 200 diaries. In this list, Olivia Cockett's diary is no. 679, Kathleen Tipper's is no. 802.

(amongst other things) the range and variety of this person's experiences, and his or her powers of observation and skill at reporting, describing, and commentating. In Kathleen Tipper's diary we find a full canvas of wartime life – a world of paid work and volunteer work; of home and family and neighbours; of travel and transport and of leisure and the arts; of conversations with friends and colleagues and strangers; of life in the streets and other public places; and of the dangers and alarums (not always, but often) of daily life in a great city under fierce attack. While this diary is a document that testifies principally to one young woman's personal experiences of wartime London, hers were experiences that were actually often shared (at least in part) with others – or that surely would have been shared with others – and that other Londoners <u>might</u> have written about, though of course with different emphases and accents. Unlike most people, Kathleen Tipper did write; she wrote with something of a reporter's eye; and, thanks to Mass-Observation and the establishment in the 1970s of the M-O Archive, her writing has survived.[6]

The Diarist and her Diary

Kathleen Margaret Tipper was born at home in south-east London on 24 May 1919. She was the first child of Alice Mary (née Rawson) Tipper (b.1890) and Charles Edwin Tipper (b.1894), who had been married the previous year. Both Kathleen's parents had worked in the Woolwich Arsenal during the Great War – her father had been invalided out of the Army and her mother was one of thousands of women who had left their usual jobs to find work in the munitions industry, one centre of which was in Woolwich. Kathleen's home birth was in a recently constructed terrace house at 7 Boughton Road (later re-addressed as 479 Rochester Way) in Well Hall, London SE9, which was then very much on the outskirts of the expanding capital, with open fields nearby. This nearly new house was neither owned nor rented by Kathleen's parents. Rather, it was a house on the Co-operative Progress Estate rented to a middle-aged couple without children, Arthur and Eliza Arnold, and Alice and Charles rented from them two first-floor rooms and had use of the ground floor facilities. Their second daughter, Joyce, was born there on 15 April 1921; and with the birth of their son, Philip, on 6 February 1925, these living quarters, even with the addition of a third room for their use after Joyce's birth, were getting unacceptably cramped. Kathleen's parents were seeking a house of their own, and in 1927 they were able to secure one – a semi-detached house, fully electrified (this was unusual), with three bedrooms – on Woolwich Council's newly-built Page Estate, just to the west of where they had been living for the previous eight years. Their new address was 50 Appleton Road, SE9, and this was to remain their home until just after the middle of World War Two. Kathleen, Joyce and Philip remained strongly attached to their first home, and the Arnolds (no mere landlords) became for them 'Auntie Lila and Uncle Arthur', whom, as schoolchildren, they sometimes visited on a daily basis, popping into 7 Boughton Road almost as if it were their own home.

6. Kathleen had for some years kept for herself a copy of her wartime diary, but it did not survive all the passages of her later life. This must be the fate of many diaries retained in private hands – and highlights the vital importance of public archives for personal papers.

Kathleen, Joyce and their mother in the early 1930s.

The Tipper family had to cope fairly frequently with straitened circumstances. Charles did not have regular, secure employment until the mid 1930s, and for a while Alice took in laundry (which Kathleen sometimes fetched and delivered) to help the family get by. Money was usually in short supply. Happily for the children's futures, both girls did well at school – they attended Deansfield Road School up to the age of eleven – and won scholarships to the recently-opened Eltham Hill School, the local grammar school, which years later became the Eltham Hill Technology College for Girls. Joyce in 2004 recalled that Kathleen was seen by her school teachers as something of 'a free spirit' and not always reliably deferential. Kathleen was a student at Eltham Hill between 1930 and 1936, Joyce between 1932 and 1938. In her final year at school, Kathleen, not wishing to be a teacher or a

Kathleen, Joyce and Philip in the early 1930s. The children, Kathleen recalled in 2004, 'saved their pennies', arranged on their own to have the picture taken in Woolwich, and sent copies to relatives and friends.

nurse (the two careers favoured by the school authorities), partly because the training required would delay her entry into the workforce, completed a programme of secretarial/commercial studies – she was awarded certificates in both book-keeping and Pitman's Shorthand (80 words a minute).[7] This training allowed her to secure a paid position promptly. In 1936, at the age of

7. We are very grateful to Marjorie Hodgson of the Eltham Hill Technology College for Girls for allowing us to inspect the school documents in her care, and for advising us on the College's archive.

17, she got her first job, at a salary of 30 shillings a week[8] – she turned over half of it to her parents – as a junior clerk with Alfred Booth & Company, a merchant shipping firm that specialised in skins and leathers and had many commercial connections overseas. This family firm – very traditional in style, Kathleen reported in 2005, and a 'friendly, pleasant company' – had comfortable, 'old world' premises at 11 Adelphi Terrace, Strand, WC2, overlooking the Thames, just east of Charing Cross station. (Adelphi Terrace also housed such notables as J.M. Barrie and, in the 1920s, George Bernard Shaw.) Initially Kathleen commuted to work by tram from Well Hall Road; later, during the war, she travelled by train from Well Hall/Eltham station to Charing Cross. Although most of Adelphi Terrace was demolished in 1936, No. 11 survived, and this is where Kathleen, aged 20, was working in 1939 when war was declared on September 3. Since 1938 Joyce had been working as a shorthand typist for the Royal Arsenal Co-operative Society in central Woolwich, and Philip was attending St. Olave's Grammar School in Tooley Street, SE1, near Tower Bridge in Bermondsey.

The Lower VI at Eltham Hill School, 1936. Kathleen Tipper is in the back row, third from the left. Photograph courtesy Marjorie Hodgson and the Eltham Hill Technology College for Girls.

8. There were twenty shillings in a pound (20s=£1); thus Kathleen earned in her first job a pound and a half a week. There were twelve pence in a shilling (12d=1s), and many everyday purchases in the late 1930s and early 1940s were paid for in pence: for example, the London *Evening Standard*, which Kathleen bought regularly, cost a penny (1d) and her local paper, the *Kentish Independent*, cost twopence (2d); 4d would buy a half ounce of tobacco or a roll of toilet paper; and for 6d one could purchase 10 cigarettes or a pound of luncheon sausage or a pound of margarine or a pair of silk hose (perhaps of rather low quality) or admission to a cinema.

Little documentary evidence exists concerning Kathleen's experiences during the first 22 months of the war. Later, on a significant anniversary, 3 September 1945, shortly after hostilities had ended, she wrote in her diary of how 'Today's date sent us all thinking of this day six years ago – with difficulty I am afraid in my case, although I shall never forget coming to town very late in the day [it was a Sunday] to put in an appearance at the office, watching the sky all the time for the enemy planes which came so much later. I was expecting bombardment all the time, and I still smile when I think of that journey.' Bombs, of course, did in due course fall, and lethally, especially between 7 September 1940 and 10 May 1941. Kathleen's place of work had to be relocated, for much of the neighbourhood around 11 Adelphi Terrace suffered serious bomb damage during a raid in mid April 1941 and Alfred Booth & Company moved to somewhat makeshift quarters at 15, 17, and 19 Kingsway, WC2 (Imperial House), where it remained for the duration of the war. The other major change in Kathleen's life related not to paid work but to volunteer work. From sometime in 1940 she began volunteering to serve refreshments to men and women in uniform for the YMCA, both out of its canteen in Morris Memorial Hall at Lee Green, 15 Eltham Road, SE12, on the edge of Lewisham, and from mobile vans. This volunteer work became a central feature of Kathleen's wartime experiences and figures prominently in her diary.[9]

Kathleen's diary for Mass-Observation begins on 19 July 1941. We do not know why she chose to start writing at that time. Mass-Observation was by the early 1940s well known, especially among the reading public; perhaps Kathleen learned of M-O's interest in encouraging wartime diary-keeping from *Picture Post* or some other periodical that sympathized with M-O's mission. Mass-Observation was adept at engaging the energies of intellectually alert and thoughtful individuals, and Kathleen was one of the small minority of diarists who wrote for several years (her diary ends on 1 February 1947). It would appear that she made handwritten notes for her diary on a daily basis and later at her office prepared a typed text of these notes (she had no typewriter at home) and posted this typescript to M-O's headquarters every fortnight. Each of these typed instalments begins on a Saturday and concludes 14 days later on a Friday, with her signature after this last diary entry. There is no diary text for significant periods in 1942 and 1944 and almost no text for 1943. It is possible that some diary entries she produced were later lost; it is also possible that, for whatever reason, she simply ceased to write a diary during these months. When she was in fact writing during the war – from July 1941 to June 1942; in August, November, and December 1942; from January to March 1944; and for most of the period from July 1944 – she produced

---

9. According to the Minutes of the YMCA War Emergency Committee for 29 February 1940,
   'Approval was given to a proposal to open Lee Green Morris Memorial Hall as a centre for troops billeted in the district. Certain repairs, additions and renovations were necessary at an estimated cost of £175.' On 9 May 1940 the fitting out and equipping of this centre was approved, at a cost of £120, half of which was raised locally (minutes of 23 May 1940). (Special Collections Department, University Library, University of Birmingham, J.125–127.) Mobile tea vans, commonly equipped with five-gallon urns and several dozen mugs, were intended to serve refreshments to those who were unable to leave their posts, such as the men assigned to anti-aircraft gun-sites.

comments and descriptions virtually daily, sometimes briefly, sometimes at considerable length. Lengthy, detailed entries, which are rare during the early months of her diary, are common by 1944 and 1945.

Editorial Practice

According to certain ideals, a scholarly edition of a diary would be presented in its entirety. If nothing is omitted, a reader is not dependent on editorial choices. For most diaries written before the twentieth century, an unabridged diary is usually both feasible and appropriate. Twentieth-century diaries, however, are commonly more expansive than those written in earlier generations. Modern diarists frequently write much more and feel less reason to be highly economical (cheap paper is one consideration). Sometimes they write regularly for years. Some of these diaries are very bulky indeed. Consequently, to publish a modern diary in its entirety is often impracticable. In preparing this edition of Kathleen Tipper's diary, we have proceeded in the following way. (a) We have given priority to selections that highlight conditions in wartime London and Kathleen's experiences there – at home, at work, while travelling and volunteering and talking with friends, acquaintances, and members of various uniformed forces. This priority applies especially to Parts One (1941–42) and Three (1944–45) of this edition. (b) Our omissions are mainly of passages in which Kathleen reports and comments on military and political news that she read about in the press or heard on the radio. These omitted passages, then, most often concern her responses to events and developments with which she had no direct experience. (c) Part Two of the diary (August 1942-March 1944), by contrast, reproduces (with one small exception) her whole diary for this period. In this section, then, a reader gets a full sense of the diary in all its dimensions. (d) On a few occasions we have summarized several weeks of the diary. The most prominent of these passages deal with July-August 1941, January-February 1942, July-August 1944, and the months after May 1945. Further details concerning our principles of selection are presented from time to time throughout the text.[10]

Our annotations to the text are mainly of two kinds. First, when brief factual information is provided – a date, a first name, a job title, a geographical location, a reference to a newspaper or magazine – we have inserted these details in square brackets within the text of the diary. Second, we have usually reserved footnotes for more substantial additions to the text: for quotations

---

10. Our experience suggests that editorial practices regarding deletions, abridgements, and additions need to be adapted to the peculiarities of each diary. Sometimes a portion of a manuscript diary might be published in full while the rest is omitted entirely. *Wartime Norfolk: The Diary of Rachel Dhonau 1941–1942*, ed. Robert Malcolmson and Peter Searby (Norfolk Record Society, vol. 68, 2004), for example, concludes at a point when the diarist's living circumstances changed significantly, with the result that the last 14 months of the manuscript M-O diary, up to February 1944, decline in interest and topical variety. By contrast, another, relatively short, M-O diary only became a book because private papers and the diarist's responses to M-O's monthly questionnaires could be drawn upon to augment the testimony of the diary itself (*Love and War in London: A Woman's Diary 1939–1942*, by Olivia Cockett, edited by Robert Malcolmson (Waterloo, Ontario: Wilfred Laurier University Press, 2005).

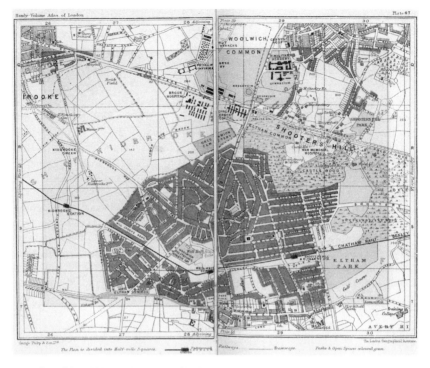

Well Hall in 1930. Appleton Road is left-centre, Well Hall Station is lower-centre. From *Philip's Handy Volume Atlas of London* [1930], map 47. Photograph courtesy Data, Map and Government Information Services, University of Toronto Libraries.

from contemporary sources, such as newspapers and Churchill's speeches; for identifying information that warrants a sentence or more; for explanations of context and background; and occasionally to refer to scholarly authorities on topics and events that Kathleen is writing about. A few of these annotations are based on information and comments given to us by Kathleen and Joyce in 2004 and 2005, though most of their testimony from these years, both oral and written, is used elsewhere, especially earlier in this Introduction, in connecting passages in the diary, and in the Epilogue.

Almost any diary is written at least sometimes in haste, with the result that some typos, misspellings, inconsistencies in usage, and minor errors in composition are virtually inevitable. Since Kathleen Tipper – like almost all diarists for Mass-Observation – was not writing with publication in mind, she had no reason to conduct the sort of careful textual scrutiny that is likely to detect those stigmata that a proof-reader is asked to search for. While we have not tampered with the substance of her writing (in fact, she wrote clearly and with precision), we have sometimes supplied or altered punctuation; made capitalization consistent (for example, 'war' rather than 'War'); silently corrected obvious mistakes (such as a missing letter or a misspelled place name); ensured that common usages are consistent (for example, we have normally presented small numbers in words except when they refer to clock-time); and supplied days of the week for all her dates. Occasionally we have used square brackets to supply a word or words that help to render a passage in the diary fully intelligible.

Almost all the persons mentioned in the original typescript diary are named, though sometimes only by either their first name or surname. Partly because anonymity was a basic principle of personal writing for Mass-Observation – many other M-O diarists did in fact conceal the identities of most of the private persons they wrote about – and partly because Kathleen herself, when she learned of our interest in publishing her diary, expressed the understandable desire that any publication not reveal the identities of many of the private individuals whom she mentions in her diary, a few of them critically, we have adopted the following conventions. We have anonymised the majority of the people she names who were friends, neighbours, acquaintances, and men and women in the armed forces whom she met in the course of her volunteer work. Thus (to illustrate with fictional names), a 'Mr. Johnson' becomes 'Mr. J.', 'Mrs. Long' becomes 'Mrs. L.', 'Edward' becomes 'E.', and 'Margaret Thorpe' becomes 'M.T.' The gender of the person spoken of is always clear or made clear. We have retained the actual names of all public figures; members of Kathleen's immediate family and relatives; children; a few individuals whose names we have chosen to preserve in order to record explicitly their personal characters as perceived by Kathleen; and a small number of people who make such frequent appearances in the diary that their actual names are important for a clear understanding of Kathleen's social network and relations. This small group comprises her two main friends and colleagues at work, Rene and Dorothy; one of her best friends, Eileen; and Eileen's fiancé, Dan. Kathleen does a lot with her sister, Joyce, and it is apparent that on many occasions when Kathleen writes of 'we' or 'our' or 'us', she means some version of 'Joyce and I'. Kathleen sometimes for brevity spoke of her brother as Phil, and at her request we consistently identify him as Philip, his preferred and usual name. Our goal as editors has been to acknowledge the convention of anonymity while providing names when they are essential for a full appreciation of the historical realities that the diary depicts.

Finally, we should mention that the division of Kathleen's diary into three Parts is entirely a function of editorial discretion. Both Parts Two and Three begin after a significant break in the diary's continuity – in the first case, a break of six weeks, in the second case, a break of over three months. Although it would be inaccurate to ascribe any clear thematic unity to each of these Parts, we like to think that Part One offers selections that launch the diary, portrays something of Kathleen's outlooks and varied activities during her 23rd year, and introduces many of the people in and the circumstances of her life; that Part Two deepens this portrait, partly by virtue of presenting almost all of the original diary entries; and that Part Three (the longest Part) offers a rich and evocative account of the last ten months of the war against Hitler's Germany, a time when victory seemed virtually certain but destruction on a frightening scale continued unabated, not least in London. The Epilogue summarises some of the major themes in Kathleen's immediate postwar life (up to early 1947) and concludes with a few words about her later experiences, between 1947 and 2005.

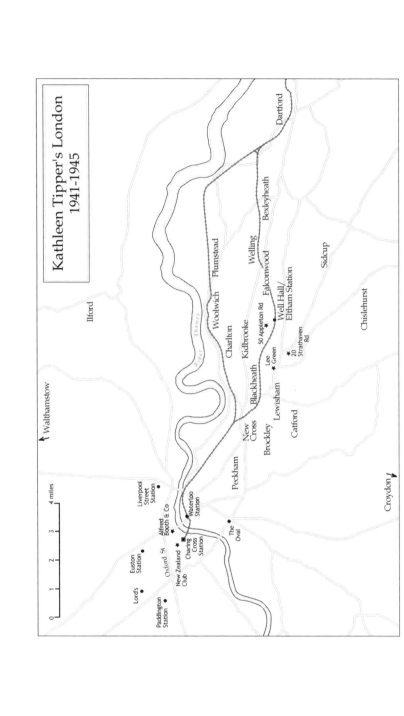

Kathleen Tipper's London 1941–1945

Map drawn by Jennifer Grek Martin

Kathleen Tipper in 1937.

THE DIARY OF KATHLEEN TIPPER
1941–1945

PART ONE (JULY 1941–JUNE 1942)

Kathleen Tipper began her diary for Mass-Observation on Saturday, July 19, 1941, some four weeks after the ferocious German invasion of the Soviet Union. With this momentous act of war, Britain had a new and vastly important ally, and the central drama of the European struggle shifted decisively (at least for several months) to the Eastern Front. From mid-May there had been little bombing of British cities, and thus the Home Front became safer and more secure, though of course nobody could know if and when air raids would be resumed. Kathleen's diary records a good deal of war news and talk about the war and its politics. During the summer of 1941 she commented on radio broadcasts; military losses; changes in the Ministry of Information; whether or not Japan would declare war; debates in Parliament and statements by politicians; the evolving policies of the United States; the attempt to assassinate the pro-Nazi Vichy politician, Pierre Laval; and the movements and speeches of the Prime Minister, Winston Churchill, whose talents Kathleen admired (though not unreservedly) and would admire more in hindsight. Sometimes it was hard to be upbeat. 'I have got into a mood of terrific depression,' she wrote on August 21. 'The war news is really getting so serious. The Russian Army

1

seems to be cracking badly and I have an awful thought that unless something is done at once the citizens of London will be in a similar position to that of the people of Leningrad.' The following day she wrote only one sentence: 'Am still exceedingly depressed and the news from Russia is not cheering.'

Some of Kathleen's diary entries in the summer of 1941 touch directly on life in London, its defences, and her conversations there. On Tuesday, July 22 she observed: 'Odd to see how fashionable it has become to read *Soviet War News Reviews*, etc., and even the nicest people can read them in public without attracting ugly looks. Outside Charing Cross [station] a young woman brazenly sells *Russia Today* – she hasn't done such business since the [Communist] *Daily Worker* was banned.' Four days later Kathleen again mentioned the Soviet Union. 'See a news reel at the cinema. I was much amused when the commentator described the Russian people as being resolutely led by Joseph Stalin (close-up of J.S.'s face), at which everybody applauded. Perhaps I am a little unfair, as most ordinary people in my part of the world have always felt quite warmly towards the Russians, even if they were not partial to their government's methods sometimes.' (July 26) There were, of course, many different attitudes towards Russia, and these differences were sometimes evident in Londoners' conversations. On Tuesday, August 19 Kathleen wrote: 'Travelled to town today with S. who still nurses communist views. Before the Russians entered the war she took the official party view that the workers etc. were being lured into this war against their interests. Now, although she supports the war, she is indignant because her department (of the civil service) has now to work 48 hours a week, which she considers an imposition. How she imagines we (as well as her Russian brothers) are going to win this war when people like her aren't even willing or anxious to work eight hours a day, I can't imagine – this despite the fact that she is always lamenting the fact that she never has anything to do after 5 p.m. I think she is quite illogical and am inclined to lose patience with her.'

London in the summer of 1941 was a very different city from the London of two years before. The sky was full of barrage balloons, which, increasingly, were being managed by women. On Sunday, July 20 Kathleen recorded that 'On my rounds with the [YMCA] mobile canteen most of the balloon men are relieved. S. says, "Let the women man the balloons (if they can) and let some of us get on to the jobs we are fitted for and for which we originally volunteered". He is a civil engineer and, as he once said to me, has been attached to the end of a pencil for two years knowing little more about balloons than that they fly and are at the end of a string, which he learned when he was aged five.' This was a time when many people were complaining of inappropriate employment, or inequitable employment, or underemployment. On Sunday, August 10 Kathleen worked 'all day in the stationary canteen [on Lee Green]. We are getting a little tired of the everlasting "browned off" complaint from the men. In their case it is caused by too much time on their hands, too little money to spend and nothing much to do.' Most people were sensitive – even ultra-sensitive – to issues of fairness, and whether or not others were doing as much as they could or should in aid of the war. On the August Bank Holiday, Kathleen and her sister, Joyce, spent the day watching cricket at Lord's: 'Apart from the hundreds of uniforms it is quite a peacetime scene. What sort of work is performed by some of these players who are in the forces? Many of them are *able to give on an average two days a week to cricket (or any other sport), yet other men are not always certain of getting their seven days leave in three months. There is something wrong somewhere with this system, if system there is.'* On July 22 there had been a debate about a different form of skilled labour: *'We had quite an argument'*, Kathleen reported, *'as to whether male ballet dancers are doing national service by ballet dancing!!'*[1]

Kathleen had a keen eye and ear for what went on around her, as she met and talked with servicemen, friends and strangers and as she commuted from Well Hall/ Eltham in south-east London back and forth to her work in Kingsway. On Monday, August 18 she wrote of how *'A blonde glamour girl amused me this morning in my carriage. She was describing her work to a friend and incidentally to all the other occupants of the train. Apparently she worked in an office with the wireless playing all day, partook of a sherry at 11, had lunch around 12, had another drink in the afternoon, and then presumably went home. Their drink bill was one of the largest office expenses, she said (and I don't wonder). A creature of this sort is nearly as good as a blitz for bringing people together and after she left the carriage everyone became quite talkative and the men, particularly, said with feeling that she ought to be in a munition factory. I don't think they liked her long red nails.'* Kathleen often wrote of other women, especially women who, like her, were in their early twenties (she was 22). On Wednesday, August 27 she met *'two old school friends. M. is down in the country, evacuated there by her firm. They live in large house, work hard from 9.30 to 5.30 and have Saturdays and Sundays free. They do no firewatching to speak of and have had no bombs near to them. She says quite honestly that she wouldn't come back to London while the war is on, but will be back like a shot when it is over. I believe the girls at her firm are going to do a spot of harvesting sometime soon – this they consider is their national service. P. is still up in town working hard from 9.30 to 5 and fire-watching enthusiastically about once a week! Both these girls are automatically exempt when it comes to registering for work of national impor-tance and they are only typical of hundreds that I and my friends know of. Yet girls who are doing their ordinary work and a part-time job of Red Cross nursing or as Air Raid Wardens are likely to be called up!'*

By late August Kathleen had mailed three instalments of her diary to Mass-Observation, once a fortnight. Her fourth instalment begins with the last Saturday of the month.

---

1. Ballet management in fact resisted arguments that male dancers should be exempted from conscription (as actors had been). 'To have done so', as one contemporary authority argued, ' … would have damaged ballet beyond recovery in the public mind. The male dancer has yet to earn the complete recognition in England that he has in Russia. His true function as a virile partner contrasting with ballerina, whose fragility and beauty reveals and enhances, has yet to be fully understood. The fact that the male dancers of Britain's ballet not only opposed all pleas of exemption on their behalf, but as volunteers and conscripts enjoy an exceptionally fine record in all the services, while it adds greatly to temporary difficulties, will, I am convinced, go a long way towards banishing any prejudice against male dancing and bringing the right type of boy to ballet. Every one of the original male personnel of Sadlers Wells is in the Forces': Arnold L. Haskell, *Ballet Since 1939* (London: British Council, 1946), pp. 15–16. Ballet remained active during the war and employed boys of 15 or 16 and a handful of foreign male dancers.

1941

Saturday, August 30. Our [YMCA] van is very temperamental today, but it is truly amazing how kind and helpful people are. Whenever we broke down there was always somebody around who could give us assistance. Finish just before 6 and manage to get a lift to Charlton to see the first football match of the season with Chelsea. The crowd is quite large, nearly ten thousand, mainly servicemen, and the football is excellent considering the fact that many of the players are doing it on their half day off.[2]

Sunday, August 31. They gave me a day off at the canteen. We go to see *Fantasia*. I cannot put into adequate words my opinion of this remarkable film. I don't however think that people who live for classical music will like it very much, because most of them have preconceived ideas of the thoughts in the composer's mind when he wrote the various pieces in this film. Nor do I imagine that it will be popular with the 'two or three times a week' film-goer. In fact I think they will dislike it. I went with an open mind, and although I love good music, I know very little about it, but I have never seen anything as completely lovely as the Disney interpretation of *The Nutcracker Suite*.[3]

Monday, September 1. According to this morning's news the Ministry of Labour is going to call up more women for the ATS [Auxiliary Territorial Service] and the munitions. If with regard to the ATS the powers that be would dispense with a few of the stupid and petty rules that make the service unpalatable for many girls and concentrate on cleaning up the moral side, I think they would get a better type of volunteer and probably the service would get a pleasanter name. Rene [a co-worker] was telling me today about some friends of hers who are now working in a munition factory. One of these, a charming middle-aged lady, admits frankly that she would never let a daughter of hers go into a factory. She says the language and general behaviour is absolutely disgusting, which seems to bear out all we have heard from other sources. With all this going on the Government still say that mothers should not forbid their young daughters leaving home to go into war work as their morals are carefully protected. Rubbish!

Tuesday, September 2. D., G. and Dy. come in to the canteen this evening to say good-bye. They are leaving within a day or so. I must admit that I will be very sorry to see them go. I have become quite fond of them. D. has been to a wonderful fortune-teller – he is full of it. This woman apparently told him accurately how his father and sisters were killed, and many other happenings which he says were perfectly true. Dy. became a little sentimental and started

2. This game – Charlton beat Chelsea 2–1 – marked the opening of the 'London War League fixtures' (*Kentish Independent*, 5 September 1941, p.2), which scheduled football games on a regional basis, partly to minimise travelling. In 1941–42 there was a Southern League, mainly though not exclusively of London teams.
3. *Fantasia* was a Walt Disney technicolour feature film that presented animated interpretations of great works of classical music.

to give us details of sundry 'low dives' in London and Glasgow. I thought that this was not quite YMCA talk and gently stopped him. I heard today that G. has now arrived in the Middle East. No doubt this will curb his impatient spirit. I wondered privately how he managed to get all his stuff taken along, as for two years now he has been going from camp to camp all round England, with a large fast sports car, hundreds of gramophone records, a miniature library and sundry sports equipment. In fact it was a joy to see the convoy leave with G. in 'Bertha' bringing up the rear.

Wednesday, September 3. Casting my mind back over the past two years, I am still amazed that so many of us are still alive, especially when I think of our unpreparedness on this day two years ago [when war was declared]. Perhaps if we had known the truth then we would have given up. The news today says that Marshal [Kliment] Voroshilov is on the Leningrad front and personally conducting the offensives. If Leningrad falls, what will become of Kronstadt?

[Intervening entry omitted]

Friday, September 5. Go to see *The Cherry Orchard* [by Anton Chekhov] which I find quite a stimulating change from the inevitable musical comedies that cram the London stage these days. Certainly only real theatre-lovers would go to see it though; it is not the sort of thing for an afternoon's spree. E., a budding-solicitor friend of mine who went off to the war two or three months ago, has written a harrowing story of his life in the Army these days. Apparently the conditions are so bad where he is that two men have deserted and the man in the next bed to himself shot his fingers off in order to get out of the Army. This is tragic because E. was filled with the tradition of his regiment and had swallowed the ideals of the Army completely. In fact, he was ideal mate-rial for the Army – keen, intelligent, and above all, he approved of all the discipline which irks most new soldiers. It is really terrible that he can't be used in some way, because his brain is definitely being wasted.

Saturday, September 6. Alistair Cooke's broadcast as usual was an eye-opener. Apparently material aid for Britain is hindered very considerably over there [the USA] by muddle and red tape, so he more or less warned us not to expect too much for quite a time. I know many people here do imagine that we are getting quite a steady stream of aid and for this we have to thank (to some extent) optimistic journalists who have painted this aspect of the war with very rosy hues.[4] All men 18–60 have to register for fire-watching. I don't think this will make very much difference; where men are determined not to do any, they will manage to avoid this duty. The authorities must be over-whelmed with forms; what with the registering of women for war work, men for firewatching and men for national service, I can imagine amusing possibil-ities if the respective papers were mixed up!

---

4.   A printed version of Alistair Cooke's *American Commentary* appeared in the *Listener*, 11 September 1941, p. 371, as 'A New Deal for American Defence'. Cooke highlighted devel-opments in the USA that might be construed as political actions in preparation for war.

Sunday, September 7. How grim this date looks. Spend the day at the canteen. What a contrast to the same day last year, the last hours of which we spent in amazed horror in our air-raid shelter. That day, I know, I thought all was finished. As we looked at the fires all around us I thought nothing could save us, and the next nights were equally horrible, bombs and more bombs.[5] T. is home this weekend and admitted, much to my surprise, that he is occasionally frightened, although he does say that they all have the utmost confidence in themselves. How everybody envies him! The *Brains Trust* was, as usual, very amusing. Isn't it amazing how popular this programme has become. Most people listen to it, but what a poor show the visitors put up compared with the resident stars, although I think the 'compere' Donald McCullock [sic, recte McCullough] is the brightest star of all.[6]

Monday, September 8. Berlin was heavily bombed last night, the anniversary of the first heavy raid on London. If this was meant as a belated reprisal, it does not seem worth the lives of the airmen taking part as last night 20 bombers failed to return which means over 100 men lost in one night's operations. The Germans say (according to the 9 o'clock news) that they have surrounded Leningrad. [David] Low surpasses himself tonight in his 'Defence of Leningrad-London-Washington' cartoon.[7]

Tuesday, September 9. We have landed on Spitzbergen [Norwegian island in the Arctic]. The Canadians must have enjoyed this first taste of action and I expect they were sorry to find the island free of Germans. Mr. Churchill makes his first War summary since the Atlantic meeting but says very little except that we are giving Russia more help than some people may be thinking. I sincerely hope this is the case! He pays tribute to the men of the submarine service, tribute which has been long delayed. Like our airmen, these men, few in number, are doing so much, at great cost to themselves, to keep the Germans from our shores.[8] D. has failed in his medical, so he can't become a rear-gunner. After passing all the written examinations and most of the medical

---

5. The Blitz on London had begun on this day in 1940. Woolwich and nearby boroughs had been heavily targeted.
6. Donald McCullough (b. 1901), the Question Master of this much listened-to question-and-answer programme, was an expert in public relations. The permanent members of the *Brains Trust* — 'the resident stars', in Kathleen's words — were at this time the scientist Julian Huxley, Professor of Philosophy C.E. M. Joad, and Commander Archibald. B. Campbell, a practical military man. At times during the war the *Brains Trust* attracted 10 to 12 million listeners. It was profiled in the magazine *Picture Post*, 30 August 1941, pp. 16–17, and written about by its producer, Howard Thomas, *The Brains Trust* (London, 1944). After 1941 other notables joined the *Trust*, including many new guest members.
7. David Low (b.1891), cartoonist and caricaturist, drew principally for the *Evening Standard*. This cartoon (see opposite), which is reproduced in his *Years of Wrath: A Cartoon History 1932–1945* (London: Victor Gollancz, 1949), p. 174, highlights the burden of war being borne by the Soviet Union, and implies that British support for her new ally was insufficient.
8. In 'The War Situation', delivered to the House of Commons, Churchill paid tribute to submariners (*Speeches*, VI, pp. 6482–83) and spoke of aid to Russia (pp. 6487–88). He and President Roosevelt had met secretly off the coast of Newfoundland – 'the Atlantic meeting' – the previous month.

DEFENCE OF LENINGRAD

Kathleen praised this cartoon on September 8. Reprinted with permission of
Solo Syndication, London.

tests he was turned down by the last doctor. It does seem a pity. Some of those
boys are so dead keen that I am sure they deserve some job, a little out of the
ordinary, to use up this excess of spirit that they possess. Otherwise they tend
to turn cynical and prematurely hard.

Wednesday, September 10. As I came up in the train today I once again
marvelled at the speed at which some of the factories destroyed or severely
damaged in the blitz are being rebuilt. Certainly this is a good way of keeping
up morale, as it gives one faith in our ability to recover from any setbacks we
may have to face. Spent Philip's last evening at home. It is incredible that
more than five weeks have passed since he came home. He is returning now
refreshed and quite willing to study much harder after his holiday. It seems
to have been a wise gesture on the part of his headmaster to let him come
home.[9]

9.   Philip (b.1925), Kathleen's brother, was a student at St. Olave's School, SE1, which had been
      evacuated to Torquay, Devon.

Thursday, September 11. We are astir very early. I went with Mother to see Philip off. Mother is exceedingly glum, but is looking forward to Christmas time. I am afraid Philip still thinks Torquay a 'dump and a funk hole' and considers himself to be the equivalent of a convict in Dartmoor. Furthermore he declares that after the war he will never go near the place again. See that Pastor [Martin] Niemöller has been moved to Dachau. I still wonder why Hitler has not had him removed long ago. With this example before them it is a pity that some of our clergy do not give more positive proof of their faith and integrity of character!

Friday, September 12. President Roosevelt makes his long awaited announcement that USA will fire on Axis ships in American waters. I hope they shoot at Germans as fiercely with their guns as they do with their speeches and press articles! If they do the Axis will have to beware. At the cinema this evening I saw a Ministry of Information short called *One of Our Pilots is Safe* which I think is a gem in its class.[10] Oddly enough I heard last night that P. is joining this rescue service and starts training in the next few days. One of the qualifications he had to possess was the ability to swim over long distances. I also saw the second part of the German propaganda film of their war against Russia which some people say is a fake. Whatever it is, this film is horribly terrifying and I hope that people who scoff at the remote possibility of invasion here will see it.

Saturday, September 13. Our last visit today to the Guards who are leaving our district for good. Many of the men in this Company are recent additions as they lost heavily in France. Raymond Gram Swing in his *American Commentary* this evening mentioned that Col. [Charles] Lindberg made a speech on the same evening as the President. He is, it seems, using all the Nazi arguments these days and has begun attacking the Jews. These views, one would imagine, would be extremely unpopular with certain Americans. But I suppose that in America as has been the case everywhere else in the world, these sentiments are lapped up by all those persons who dislike Jews for one reason or other.

Sunday, September 14. A wing of the RAF is in Russia. I have been wondering for some time now what the Russians (who until the Germans invaded their country obviously knew little about the outside world, particularly capitalistic Britain) will think of our pilots. I should imagine that they will be amazed at their spirit and dash and devotion to their cause, because one presumes that the Russians have been taught that such spirit of devotion to a cause can only be inspired by Bolshevik teaching. In the same way I expect our pilots and men will find many of their preconceived ideas of Russia swept away when they actually work and fight together. Almost to a man on our rounds today, they envy these RAF who are at least seeing some action. Frank Owen of the

---

10. Kathleen probably meant *The Pilot is Safe*, a seven-minute short about air-sea rescue produced by the Crown Film Unit and released in 1941.

Evening Standard gave the *Postscript* tonight. His talk like all his articles since the real war started was urgent and full of admiration for the Russians.[11]

[Intervening entry omitted]

Tuesday, September 16. I have just finished reading *The Spanish Farm Trilogy* [1927] by R.H. Mottram, one of the best books I have read about the last Great War. Without using flowery or flamboyant language, the author presents an impressive picture of the trenches in France. Somehow reading it now it is easier than it would have been two or three years back to visualise it all – and in some way helps one to understand the war as it is being fought in Russia now. I don't suppose many men who saw the whole of the last war in its frightfulness ever imagined that in 12 weeks about four million men could perish, as has in fact occurred. I should not think they can even attempt to bury most of them and it is incredible that terrible plagues are not spreading all over the battle front.

Wednesday, September 17. Mother woke me this morning with 'Well, we'll be bombing Rome soon now' in quite a pleasant voice. I contend that this is one of Hitler's worst crimes, to have turned nice, kindly women like our mothers into hard revengeful women who delight in seeing the Germans and Italians given a taste of their own medicine.[12] It is announced today that Sergeant Ward is posted missing from a flight over Germany. This sort of news is becoming increasingly familiar these days.

Thursday, September 18. J.M. Keynes is to be a Director of the Bank of England. One would think that pressure has been applied in certain quarters because Mr. Keynes has said some fairly unpleasant things in the past about the Bankers of the City. Perhaps this super-critic has some revolutionary plan to clean up finance!! He will probably lapse into obscurity in the same way that all 'fire-brands' do when they obtain a position of authority.[13] The Germans report having cut off the Crimea. That peninsula has seen some varied conflicts over the past two thousand years, all to no purpose it seems. The same old

---

11. *Postscript* was a programme that followed the 9.00 p.m. news on Sunday; it offered fifteen minutes of commentary by some (as a rule) noted individual, chosen by BBC producers. It had been made famous by J.B. Priestley in the summer of 1940, who spoke regularly during those critical weeks. Frank Owen (b. 1905) was editor of the *Evening Standard* 1938–1941.
12. On the evening of Monday, 25 August, Kathleen had gone to the cinema to see *Target for Tonight*, an account of a British bombing raid on Germany: 'Whilst I was watching the film … I felt most bitter against the Germans because they have made our fundamentally decent young men take part in such a fiendish business.' The following day, 26 August, she spoke of how German 'crimes' had succeeded in hardening British sensibilities.
13. John Maynard Keynes (b.1883), the already celebrated economist, had often been critical of Britain's financial orthodoxies. His biographer offered a succinct comment on Keynes' relations to power. 'He was a rebel who entered the Establishment, not by succumbing to it, but by shifting it toward his own ground': Robert Skidelsky, *John Maynard Keynes: Volume Three, Fighting for Britain 1937–1946* (London: Macmillan, 2000), p. xvi.

enemies are fighting the same old battles and for all we know will still be fighting there a thousand years from now.

Friday, September 19. The Russian situation is getting still more serious. The Germans seem to be throwing endless thousands of men into the battle. If we can't do anything to help ourselves now, when the Germans are fighting so hard with most of their resources concentrated on this far front, what shall we do if Russia goes down and the whole weight of this giant war machine turns on us alone!! Even if we are morally supported by the USA it is useless to think that we can put equal numbers of men in the field against the Germans. Go to the cinema in the evening – see a newsreel showing tanks on manoeuvres and in production. The commentator made the extraordinary statement that although production was quite good now, it would really put a spurt on when we personally got to grips with the Nazis. This I think is a particularly unfortunate statement in view of the fact that the Russians need tanks so desperately, and if we supply them in large enough numbers, we may never have to meet the Germans on our own soil. I suppose we shall really start doing something desperate when the Russians have been beaten and it is too late. Or are people in this country still optimistically thinking that millions of Americans are suddenly going to appear here to save us?

Saturday, September 20. On the van today with a female of the 'we have practically won the war – look at how the Russians are flinging the Germans back' school of thought. She was furious when some of the men (all of them strangely pessimistic today) said that they wished we would do something active to help Russia instead of waiting until it is too late. We receive an emergency call at lunchtime and dash out to serve 400 men just arrived from the North. Are they glad to see us after their long journey. These emergency calls, on top of our ordinary runs, mean a lot of hard work, but they are well worth while.

[Intervening entries omitted]

Wednesday, September 24. I go to Fulham Hospital with Mother this morning. She has to have another course of treatment [for cancer]. As I waited inside the hospital I realised once again how futile is all worry about one's own safety these days. Apart from the danger of bombs there is all this illness which is still carrying people off in great numbers. In fact one has only to think in order to realise how frail is human life. But I do think it is wonderful that this great fight against disease is still going one even amidst the ever-increasing death and destruction.

Thursday, September 25. Mother is quite knocked up by her first dose of treatment. It is extraordinary how relatively unimportant world affairs become as soon as you have some personal worry. Somehow even the Russian war seems quite remote already.

Friday, September 26. Hear today that D. is to be 'screened' quite soon. He has almost finished his 30 raids over Germany again. I think he has to make another three.

Saturday, September 27. The end of the 'Tanks for Russia' week. M. Maisky broadcasts his country's thanks for this record output.[14] I do the stationary canteen all the morning and have a terrific time – 80 men come in from a convoy, all very hungry and all in a hurry. In the afternoon I do a busy run down in the dockyard. Hear the air raid warning during the night. The gunfire was apparently quite heavy but I didn't hear that.

Sunday, September 28. The Sunday papers are filled with the very interesting news that the Prime Minister's daughter [Mary] is in the ATS. No doubt this will stimulate recruiting. Oddly enough I noticed in the paper a few days ago a statement to the effect that ATS girls are being trained as officers after only two or three weeks in the service. Was this specially for Mary? Spend a musical evening with Mrs. T. A. has just bought the whole of the *Pathetic Symphony* [Tchaikovsky's Symphony No.6]. We heard it all through twice. As well as this symphony we played all my favourite Chopin and it made the war seem very remote.

[Intervening entries omitted]

Wednesday, October 1. I am always astonished at the bad manners some men and women display in restaurants. The men seem to be divided into two classes – those who are very familiar with the waitresses and the others who go out of their way to be as rude as they can to these hard-worked girls. Today a man at my table was so impolite that I longed to butt in and take the girl's part. These men are probably working terribly hard. Perhaps they are over-worked. But it does seem a little unkind to take it out on the poor waitresses. The rudeness now, however, is not confined to one side of the counter. Some shop assistants are making up for all the insults they had to endure before the war and the maxim these days seems to be 'the customer is always wrong'. But I do think some of them go too far. We poor shoppers now can only mutter to ourselves 'there will be an after the war'.

[Intervening entry omitted]

Friday, October 3. Lady Astor in a speech yesterday is reported as having said 'The time has come when men should hand out white feathers to girls of their

---

14. Ivan Maisky (b.1884) was Soviet ambassador to the UK from 1932 to 1943. Churchill and Lord Beaverbrook, the Minister of Supply (previously the Minister of Aircraft Production) and owner of the *Daily Express*, agreed to promote a 'Tanks for Russia Week' whereby all tanks produced in Britain during the seven days up to 27 September – just as Beaverbrook was due to arrive in Moscow – would be delivered to the USSR: Anne Chisholm and Michael Davie, *Beaverbrook: A Life* (London: Hutchinson, 1992), pp. 406–07.

acquaintance whom they meet in the streets and who they know refuse to join the women's services'. I can't imagine that any girl so referred to would be lured into any of the forces. Perhaps Lady Astor does more harm than she thinks by this sort of remark.[15] I saw two grand documentaries this evening. One, *H.M. Minelayer*, was an MOI [Ministry of Information] weekly short. The other, called *The Gun*, was a longer film made by the Admiralty and Edward Murrow of the NBC [actually, CBS: Columbia Broadcasting System] and apparently this film has been used in America to speed up the production of AA [anti-aircraft] guns for use on merchant ships. The first shots taken inside the Admiralty during a blitz are calculated to impress any American. Walls rock and ceilings and chandeliers shake as bombs drop all round, but the conference and meetings inside the various rooms go on as usual. During the interval, a collection was made for the Russian Red Cross and whilst it was taken a young man (I knew him to be a member of the local Communist party) proceeded to harangue the audience on the subject of the conflagration in the East. He had obviously learned his speech off by heart and faltered every now and again, on these occasions saving himself (and amusing me) by referring in hushed tones to this flame burning in the East. I am afraid that however ardently I support an idea, this type of person turns me against it and I am certain they do a great deal of injury to the cause which they are supposed to be helping. Anyhow, I don't think many people here (or in Russia for that matter) admire the various attitudes taken by the British Communists.

Saturday, October 4. S. and I had a terrific day. We had to serve [in the YMCA canteen] about 600 Scots Guards in a very short time. One of their officers, who made himself very pleasant, turned out to be one of England's premier barons. I thought him very charming although he did say that he thought the men 'would love us dearly', which I thought an odd phrase! There has been some hitch in the arrangements for repatriation of wounded prisoners. Rumour has it that Hess was demanded by Hitler.[16] Mother and Joyce went up to St. Olave's to hear a statement by Philip's headmaster, Dr. Carrington.[17] He says among other things that the boys he has now of 16 and 17 are the cleverest he has ever come into contact with during his teaching days (and the same is true, he said, of boys all over the country). This to my mind is very comforting because in 10–15 years time these boys will be in the thirties and so perhaps we may then have a young generation running and governing the country with real intelligence.

---

15. Nancy Astor, wife of Viscount Astor, was the Conservative Member of Parliament for the Sutton Division of Plymouth. She was outspoken, something of a loose cannon, and not always an asset to her party. (See also below, 4 December 1941 and 6 August 1942.) From December 1941 single women aged 20–30 (and childless widows) became liable to conscription.
16. Rudolf Hess (b. 1894), Hitler's Nazi Party deputy, had been a prisoner in the UK since his extraordinary flight there from Germany on 10 May 1941.
17. Robert Clifford Carrington (b. 1905), M.A, D.Phil. (Oxon), had been headmaster at St. Olave's School, Tower Bridge, SE1, since 1937. He was a classical scholar and author of *Caesar's Invasions of Britain* (1938).

Sunday, October 5. As I am on all day in the canteen I can't go to hear A.V. Alexander, who is speaking [at the Polytechnic] in Woolwich. Mother and Father went. The meeting was packed and A.V. was apparently in good form. Among other things he told the audience that there were more German and Italian submarines and U-Boats operating now than at any other time during the war. Mr. George Hicks, M.P., a popular speaker at any time in Woolwich, caused everyone at the meeting to think hard when he asked them 'Would you burn your home as the Russians have done if the Germans landed here?'[18] B. was telling me today about one of the Polish army who is billeted in his house in Scotland. This Pole and his brother were captured when the Germans over-ran Poland and they were thrown into a concentration camp. The brother died after he had had his hand cut off publicly as a punishment. B.'s Pole escaped into France and then to England. His father is in a concentration camp, his mother managed to get to friends in Switzerland, his sister has now married a German in Poland, and he is just longing for a chance to kill at least a dozen Germans before he dies. B. says that the people in his part of Scotland think a lot of the Poles and I expect the Poles think a good deal of the Scotch.

[Intervening entries omitted]

Wednesday, October 8. Two well-dressed business women were discussing the wireless in the train today. One said to the other 'I never listen to the news these days, it upsets me so'. The other added 'and the talks after the news, they are so horrible, they shouldn't be allowed'. I should have thought that the super-optimism of the BBC news would have suited these women perfectly. The news of the fighting as given on the radio and in the press is strangely reminiscent of the news that we were filled with when France was collapsing. Go to see *Lady Hamilton*. The acting was first-rate, particularly that of Laurence Olivier ....[19]

18. This rally was held under the auspices of the National Council of Labour, in association with the Woolwich Labour Party. Albert Victor Alexander (b.1885), Labour MP for the Hillsborough division of Sheffield, was First Lord of the Admiralty. (Ernest) George Hicks (b.1879) was Labour MP for East Woolwich. Alexander mentioned various issues, including the need to avoid work stoppages. 'If there was a matter for discussion let it be dealt with through the shop stewards, but let the work go on. Every sectional stoppage held up munitions and help for Russia. The work of the Navy was such that people should see to it that work went on without interruption, and [without] that nasty little habit of breaking off a quarter of an hour before time.' (*Kentish Independent*, 10 October 1941, p. 4.) 'The meeting passed a resolution acclaiming the unity of the British people against Nazi aggression; recording thanks to all carrying the burden of national service; conveying admiration of the Empire's contribution; saluting the Atlantic Charter; paying tribute to the people of Europe resisting the Nazis; rejoicing that the great Russian people are fighting as our Allies; paying homage to all who have died in the common cause; and pledging increasing efforts to provide equipment for all Allied Forces.' Kathleen's parents were strong Labour supporters, and her father read the *Daily Herald*, the principal journalistic voice of the labour movement.
19. This morale-boosting film (titled *That Hamilton Woman* in the United States) pitted Admiral Nelson against Napoleon. The former was portrayed in Churchillian style, the latter was likened to Hitler. The film pointed vividly to Britain's historic triumphs over autocratic warmongers. Churchill was said to be very fond of the movie and liked to screen it for guests. It also featured Vivien Leigh as Emma Hamilton.

[Intervening entries omitted]

Saturday, October 11. I go out today [in the van] with Mrs. W., a charming middle-aged woman, never ruffled by events, however disturbing. I remember very clearly last year how she never flickered an eyelid when we were serving right beside ack-ack guns belching forth at Jerries. The men like her too – she is so sensible. Have a very serious talk with F. at lunchtime today. He is French, born in England of French parents, but as he was sent to France when he was quite small in order to be educated there, he has a pronounced accent. He came back to England five years ago, his parents never leaving this country, and he is ferociously anti-Nazi and is glad to be in the RAF. He is not allowed to communicate with his relations in France as he is serving, but his parents get occasional cards to the effect that all is OK there.

Sunday, October 12. Have the afternoon off from the canteen in order to relieve Mother of the housework. I quite enjoy doing this but stop fairly often to do a bit of reading, or look in odd cupboards. Lord Beaverbrook makes an extraordinary broadcast this evening, raving like a maniac. I should imagine that Stalin was amused by him as Beaverbrook was impressed with his strong sense of humour. I expect Stalin thought he was a peculiar Britisher.[20]

Monday, October 13. In town today I saw about 20 men in odds and ends of clothes, skiing boots and hats, all wearing the little flag that the Norwegian pilots wear on their shoulders. I wish I could have stopped them and asked them to tell me of their adventures. I am certain that I should be thrilled. We hear the Voice [German intrusion into a BBC broadcast] for the first time.

Tuesday, October 14. The Voice is practically silenced. In the evening we listen intently but as the canteen wireless is always on at the maximum volume, no voice could get a word in edgeways against the din. According to the papers 'Paddy' Finucane [a famous fighter pilot] and some friends were celebrating outside Croydon Town Hall last night – he tried to dance on a parapet together with a colleague and succeeded in falling about ten feet. Both were taken to hospital. One can imagine the dance they will lead the nurses who have the job of looking after them.

[Intervening entries omitted]

---

20. Beaverbrook's ebullience and extravagant pro-Soviet rhetoric this weekend – he had just returned from talks in Moscow – are reported in Anne Chisholm and Michael Davie, *Beaverbrook: A Life* (London: Hutchinson, 1992), pp. 420–21. 'Perhaps this was the most important speech of Beaverbrook's life' is their verdict on the words Kathleen heard. At this time he was Minister of Supply. See also below, 23 October 1941.

Saturday, October 18. Today the gale continues. The men manning the balloons are very sarcastic when we visit them, at the expense of the girl balloonists. The gale made the balloons practically unmanageable during the night and I could not imagine girls, however tough, handling these things at night with no lights. When there are so many men in the services still doing office jobs, it seems strange to give the girls difficult jobs, like ballooning, when they could tackle simpler tasks.

Sunday, October 19. Our day at the canteen today was 9 a.m. to 10.30 p.m., which would satisfy even Mr. Bevin [Minister of Labour] I think. T. is in again today and he is very sarcastic about the number of WAAFs [Women's Auxiliary Air Force] at their aerodrome. He says there are hundreds of them doing odd jobs, many of them with practically nothing to do. All the men they have released are now idle with nothing to do. He says that the flyers wax quite indignant about them, particularly when these women swarm around them at meal times. T. also says that at their 'drome there is no place where a man can really be alone to read or to be quiet. There is no rest room. The crews' rooms are noisy and lacking in comfort, the wireless is permanently on in the mess, and the canteen is usually one fighting mass, so in order to read quietly they have to sit on their own bunks. It does seem scandalous that these men should have so little comfort when one thinks of all that they are doing.

[Intervening entries omitted]

Wednesday, October 22. One of the Lyons teashops in the Strand is now a 'help yourself' and it seems to have caught on quite nicely. Customers' time is saved and of course a number of girls will have been released for other jobs.[21] During the course of my lunch today, my neighbour, a Canadian girl, told me quite a lot about herself, which naturally passed the time quite pleasantly. She had been here six years and she is of the opinion that people here do not take the war seriously, saying to themselves 'England can't lose', and letting their lives follow the lines of this hope. Heard gun-fire during the evening, warnings too, but it had all finished by 10 o'clock.

Thursday, October 23. Lord Beaverbrook's speech in the Lords [today] is an 'eye-opener' and I am now almost convinced that we are doing a good deal to help Russia. Anyhow no sacrifice is too great and I am sure the mass of the people here producing these weapons of war would wish that they could go to

---

21. On Friday, 15 August, Kathleen had remarked, 'How difficult it is to get lunch these days. Apart from the queues, food usually gives out soon after 1 o'clock, so most people are trying to get out earlier.' The first Lyons Teashop to adopt this help-yourself service, on 8 September 1941, was at 108 Oxford Street, and the new practice spread rapidly, largely because of the impressive savings of labour (around 50%). The 'nippy' server virtually disappeared. Details are provided in a typescript entitled 'Lyons Teashops in Wartime', London Metropolitan Archives, ACC/3527/230.

Russia as soon as possible.[22] Mother gets a letter from Philip's headmaster asking for permission for him to go to an aerodrome with the ATC [Air Training Corps] as part of their training and also for permission for him to make a flight. What opportunities these boys have. I do envy them and on occasions like this I most wish I had been born a boy. Two men come into the canteen this evening. They have come up from Bath this afternoon with some stores and are on their way back tonight. Neither of them are very sure of the way, so I expect they will have a job to get back in time.

Friday, October 24. In the train on my way to work a girl was holding forth on the subject of her new job as secretary to Frances Day [a popular singer and comedienne]. She didn't have any fixed hours, just worked when she was told to. She also enlarged on the 'sportiness' of 'Buddy Flanagan' [a comedian and singer] who was always popping into her room. I am afraid that she didn't create the impression she was trying to. I go to the dentist today, and have got to pay several more visits. The practice has been taken over now by two alien dentists as the original pair are now in the RAF. Why is it that we are so scared of the dentist? J., our office boy, who is now a 'Snotty' in the MN [Merchant Navy], came in today.[23] He is quite annoyed because he has not met any German submarines or raiders yet, and hopes that they will get some excitement before long.

Saturday, October 25. We have a terrific day with the van today, serving about 600 men, consisting of RAF, Scotch Guards, RAOC [Royal Army Ordnance Corps], RASC [Royal Army Service Corps], London Scottish, REs [Royal Engineers], RAs [Royal Artillery] and Rifle Brigade as well as a large number of sailors in the docks and thereabout. It is quite interesting, too, listening to their various opinions and grumbles. So many of these men are bored these days, longing for some action and wishing they could take some part in the Russian war. I can see trouble ahead if they are not given a big job to do, because this feeling seems to be universal, and this 'browned off feeling' could quite easily lead to discontent, which might do us a lot of harm when our hours of trial came.

Sunday, October 26. We spent a lovely day today as we took Mother to see *49th Parallel*, despite her orthodox views on Sunday entertainment. I was a little doubtful about this film, as so much ballyhoo surrounded its production, but my fears were not justified as it moved me very considerably. The scenery

---

22. Beaverbrook, who had conferred with Stalin in Moscow, gave a speech that was designed primarily to demonstrate that robust efforts were being made by Britain to aid her Soviet ally (*Parliamentary Debates, House of Lords*, 5th series, vol. 120, cols. 396–408). He presented evidence to show that 'every conceivable thing has been done, every effort has been made, every purpose has been carried through in order to bring assistance and relief to the Russians in their battles' (col. 406). He even claimed that 'We simply gave what Stalin asked for in full measure' (col. 399).

23. A 'snotty' was a junior midshipman. His uniform jacket had three buttons on the cuff, allegedly, according to naval lore, to stop him from wiping his nose on it.

alone was terrifyingly beautiful and was a perfect background for working out the story. I don't think I liked any one particular sequence better than any other; they were all perfect in themselves. The acting is superb. Eric Portman's portrayal of the Nazi is almost too accurate [Portman was a noted Shakespearian actor]. I think that in a subtle way the makers of this film want to convey to audiences the character of the real Nazi we are fighting – the enthusiastic and sincere Nazi who will never realise that he is beaten (or maybe he hasn't had an opportunity yet to see that he may be beaten). The rest of the cast are no doubt very proud of their parts in this film. ... The audience was almost completely composed of service men, dozens of Canadian soldiers and airmen being present – mustn't they have felt flattered!! On our way through London, the comrades were dispersing from their great 'Aid for Russia' meeting in Trafalgar Square.[24]

[Intervening entry omitted]

Tuesday, October 28. Dorothy [a co-worker] went to see *49ᵗʰ Parallel* yesterday and she enjoyed it as much as I did. Most of the enjoyment of a film or play, I find, comes afterwards, when you are able to discuss and criticize it with friends who have also seen it and whose views you respect even if you disagree with them. E. (who is home on leave for a few days) went to see it too and not surprisingly was bored stiff – 'two hours of unadulterated propaganda' he called it, yet he is the most patriotic of individuals.[25] E. also told me about the women 'navvys' who are helping to build their aerodrome. There are, it seems, several hundred of these women and he says they are huge females with bulging biceps and triceps, every one of them as strong as a man. I should imagine the soldiers keep clear of them!

[Intervening entries omitted]

Friday, October 31. We do the stocktaking at the canteen in the evening. This job has to be done every month and involved a good deal of work, which almost inevitably falls onto me. T. arrives home on 11 days leave and helps me to do most of it. When we have finished the job T. and I argue for quite a while, finishing our arguments at around 12.30. He thinks most people in England are

---

24. At this labour demonstration, attended by some 10,000 people, 'A resolution was carried assuring the Soviet Union of the British people's determination that the greatest practicable help shall be given her with all possible speed'. (*The Times*, 27 October 1941, p.2.)
25. *49ᵗʰ Parallel*, a star-studded feature production (123 minutes long), was the first feature film of the war to be directly funded by the Ministry of Information. It tells a story of the survivors of a German submarine who fight their way across Canada (where most of the film was shot) in an effort to escape capture. The plot pits democratic values against Nazi brutalities, and serves to reveal Britain's and her Dominions' reasons for being at war. The film was deemed a major success. For further details see Anthony Aldgate and Jeffery Richards, *Britain Can Take It: The British Cinema in the Second World War* (Edinburgh: Edinburgh University Press, 2ⁿᵈ edn., 1994), chap. 2, and James Chapman, *The British at War: Cinema, State and Propaganda 1939–1945* (London: I.B. Tauris, 1998), pp. 70–74.

complacent and this is the only point on which we agree at all as T. is the genuine 'Tory' and when we get onto the subject of Labour and the war the fur flies with a vengeance. Joyce thinks his outlook is the result of a spoilt and indulgent upbringing, and I think that certainly had a lot to do with it, realising nevertheless that he is giving everything he can to his country and therefore has far more right to criticise the country's war effort than I have (although I didn't tell him this).

Saturday, November 1. We spent a very busy morning on the van and in the afternoon we have to get back fairly early in order to pack vans ready for tonight's manoeuvres – the vans are to be attached to the invaders and the defenders [in this military exercise]. The Guards are rather contemptuous when they mention tonight's 'do' to us. One summed up their feelings with 'fancy getting us up at —— hours to play soldiers with the Home Guard' and we knew quite well that if it was Germans they were to fight they wouldn't worry at all about any hardships they might be called on to suffer, as indeed they proved in France. Spent a very pleasant evening at the cinema. We saw *Billy the Kid* and I was really able to forget the war and even forgot that such a person as Adolf existed. We hear fairly heavy gunfire over a period of two hours from 9.30 and there are several planes about, but I was fast asleep before the 'all-clear' went.

Sunday, November 2. We brought down six planes last night according to the news this morning. The raids must have been on a heavier scale than recently. Joyce and I are on all day at the canteen. We are terribly busy, mainly because convoys make it their business to pass our way now, and the canteen is a regular stopping-place for route-marchers. I am much amused during the afternoon by a Scotch lad by name, Philip – he is very young and possessed of a droll sense of humour. He is very hurt because, as he says, old ladies down here say when he passes them 'Isn't it a crime to put such young boys in the RAF'. Personally I am inclined to agree with the old ladies, as these lads are really not fit to be sent into the wicked world on their own. They should still be at school.

Monday, November 3. On Monday evenings the BBC now send out a programme for all women in uniform under the title 'Calling all Women' which includes a puzzle corner and an advice column presided over by [the novelist] Pamela Frankau. Carol Gibbons 'sings' requests from women in the forces and to conclude this brilliant programme a famous actor or film-star is interviewed by one of the golden-voiced women announcers. No wonder sarcastic critics of the BBC attack the programmes when trash of this type is heard. I think this sort of thing is an insult to the intelligence, but I suppose some listeners must like it or they would not broadcast it week after week.

Tuesday, November 4. …P. is in the canteen this evening and he is very ill, but as he is in a billet and a very uncomfortable one at that, he prefers to lay in an arm-chair by the fire here rather than go home. Some people who have the job of billeting servicemen seem to be lining their pockets very considerably, and

I could name quite a few of them. 'R——' failed today to pass his medical for air crew; he is apparently colour-blind. However, he is to take a commission in the RAF just the same.

[Intervening entries omitted]

Friday, November 7. Go to the cinema in the evening to see *The Great Lie*, a dramatic tale relieved by some first-class acting. I was much interested in a Ministry of Information film about the WRNS [Women's Royal Naval Service], which I think will tempt many girls into this service. However, I understand from friends who have tried that the only vacancies in this service are for cooks, which I think is a pity because it is the only women's service with anything like a good name.

Saturday, November 8. The news is very ghastly today – 37 bombers lost last night in extensive raids over Germany, and today we lost 15 fighters. It is an odd thing too – you can feel the depression everywhere and read it on the faces all around. We have a very busy day and I dash up to town to see *Jupiter Laughs* [by A.J. Cronin]. I enjoyed the play quite a lot. The dialogue is extremely witty, but I don't think it will rank with the greatest. I found Dr. Mary Murray, Dr. Cronin's religious heroine, rather a prig. James Mason takes all his chances and makes the most of this opportunity to establish himself as a recognised leading man in the West End.

Sunday, November 9. We are on all day at the canteen. During a slack period around teatime, Ian gives me a lesson at billiards. I am not a good pupil, but he is far too polite to tell me so. We are all put in good spirits when the news of the action in the Mediterranean comes through – four of our ships sunk two Italian convoys. What on earth were the Italian escort ships doing all this time? Did they run away or did they imagine that the whole of the battle fleet was after them?

Monday, November 10. Today is Lord Mayor's Show Day.[26] Although I have lived in London all my life, I have never seen a show, but as I was going to lunch today the procession came along the Strand. I don't know why it is, but the Navy inevitably steal processions. There is something stimulating about the way in which they march. They seem to be a service apart. I was glad that the AFS [Auxiliary Fire Service] led the line, with their band in front. They surely deserved the premier place in a show of this kind; but for their work, there would have been no London to 'process' through. The Dominion navies, armies and air forces looked fighting fit, particularly the Indian troops who got

26. 'The Lord Mayor's luncheon today retained a good deal of its former pageantry', according the *Evening Standard* (10 November 1941, p.2). 'The majority of the Cabinet were there', including the Prime Minister. 'The tables were decorated with gold urns and vases of chrysanthemums.' It was apparently assumed that ordinary citizens would approve of these efforts to preserve colourful traditions in times of peril and sacrifice.

a special cheer. There were crowds of Dominion and Allied servicemen lining the Strand. I was near a group of Poles who cheered and shouted words of encouragement to their men. I think Britain got a first place, however, for bearing and smartness when the final batch of troops marched past. They were men from the Brigade of Guards, picked men I should say, so tall that they towered over all the others in the procession. *H.M. Cossack* has been sunk. This destroyer has become almost a household word, and I think most people now could tell you a certain amount of its history.

Tuesday, November 11. Joyce told me a tale today which I thought rather amusing. Last Saturday P. (Joyce's friend) was driving home from Woolwich with her parents when they were stopped by Home Guards, armed with Bren guns, machine guns, etc., challenged, and her father asked for his Identity Card. He produced it and then for some reason (probably because she can't help being stupid) P's mother sang out from the back of the car 'I haven't got mine though', to which the Home Guard replied 'Oh well, that doesn't matter, I was only told to look at the driver's card, nothing was said about the passengers', this despite the fact that in actual fighting P's father would prob-ably have a carload of fifth columnists. During the evening at the canteen [the manager] 'R—' interrupts for a short service conducted by the camp chap-lain, and as soon as the fellows got to know of this, they found appointments elsewhere. However, a certain number were trapped and some were suffi-ciently loyal to us to stay. Personally I think that the men should willingly stay to a service – they are glad enough of the other facilities of the canteen. Whilst the final prayer was being read, L. and I. burst in rather noisily, but they caused themselves most embarrassment when they realised what they had done.

[Intervening entries omitted]

Saturday, November 15. Out all day on the van. We had to serve some Cana-dians up in London on a job. They have plenty of money to spend and they are the worst paid of the Dominion troops. I can understand why our men are so bitter about this inequality. I do think it causes a great deal of unpleasantness when these troops, most of them doing exactly the same as our own men, are paid on a much higher scale.

Sunday, November 16. Joyce and I are on all day and I don't think we have ever been busier. Towards 8.30 there began a general exodus. Sergeant G. and several others, however, had their line of retreat cut off by the rector himself and they were obliged to stay. The service was quite informal and I don't think it can do any of us any harm. Tonight's clergyman was a Church of England converted atheist. Joyce whispered to me that it was unusual for a Church of England clergyman to admit that he had been converted, although in most of the more peculiar religions it has become part of the weekly sermon for the minister to reveal how he first saw the light. 'R—', who usually says a few words at the beginning of the service, is really very good and I must admit he has just the right touch. He knows when to joke with the men and when to preach and they seem to like him. I realise now how clever the YMCA authorities are, because the several men I have met who run organisations like ours are of a very good type and certainly know their job.

Monday, November 17. I went into Mrs. Steptoe's sweetshop on my way to the station this morning. She is very old and much of this war has rocked her little shop, but she is determined not to leave London. I have gone into her little shop over a period of 15 years and consequently know her well, but she still thinks of me as a schoolgirl. This morning two very tough bus drivers came into the shop and one of them said to her 'What was the name of the little boy in *David Copperfield* who ran away from home?' I was so surprised at this question coming from such a tough man, but not so Mrs. Steptoe. She proceeded to quote long passages from the book and told me afterwards that she knows several of Dickens' books more or less by heart. I suppose she was made to read them when she was a girl. Anyway her knowledge made me feel quite ashamed, and I said to myself, I must read these books again soon so that I can answer questions from bus drivers. Incidentally, Mrs. Steptoe told me she has children in her shop aged about ten who can neither read nor write. Some can't read the time from a clock face. Of course the children she mentioned haven't been to school for two years. Fortunately, for the good of the nation, they are now compelled to attend for at least a few hours a day.

Tuesday, November 18. Mrs. S. told me today about a friend of mine named I. A few months ago she was married to another friend of mine, one R. who works in the [Woolwich] Arsenal. Like everybody else she registered early in August and in due course was called up for an interview. The official at the Labour Exchange told her that she must work, whereupon R. sallied off to the Exchange and told them that his wife was not going to work as he didn't want her to. The Exchange officials, apparently numbed by this outburst, agreed that I. should stay at home. I do not wonder that women will not go forward for war work when they know of instances like this one. I. is a lazy girl and never liked work. She now wanders around doing odds and ends of shopping and has a good time generally. I know of a good many cases of this type and I am sure there are hundreds of girls who are doing as she is doing.

Wednesday, November 19. The weather today is real November weather and as evening draws on it is really thick. 'R—' has a terrible job finding our house. He knocks on every door but ours. What a great responsibility it is to drive any sort of vehicle in the blackout hours. It is almost impossible to see pedestrians even when you are on top of them and it is almost as difficult to see cyclists. I realise very clearly now, having done a good deal of blackout travelling, how the casualty lists rise so rapidly. In fact I am astonished that they are not a good deal heavier.

[Intervening entries omitted]

Saturday, November 22. We are fairly busy today. I went out with P., one of the most interesting girls I have met since the war began. She does a whole-time job of driving a car for a big local firm. Four nights she does ambulance-driving and two nights and a day she drives for the YMCA. She drove all through the Blitz last year and had some ghastly experiences with her ambulance – one when a child was born en route for hospital was I think the most terrifying. P., however, is never ruffled and is amazingly strong, much stronger than most men. Just as I was going to bed the news came through that the New Zealanders have captured Fort Capuzzo [in Libya].

Sunday, November 23. Today I finished reading *Talking about Cricket* [1941] by William Pollock, one of the best writers on the subject. This is a delightful book, written in his very amusing style and containing one or two fresh stories .... I think I shall buy this book for DKH [Mrs. Hendry] in Scotland. It will take her back to the marvellous days we spent at the Oval during the six or seven summers preceding the war.

[Intervening entry omitted]

Tuesday, November 25. This morning I met S. A week or so back I told her of the difficulty I was experiencing in my endeavours to join the Home Guard for instruction in shooting, and although she expressed contempt at the time, I now find that she has joined the Home Guard section of the Ministry of Information. How people change. She also told me of an urgent telegram which took two days to pass from one floor to another at the Ministry.

Wednesday, November 26. L. tonight told me that he definitely supported the conscription of single women and opposed the calling-up of serving-men's wives. I think this is a selfish attitude, but I realise that most married men share it. They say that other women can go, but their own wife must be at home, looking after it, in order that it may be comfortable when they go home on leave. I don't think L. had thought of the fact that many single girls have ties quite as strong at home as those of a wife.

Thursday, November 27. The press has almost forgotten the debut of Wilfred Pickles last night, this despite the fact that various writers were continually urging the BBC to engage announcers with 'accents' [Pickles was from Yorkshire]. Personally I thought he was less good than our usual announcers, but probably he will improve with practice. I expect Yorkshiremen and women who expected to hear a man with their broad dialect were sadly disappointed, as he has very little accent. Why people get so excited on the subject of announcers and their accents, I can't understand, because I have never heard anybody (no matter which part of Britain they have come from) say that they couldn't understand Alvar Liddell [an established BBC announcer] or any of his colleagues and surely if any of them possessed a rich dialect it would definitely limit the number of listeners who could understand the news and this is the one programme that nearly everyone in Britain and many people in other parts of the world listen to.

Friday, November 28. Apparently Mr. Churchill is to speak next week on the subject of man and woman power and the use thereof. I hope that before the Government begin tearing women from their present jobs they will first take all the men who are avoiding calling-up on one pretext or another; and then the thousands of idle young married women without children who apparently can waste their time legitimately as long as they are available when the husband comes home on leave.[27]

Saturday, November 29. I go out all day on the van with a man on sick leave from the AFS. He broke his thigh over a year ago when a local fire station was destroyed by a land-mine and, without realising what he had done, walked across the road with this wound thereby complicating it considerably. Although he has been in hospital for 12 months he only received his pay for 13 weeks and, but for the generosity of an American benevolent society which has been paying him his wages, from that time he would have been without means – and this for a man who gave everything for his country. He lost his home in the same incident and much of that was stolen whilst he was in hospital. What I think is so unjust is that an ordinary fireman gets his pay in full for (I believe) six months even for a minor illness, yet this man who was so terribly injured in the service of his country has to depend on foreign charity in order to live.

Sunday, November 30. Joyce and I are on all day at the canteen and we take more in our 12 hours than any others have taken this year. Nowadays we have hundreds of Scotch soldiers and airmen stationed nearby and I am amazed at the numerous accents to be found amongst them and all completely different. I can now distinguish a Glasgow accent I think, but the others completely baffle me. In fact many of them might be foreigners from central Europe, so unintelligible are they. When we got home the news had just come through of the recapture of Rostov by the Russians.

[Intervening entries omitted]

Wednesday, December 3. The full report of the debate [on the conscription of women for the ATS] makes interesting reading, particularly the speech by Miss Eleanor Rathbone who defended the morals of the ATS and also said that she had little patience with the 'over-placid' parent or the 'over-cautious' girl, and added that girls have to take their chance in the same way that boys have to. Personally I think this lady was expressing the opinion of the Government

27. Churchill's speech in the Commons on 2 December concerning manpower and womanpower is printed in his *Speeches*, VI, pp. 6514–23. Action was promised to address Kathleen's first hope, none to address her second hope. Men (usually in the forces) with young wives were adamantly hostile to the conscription of their women, and the Government was disinclined to ignore their views and risk weakening their morale.

when she voiced these views and I think they are pretty revolting. I was under the impression that we were fighting for Christian principles and an upright way of living – and then we hear statements of this sort. Does Miss Rathbone imagine her words will make any impression in the minds of those who know the truth about much of the immorality in the women's services.[28] During my lunch hour today I saw [the actor] John Gielgud in Kingsway, which brought back to my mind the fact that the serious people of the stage lost a great opportunity this summer, when they failed to put any serious plays on. Not until the days became very short did any straight plays appear in the West End and I do regret that they wasted the long summer days.

Thursday, December 4. Lady Astor's speech in the Commons yesterday put the case of the unmarried women extraordinarily well. Now that I have lost faith in the integrity of everybody in positions of authority I wondered 'Was she bribed by the Spinsters' League to make this speech?'[29] We have a frantic evening at the canteen – don't have time to stand still once during the five hours we are open.

Friday, December 5. We hear today of Fred's death and we are all very upset about it. He was one of my best school friends and I still remember how patient he was with me – how he would bowl to me for hours in the field just near our home and how I kept watch for him when we all went 'scrumping' in an orchard nearby. I was shaking with fear all the time – Fred never caring how near the farmer or his dogs were. Well, Fred became a bomber pilot and had been screened after his 30 or so operational flights, and he was killed whilst testing a new American bomber. I have to go to the dentist again, not a visit I enjoy.

Saturday, December 6. I am out all day on the van with the AFS man again. Many of the men are unsettled these days, not knowing quite what is to happen to them, yet all wanting to do something active. At one of the gun-sites I was talking with a Sergeant about the girls on the guns. He was rather superior about them altogether and took the attitude of many other soldiers. He

28. Stories of sexual promiscuity in the ATS abounded and deterred some young women from signing up. Eleanor Rathbone, MP for the Combined English Universities, thought that much of this talk was 'wholly untrue' or 'grossly exaggerated' – and downplayed its importance and the grounds for concern. 'Not that I have myself much patience either with the over-cautious girl or the over-cautious parent. Girls, like boys, have to take risks in these days, and if the Army wants a bigger and better ATS, the Army has to get it.' (*Commons Debates*, 5th series, vol. 376, col. 1089, debate of 2 December 1941.)
29. Viscountess Astor argued that the proposed policies on the conscription of women were biased in favour of younger married women. 'Very often the married woman lives with her "in-laws," and has enough to keep herself very well without working, unless she wants to work. But the Government intend to conscript an unmarried woman who may be the sole support of a father or mother; she will have to go into the Army. It is very unfair in comparison with married women … I believe it would be much fairer if there were conscription of girls and women from the time they left school until 30 years of age, with generous exemptions.' (*Commons Debates*, 5th series, vol. 376, cols. 1205–06.)

wondered how they would face up to months of continuous action like the men endured last winter, when many of them were on the guns for weeks on end, sleeping near them if they got the chance, often not getting any sleep for days. Maybe we will be surprised, but the Sergeant agreed that the Germans may wait until the girls are manning the guns in large numbers and then launch a terrible blitz on them.

Sunday, December 7. What a day. The morning papers report huge concentrations of Japanese troops in Indo-China and by the time the evening comes the Japs have bombed several of the American bases in the Pacific. I suppose this really does mean America [is] in the war. Mother is convinced that the war will be decided in the East. I wonder.

Monday, December 8. Mother's birthday [her 51st] – certainly one she will remember for a long time. The news at breakfast-time caused me to forget to wish her 'Many happy returns' so I had to send her a telegram instead. The telegram took under half an hour to reach her, which I thought extraordinarily good in these times. The news today is really serious and the Americans can do nothing but declare war on Japan. The raids on Pearl Harbour were apparently terribly bad and President Roosevelt admits that the casualties were great. It seems absurd that these places – Hawaii, Waikiki and Honolulu – associated in many of our minds with American films of singing girls and white-clad USA marines, should be the scene of this most terrible of wars. We hear the speech of President Roosevelt to Congress and a fine speech it is too, such a contrast to that of Mr. Churchill later in the evening, which is stilted and disjointed. But I suppose he is tired after his strenuous weekend [at Chequers].

[Intervening entry omitted]

Wednesday, December 10. I was in the middle of the road at lunchtime today when I saw the newspaperman writing on his board the terrible news *Prince of Wales* and *Repulse* sunk [in the South China Sea], and so surprised was I that a car nearly ran me down. The driver was furious until he saw what had caused my lapse. What a ghastly difference this will make to our power in the East and it seems that it will be some time before the Americans can do anything at sea there. The Chinese have launched an offensive against Canton in order to relieve pressure on our forces in Hong Kong, but we are assured that the Japanese will have to fight for a long time before they can take the island. Nevertheless there will be many thousands of homes in this country tonight whose occupants will get little sleep. We can only hope that some of the crews will be saved.

Thursday, December 11. The lunchtime news placards say that over 2,000 men have been saved and landed at Singapore. Admiral [Sir Tom] Phillips and Captain Leach are still among the missing. An extraordinary thing has happened – General [Sir Alan] Cunningham has been sacked in the middle of the battle in Libya! Officially, he is over-strained!

Friday, December 12. This evening we saw *The Man Who Came to Dinner* [by George S. Kaufman] at the Savoy and for three hours the horrible reality of the war seemed as far away as Mars. The play is extremely witty and quite vulgar. The audience was particularly intelligent and followed the dialogue very quickly. The hit of the show in my eyes was Edward Cooper's brilliant impersonation of Noel Coward, which was both kind and cruel.

Saturday, December 13. The Japanese admit that 30 planes were shot down in the raid on Pearl Harbour, so apparently the USA defences did go into action. Mother and Father went to Colchester to spend the weekend with my Grandmother, who is losing her sight. She certainly has had her fair share of trouble. She lost one of her sons in the last war and since the beginning of this one my Grandfather has died and her youngest son, aged 27, was killed in France. No wonder her health is failing.

Sunday, December 14. We spend a busy day at the canteen and at 10.30 in the evening have to spend over half an hour waiting for a tram home after spending 13 hours on our feet. We were pushed off the first tram by men and women who had spent the evening in public houses. We were mad. One of the men gave Joyce some grim details of murders etc. which he photographed in his peacetime job of news-photographer. The vicar this evening was very annoyed because none of us joined in his unaccompanied hymn-singing.

[Intervening entries omitted]

Wednesday, December 17. Despite the miserable news [from the Far East] we spent the evening fastening up Christmas presents in order to get them off tomorrow. Shopping has been a real task this year as the shops have been absolutely crammed with pushing individuals, all intent on spending their money on anything available in the shops. I have managed to get two or three decent presents. The few others that I have had to buy, I have just picked up wherever I have happened to be. We had some carol-singers round this evening. They were quite good too.

Thursday, December 18. We are at the canteen all the evening. The Duke of Kent [younger brother of the King] was at the camp today and the men are full of it.[30] He spoke to quite a few of my friends and they all admitted that, whilst he smelled rather strongly of scent, he appeared to know quite a lot about the actual work in the workshops. Mrs. O., who was up at the camp with the van this afternoon, spoke to the Duke's chauffeur. He said that he rarely drove the car himself – merely kept the engine warm for the Duke, who was furious if it

---

30. The camp that Kathleen was referring to was the RAF Station on nearby Kidbrooke Park Road. It encompassed land on both sides of the road, north and south of the Kidbrooke train station, where there had been as yet no residential development. The camp was used by the RAF as a depot and maintenance unit and a balloon centre.

got cold. 'R—', Joyce and I stopped rather late talking to Jimmy about the variety of accents to be found in the Scots. He maintained that there were more accents in England than in Scotland, but as far as I can make out every Scotchman possesses a different accent.

[Intervening entry omitted]

Saturday, December 20. P. and I are out together today, and we did some new khaki sites out in the country. At the first one we had a dud shilling passed on to us. The officers at this site were exceedingly mad about this and insisted on refunding the shilling. I do think this sort of trick is quite the meanest way of getting things for nothing.

Sunday, December 21. Apparently Japanese submarines are out in the Pacific off America and are sinking American ships. This will mean that the USA will withdraw more of their ships from the Atlantic patrol, I suppose. It is announced today that the King is to broadcast on Christmas Day. I wish he would not speak. I always spend a most uncomfortable quarter of an hour whilst he is on the air, wishing the whole time that I could do it for him [George VI stammered]. The service this evening was from St. Martin's in the Fields, although the announcer called it 'a well-known London church', coming from the crypt. The new vicar seems to have followed perfectly in the steps of his famous predecessors. The BBC today broadcast a concert in honour of Stalin's birthday. If anybody had said that this would happen, even a year ago, we should have said that it was insane, and I can easily imagine the wrath with which the Archbishop of Canterbury would have denounced it.

Monday, December 22. Philip comes home from Torquay. He has travelled by coach in order to avoid the crowded trains. I have been trying to buy *Berlin Diary* [by William L. Shirer, 1941] for Joyce, and it is really an impossible task because the book has been sold out several times and the book-sellers do not know if it is being printed again before Christmas. I didn't know that it was in such demand.

Tuesday, December 23. The headlines this morning say 'Mr. Churchill in USA'. Certainly this visit has been kept secret very well. How the Germans must rave when they hear of it, because whilst Hitler can go across the frontiers of the countries surrounding Germany, I can't think that he would dare to travel to, say, Japan, his ally in the Far East, yet Churchill goes everywhere he pleases and exactly when he pleases, despite Nazi U-Boats and planes.

Wednesday, December 24. Finish my Christmas shopping with Philip. The shops by now are almost empty. We are very busy in the evening preparing for tomorrow's 'do' in the canteen. I made 70 trifles and Mother made seven dozen cakes. She became rather fed up as the evening progressed. There seemed to be trifles, trifles, everywhere and nowhere to sit down. President

Roosevelt and Mr. Churchill broadcast short messages from the White House party this evening. The speeches were short and not very well received on our wireless.

Thursday, December 25. 'R—' announced his engagement to I. today. I spent the morning visiting old relations. Then we sat down to a grand peacetime dinner – goose (rather tough), chicken (wonderfully tender), Brussels sprouts, potatoes, etc., followed by Christmas pudding and mince-pies. I felt a stone heavier after this dinner. As transport stopped early we had to walk to the canteen with some of our stuff. Some went earlier in the day by van. Fortunately Pop[31] and Philip wanted a stroll so carried what was left for us. We had a grand evening and gave the men a wonderful time. We had sponges, trifles, cakes, mince-pies, sausage rolls and various drinks, which made a fine spread for the men. This was all paid for by subscriptions by the voluntary workers and friends, as was the entertainment we provided for the men of a nearby gun-site. The several hundred men there were confined to the site so 'R—', aided by six or seven of the YM ladies, went up there and gave them a buffet supper and kept things going generally. In all we were very pleased with our day's work. I think we gave many hundreds of men a little enjoyment, because as well as the activities mentioned, seven vans went out morning and afternoon with free goodies.

The news that the resistance in Hong Kong had come to an end did not register much, as everybody was bent on enjoying themselves, but I thought myself that if our Navy out there was as powerful now as it was months ago, we should have been able to sustain Hong Kong as we did Tobruk [in Libya].

Friday, December 26. I am off duty at lunchtime so go with the family to the cinema. The programme was not much good. I do think cinema managers show up very badly at holiday times. They never have good films, because they know that any old tripe will get an audience when people have nothing else to do. Mr. Churchill's speech to the Senate and House of Representatives in Washington was broadcast tonight and was an extraordinarily fine speech [*Speeches*, VI, pp. 6536–41] – one of the best he has made recently – and did he get a fine reception! Manila has been declared an open city and I suppose troops etc. have been moved out – a lot of good that will do the Americans. I expect the Russians are much amused by the 'scorched earth' methods of the democratic powers – not much like theirs!!

Saturday, December 27. We spend a very busy day on the van today. The men are still recovering from their holiday jollifications. Most of them seem to have had a good time and those whose Christmas was made pleasant by the YM staff are really grateful, which is all that those who worked so hard ask. ...

---

31. In 2005 Kathleen was surprised by her use of the name 'Pop' for her father, and remembered that 'We almost always called my father 'Father' or 'Dad', but early in the war a new friend – later a very good friend – started calling him 'Pop' and it somehow spread. After the war years it petered out.'

[Intervening entries omitted]

Wednesday, December 31. Details of yet another Commando raid are given out today – this one took place in Libya. The Commandos stormed Gen. [Erwin] Rommel's headquarters with the object of taking him alive. During this action Col. Geoffrey Keyes, son of Admiral Sir Roger Keyes, was killed. These acts of great courage and daring seem to be everyday occurrences now. Scarcely a day passes without news of a Commando raid, a great deed by the Navy or Merchant Navy, or the usual bravery by members of the RAF. We did the stock-taking at the canteen this evening. As we came home the population seemed to be drawn as if by a magnet to all the local public houses, celebrating Hogmanay I suppose. Certainly 1941 is a year I am not sorry to see pass.

1942

During the first nine weeks of 1942, London and her own daily activities there receded in prominence in Kathleen's diary. Some of her entries are brief. Her descriptive passages are meagre and her observations of incidents in the capital and reports of London-centred conversations and occurrences are less frequent and less noteworthy. She wrote mostly of news she had heard from other parts of the country; of films, journalism, and radio programmes and her opinions of them; of political wrangling and debates in parliament; of news from the United States; of gossip, rumours, gnawing physical ailments, and the cold weather; of people she liked or disliked; and, in particular, of military events around the world, mainly in the Pacific, Russia, and North Africa. This was a time when the war was not going well for the Allies, especially against Japan, and Kathleen's diary, which was highly sensitive to news from the various battlefronts (most of it censored, of course), recorded some of her concerns, questions, criticism, and praise. The fall of Singapore in mid-February was a particularly bleak moment for British morale. 'The one bright feature of the news these days is the Red Army', Kathleen declared on 2 March.

Perhaps the most significant facts she notes about her own life came from late January. 'Went this morning to the Labour Exchange to volunteer for the WRNS', she wrote on January 26. 'My employers told us last week that we could volunteer if we wanted to. The interviewer was extremely helpful and was not the hostile dictator I imagined she would be.' Kathleen did not have to wait long to hear the verdict. 'Had no luck with the WRNS yesterday', she reported on January 30. 'They are not taking any more volunteers with my qualifications, and I did not get a chance to tell them that I have worked for a shipping firm for five years, and would, I think, find the work slightly similar.' In the summer of 2004, Kathleen recalled that an injury to her left arm, sustained playing tennis at school – she was unable fully to straighten her arm – was, she thought, a reason that she was rejected by the WRNS.

London and events and activities there return to greater prominence in the diary from early March.

Thursday, March 5. ... Joyce was on duty at the canteen this evening; D. deputised for me. Just recently we have opened a room upstairs as a study room, where the RAF can read and study in comfort and peace – a very pleasant room with sofas, etc. Unfortunately some of the WAAF have abused this privilege and have used this room during the past week as a romantic rendezvous. 'B—' [the new – and disliked – man in charge of the canteen] and Joyce made an entry during the evening and discovered several WAAF enfolded in the manly arms of sundry soldiers. 'B—' promptly ordered these 'naughty' girls out and has put up a notice to the effect that the privileges of the YM have been abused and they will please reform, thank you. Personally, from my experience of the WAAF who use our canteen, I find 90% of them lacking in ordinary morals. They use the YM merely as a place for picking up uniformed members of the opposite sex. I suppose in peacetime they used the street corner. The WAAF Corporal who is in charge of a large billet nearby is an ex-welfare worker from the North. She has now taken to drinking and is almost always a trifle 'merry'.[32]

[Intervening entry omitted]

Saturday, March 7. 'R—' [the previous manager of the canteen] is on leave. He came down to the canteen today and everybody begged him to do something about removing 'B—'. When 'R—' left [around January 10] he knew that 'B—' would turn out to be completely incompetent, but he was unable to do anything about it. I think however that he is going to try to do something now. 'R—' is now a tank driver and is enjoying himself immensely. I drove a two-ton van for the first time today and I wasn't nervous in traffic, which surprised me. The ATS on one of the gun-sites are now much happier. They are getting good food and conditions generally have improved, mainly due to agitation on our behalf with the officers, I know.

Sunday, March 8. The fine weather continues today. I think this is the best day we have had for six months. We were quite busy at the canteen today, although the WAAF continue to give trouble. It is quite pleasant to listen to the wireless again. Ours has gone to be repaired and we have been without it for over a fortnight and it is rather like I imagine it would be on a desert island. Mother misses it dreadfully during the day too – she is a great *Colonel Britton* fan.[33] Joyce and I were furious, [for] after standing on our feet for 14 hours at the canteen, we

---

32. 'What a shock to read something one had written 60 years ago', Kathleen remarked in a letter of 17 July 2005, after re-reading much of her diary. 'I didn't recognize the ghastly, judgmental writing in these pages.' With regard to some of her wartime comments on the behaviour of women, she recalled that 'I grew up in Well Hall (one of the few districts in the country with no pub). Life was entirely family/church/school orientated. We were not much exposed to the seedier side of life, so it came as a great shock to see, for instance, girls the worse for drink, etc.'
33. Douglas Ritchie (b.1905), the Deputy Editor for European news at the BBC, broadcast anonymously on the English-language European service (many listeners were in German-occupied countries) in the role of 'Colonel Britton'.

had to walk home, a decent step which took us nearly an hour, because a crowd of drunken men and women crowded us off the last tram home.

[Intervening entry omitted]

Tuesday, March 10. Mr. Eden's speech in the Commons today should be broadcast the world over and read by every officer to every soldier in the Allied armies. I should repeat it so often that people would have to take notice of it.[34] I listened to the news at the canteen this evening and made a point of watching the reaction of those listening. Very few of the 50 odd men and women in the room listened. I didn't see one girl seriously attending and during part of the speech they all giggled violently. The attitude of the men (some of whom I know came through Dunkirk) seemed to be 'Oh Hong Kong is a long way off' and one or two usually sensible men said to me 'Don't believe that, it is only wireless talk'. I couldn't find words to answer them. A friend of Joyce's left his wife and baby in Singapore when he was moved some months ago (he is in the regular Air Force and has been in Singapore with his wife for four or five years). Last week he heard that his wife was still on the island and now he has received news that she was last seen embarking with her baby onto a smallish ship which left Singapore just before the Japs landed there and has been given up as lost. I expect when he heard Eden's speech he was almost glad that she did at least leave the island, and maybe felt that it was better that way.

[Intervening entry omitted]

Thursday, March 12. Mr. [Herbert] Morrison [Home Secretary and Minister of Home Security] spoke on the radio last night about his new measures to clean up the black market. I am certain that some very important people are behind this traffic, but I can't imagine that they will ever be brought to justice. Our canteen was burgled last night. When I arrived there this evening, everybody was quite excited about the crime. ... Actually, whoever was responsible is really a downright crook. I think it is a wretched trick to rob a place like the YMCA, because it is there for the convenience of the troops and all the workers are doing jobs there out of the goodness of their hearts, [and] certainly not for anything they may get out of it. I find myself looking suspiciously at everyone this evening, quite unjustifiably I know.

Friday, March 13. D.P. has been missing for five days – he is in Bomber Command – but Mrs. P. told me this morning that he has turned up, complete with a week's growth of beard and looking extremely grubby. We went to see *Blithe Spirit* [by Noel Coward] this evening. I thought it one of the wittiest

---

34. Anthony Eden, the Foreign Secretary, spoke about Japanese atrocities at Hong Kong, comparing them to those in Nanking in 1937. 'The House will agree with me that we can best express our sympathy with the victims of these appalling outrages by redoubling our efforts to ensure his utter and overwhelming defeat.' (*Commons Debates*, 5th series, vol. 378, col. 932.)

plays I have ever seen. I should love to see it with a confirmed spiritualist – that would certainly be an experience![35]

Saturday, March 14. I drove quite a bit when we were out on the van this morning. Had lunch with P. – he is home on 48 hours [leave] and is in the middle of his Commando training. It seems that most of our armoured divisions are receiving a certain amount of severe training. He also said that there is a company of Guards training with them. They occasionally have something of a brawl, usually started by a Guardsman talking of what they did at Dunkirk to which all good Riflemen reply 'Calais to you' and I gather that this is when the fun begins. Two of the men in P.'s company have served long stretches at Dartmoor [prison]. He claims that they can remove a plate of dinner from the table without a soul being aware of the fact. They usually find out, however, when somebody is a dinner short.

[Intervening entry omitted]

Monday, March 16. The air raid warning was sounded around 11 o'clock this morning and it lasted for about half an hour. I was quite surprised to hear it in daytime, but noticed as I walked along the Strand that very few carried gas masks. I must admit that I did not have mine with me.

[Intervening entries omitted]

Friday, March 20. … We heard today that Frank is missing, believed killed in Malaya, together with several dozen local boys who were out there in one of the local regiments. It is very tragic because Frank was the type we need in the new world – socially minded.

Saturday, March 21. London's Warship Week starts today with sundry processions etc. We went today to the Scotch Guards who were preparing for the procession through the City and Westminster on Monday, getting uniforms, tanks, etc. polished up – not that they needed it.[36] The *American Commentary*

---

35. *Blithe Spirit* features a ghost – and deals humorously with death at a time when death for Londoners was felt to be an everyday possibility. The play opened on 2 July 1941 and 'ran in the West End for nearly 2,000 performances from 1941 to the end of the war'. Coward 'seems to have captured the spirit of Londoners (or London theatregoers) in his song of that year: "London pride has been handed down to us, London pride is a flower that's free".': Stephen Inwood, *A History of London* (London: Papermac, 2000), p. 813.
36. 'If Nelson could have been looking north instead of down Whitehall today,' declared the *Evening Standard*, 21 March 1942, p. 8, 'he would have witnessed a scene such as, in his own time, would have gladdened him greatly. He would have seen London men and women paying money to buy ships for the British Navy to sweep the King's enemies from the seas. They had flocked to Trafalgar Square bringing their savings – London's target for the week is £125,000,000 – and they besieged the sales vans for National Savings Certificates, Stamps and Defence Bonds.' (The target was reached the following week.)

this evening was by Edward Murrow. I thought it came at an opportune time and any criticism in it I think we can take as the candid opinion of a very good friend. I feel that I know Mr. Murrow, having just read [William L. Shirer's] *Berlin Diary*.[37]

Sunday, March 22. ... We were very busy today at the canteen. We harboured a deserter – at least we didn't know she was a deserter until we asked to see her pass. She was stranded down here and wanted somewhere to sleep. She refused to go to the police and we tried several local hostels, but they wouldn't take a deserter, so finally I sent her to Gatti's, where at least she would find a bed.[38] It is a very ticklish problem because we get into serious trouble if we assist those who have deserted and have been warned several times about it. Anyway the girl told us several different stories so I think she was up to no good. All the same we felt obliged to do all we could because it is no fun being marooned in the London suburbs.

Monday, March 23. I watched the procession [for Warship Week] pass along the Strand at lunchtime today. The crowds were eight or nine deep, more than usually gather for processions. I was much annoyed and so were many others at the hundreds of sightseers who thronged the restaurants with their children. The waitresses where I had my lunch were fuming at these women, who clamoured to be served quickly in order that they might get out in time to watch the procession. I can well imagine that many workers went without lunch today. The procession was not as impressive as the Lord Mayor's Day procession this year, but I have never watched a national show before, knowing so many of the men in it. As they all passed by I thought of what they were saying about it on Saturday. Actually the other infantry regiment in the show – the Warwickshires – are all men we serve on the vans. The highlight today I thought was the parade of pilots who led the RAF contingent. They all wore medal ribbons and personally I would not have cared to walk behind them as nobody had eyes for the rest.

[Intervening entry omitted]

Wednesday, March 25. ... We went to see *A Yank in the RAF* this evening and I enjoyed it quite a bit. The aerial photography was wonderful. The reconstruction of the Dunkirk scenes too I thought absolutely convincing, but all the time I was remembering a report which appeared in the press during the making of the film which said that the actors taking part in the Dunkirk scenes claimed extra pay because their work was dangerous – and the water was warmed for

---

37. In 'Questions America is Asking', *Listener*, 26 March 1942, p. 391, Edward Murrow, the European Director of the Columbia Broadcasting System, reported some American doubts about Britain's war effort, such as why 3½ million soldiers were in England when they were so badly needed throughout the British Empire. Murrow, whom Kathleen much admired, is mentioned in Shirer's *Berlin Diary* (1941) more than three dozen times.
38. In 1940, Gatti's Restaurant had premises at 436 Strand, WC2; by 1941 these premises were occupied by the YMCA Metropolitan Union.

them. The MOI film called *The Diary of a Polish Airman* was one of the most imaginative I have seen in months and was really moving. I do think that the men who make these films are to be congratulated. They rarely turn out a bad film now.

Thursday, March 26. I met A. today. She is a young friend of mine whose husband left her after their wedding service to rejoin his ship and was subsequently lost at sea. Some months ago she volunteered to go into the WRNS and last week she was called up. However, she returned home after three days. It appears that the authorities had nowhere to put her so she has to wait at home indefinitely until she is wanted. Now I know girls who have joined all three services and are in the same position. Surely the powers that be could suspend calling up girls until they have jobs for them to do.

Friday, March 27. The press this morning is divided on the question of the *Daily Mirror*. The debate in both Houses yesterday was at times stormy. Whatever the general public feels about the quality of the material contained in the *Mirror* I don't think Mr. Morrison would get away with a complete banning of the paper. The principle of the complete freedom of the press is at stake and I think that all newspapermen would stand together in defence of the *Mirror* for their own interests – that is except the *Telegraph*.[39] Sir Stafford Cripps is to see Mr. [Mahatma] Gandhi today. I wonder if he has any hopes of convincing this Indian who has suffered so much at the hands of the British Government of its sincerity.[40]

Saturday, March 28. T. rang up today. He said it was hell on Thursday night and they came back with a terrific hole in their plane. He said, however, that it would be easy tonight. I wonder!! The King broadcast tonight [*Listener*, 2 April 1942, p. 425]. I thought it was his worst broadcast – and once I thought he would have to be faded out. It is a great pity because his voice, when he gets going, is very pleasant. I wonder if he realises the agony he inflicts on his listeners every time he speaks.

Sunday, March 29. Details of a combined raid on St. Nazaire were given out today. *HMS Campbeltown* rammed the lock gates and troops demolished various installations in the docks. I don't think this raid has been accomplished without casualties, because the news is only trickling through.[41] The *Postscript*

39. The *Daily Mirror* had been bombastically critical of certain actions and inaction of the Government, and there were threats to silence it (under Defence Regulation 2D) on the grounds that what it printed was 'calculated to foment opposition to the successful prosecution of the war'. The paper was widely read in the Army. There had been a debate the previous day in the House of Commons on 'Freedom of the Press'.
40. Sir Stafford Cripps, at this time Lord Privy Seal and a member of the War Cabinet, was offering India total independence after the war, partly in the hope of strengthening Indian support for the war in progress (Japanese threats to British interests in India were very real). Gandhi was not convinced by Cripps' advocacy.
41. In fact, some 169 men were killed in this raid and 200 captured.

tonight was most moving. Admiral Evans recalled the life of Captain Scott and recounted the story of that last adventure. He pointed out the multitudinous sufferings of Scott and his friends, and showed how far below that standard most of us are, grumbling as we do at each irksome restriction on our own pleasure. Admiral Evans certainly made me feel exceedingly unworthy and I expect this talk had the same effect on many other listeners.[42]

[Intervening entry omitted]

Tuesday, March 31. I heard today that Mrs. F.'s husband is missing from Friday night's raid. He was a P/O rear gunner and had completed about 50 trips over Germany and France. Mrs. T. and A. are going to Herne Bay [on the north Kent coast] on Sunday and have asked Joyce and myself to go along too. Their bungalow has been slightly damaged and they want to inspect it and it will give us an opportunity to visit Mrs. R., who now lives at Chesterfield, quite near Herne Bay. The RAAF [Royal Australian Air Force] seem to be holding their own over Darwin. Another six Japs brought down yesterday. 'Tis thought that [Pierre] Laval is to return to the Vichy government. This bodes ill for us [Laval championed collaboration with Germany].

Wednesday, April 1. It is announced today that the ATS are to man searchlights. I expect this will amuse the Germans. When it comes to testing time, our defences will be manned by the Home Guard (if available), schoolboys, and women. Heard today from Miss L.C. about the Women's Defence Army which she runs in Eltham. Unfortunately they meet on Thursdays, a great shame as I am always on duty at the canteen then. The women learn the rudiments of shooting etc. which I imagine would be great fun. There is an account in today's paper [*The Times*, p. 4] of a VC posthumously awarded to Lt. [James Bernard] Jackman for bravery displayed in Libya. Certainly whilst we have men like him fighting for our cause we cannot lose – that is, if we back them up properly.

Thursday, April 2. Philip came home from Torquay today. He looks very well and says they had a raid there recently. A German fighter came down over the streets and let off his cannons quite happily. Philip says that all the locals stood and stared. Only one man was slightly hurt. He says that the din was terrific and the people were really frightened. In India General [actually, Field Marshal Sir Archibald] Wavell is taking a hand. He is to see Pandit Nehru and Sir Stafford [Cripps] is staying on a little longer.

Friday, April 3. What a peculiar Good Friday. I came up to London with Joyce. She never gets time off to do shopping so we made the most of the day. The

42. Admiral Sir Edward Evans (b.1880) had been second-in-command of the British Antarctic Expedition 1909–1913. He wanted to remind his listeners of 'the spirit of Scott' and encourage in them qualities of stoic endurance and resilience. (*Listener*, 9 April 1942, pp. 459–60.) At this time he was a regional commissioner for the civil defence of London.

West End was far more crowded than it was at Christmas time and those shops which were open were packed to suffocation. Later I went to the canteen to count the money for banking ('B—' has gone away). H. is home on 14 days embarkation leave and is to accompany us on Sunday. He does not mind going abroad again – in fact, is rather looking forward to it.

Saturday, April 4. I am helping Mrs. T. to do the office work at the canteen today – not that it is very difficult for anyone who has any experience of book-keeping at all. H. and I went to collect the stores – quite a job this. We had to come back at 10.30 p.m. to lock up and had a terrible job finding our way in the dark. It was completely black and pouring with rain. I expected to meet my doom at any moment as he drove at a steady 45. I think that driving in the blackout is a nerve-racking job, and am often surprised at the number of cars out at night.

Sunday, April 5. We drove down this morning to Herne Bay and were stopped several times, each time for Identity cards, Insurance, and H.'s pass, but not once were we questioned about petrol. I was under the impression that inspectors were around and were going to ask all motorists about their petrol, but I imagine that this was just so much Government talk. The wind was blowing a gale when we arrived and the sea was rough. Joyce and I spent the night with Mrs. R. at her lovely house at Chesterfield. Mrs. R. left the canteen about six months ago and came down here to live. She is still doing a terrific amount of work. The warning sounded around 9.30. We heard lots of planes and gunfire, but I was too tired to care about them.

Monday, April 6. We spent a lovely day today walking in the wind. Hurricanes have lots of fun down here. They skim the housetops and come down over the heads of anybody walking in the fields. We got a grand 'roll' from one of them whilst playing cricket on the beach.

Tuesday, April 7. T. was home this evening – he took French leave. They had a terrible trip last night. S. (his New Zealand pilot) brought the plane back but was very badly injured by shrapnel and is in hospital. T. says that the fires at Lübeck last weekend were wonderful, and the damage done was really grand. Their navigator hangs over the target for ages, T. says, before he releases the bombs and by the time they drop the language of the rest of the crew is really red.

There was a touch of melancholy in Kathleen's writing during the middle of April. On April 12 she wrote only: 'Spent a quiet Sunday. Went out walking all day in the wind and forgot about the war and news bulletins.' She still had a desire to contribute to the war by serving in uniform, but this was not to be. 'I went to the Labour Exchange again to see about joining the WRNS. They can't help at all. In fact they don't think I can do much until my age group [those women born in 1919] is conscripted in a week or so. I have got to the point of not caring what I have to do.' (April 18). Some of her acquaintances had succeeded in joining the forces, as she noted the next day. 'R. and B. are up for the day from Dover. They are enjoying life in the WRNS and don't seem to be hard worked. R. says that all their colleagues are girls who come from the highest society. Her room-mate was complaining because the 1s 6d a day which she is paid will send her husband's salary up to surtax level.'

From the last third of April, Kathleen's daily entries become, for the most part, more positive – and sometimes longer.

Tuesday, April 21. At the canteen this evening, we had a visit from two boys who left our part of the world about six months ago. They were passing through London on embarkation leave and decided to call in to see us. It is very pleasant to see familiar faces again and obviously they must have nice memories of our canteen or they wouldn't bother to come back.

Wednesday, April 22. This morning Commandos landed on the French coast near Boulogne, carried out operations there for two hours, and then were evacuated without casualties. This evening I saw a documentary called *Knights of the Air*. It was an appeal for funds by the RAF Benevolent Fund. Personally I think it absolutely scandalous that the future life of airmen's dependents and airmen themselves if disabled should depend on the amount collected by means of charity. Surely they and their folk should never want. They have given their lives and their limbs in the service of their country; can their country not do as much for them? No, funds of this kind exist and are in many cases the only source of income for these brave men. Every now and again the question is brought up in the Commons but somehow is always side-tracked.

Thursday, April 23. St. George's Day. Some Government department has put out an appeal to the population to hang out flags today. The raid yesterday seems to have been quite successful. In fact as some curious people point out, it seems incredible that the beaches and seas round the French coast are not mined. If it is so easy to land there, why can't the Germans land here as easily? Or can they?

Friday, April 24. R. was called up today for her medical and she expects to go into the ATS in a week or so. She is not pleased about this at all as she wanted to get into the WAAF as a Wireless/Op. I can't possibly see the method the Ministry of Labour employ in calling girls up. They seem to pick here and there in a completely haphazard way. We all went to see *The Doctor's Dilemma* this evening and enjoyed it terrifically. It really seems unbelievable that [George Bernard] Shaw wrote this play nearly half a century ago – it is so topical and the wit so modern. The acting was first-rate, particularly that of Austin Trevor, but Vivien Leigh, who looked ravishing, does not move me as an actress.

Saturday, April 25. At one of the gun-sites this morning a 'Defiant' fighter was giving the girls practice with their predictors. For about an hour he dived down over them, skimming the trees and at times almost knocking the top off our van. G. didn't like it. He said it reminded him too much of the night when the land-mines were dropped by a dive bomber. Personally, I thought it was great fun. Sometimes it seemed that he must come crashing down, but always at the last moment the pilot pulled out of his dive.

Sunday, April 26. Took Philip to see *One of Our Aircraft is Missing*, which I think is a finer film than *49th Parallel*. The story is better constructed [a British bomber is shot down over Holland and its crew is helped home by the Dutch resistance] and the characters have so much charm. The atmosphere in the plane too is well brought out, not self-consciously as it was in *Target for Tonight* but absolutely naturally, maybe because genuine actors are taking the parts – amateurs are always inclined towards over-emphasis. Eric Portman, who was so brilliant as the German in *49th Parallel*, is even better in this film as the Yorkshireman, bringing out all the pleasanter characteristics of his breed. Godfrey Tearle somehow dominated the film. I couldn't decide whether it was his voice, his presence or just his acting ability which dwarfed the rest of the cast. As a Dutch Burgomaster, Hay Petrie contributed a gem of acting to the film. The newsreel was quite exciting too; the Commando raid was very real. The *Postscript* tonight was given by Oliver Lyttelton and seemed too good to be true, and contained a good deal of talk about the wonderful new world etc. after the war. I wonder if he was expressing his real views or whether this talk was merely 'Sop'.[43]

Monday, April 27. Rostock was raided for the third night last night and it is announced here that Bath was raided on Saturday and again last night and obviously a good deal of damage was done. I think we in London feel more for the people in the provincial areas who suffer bombing than they did when we were enduring it. ...

[Intervening entry omitted]

Wednesday, April 29. Philip went back today – he didn't want to go but I am afraid he had no choice. I expect some of the parents kept their boys home, wondering no doubt if Torquay is a two-star town! ... The RAF are continuing to hammer the German naval bases. Trondheim and Kiel are the latest to feel our strength. York was the fourth 'Baedeker' starred town to be blitzed last night. I wonder if the Germans really expect to break our morale by these means.[44]

43. Oliver Lyttelton, Minister of Production, spoke about 'Planning the Course Ahead' (*Listener*, 30 April 1942, pp. 547–48). He argued that there are three things that everybody wants after the war: a cheerful, active, and enterprising country; no mass unemployment; and the modernisation of capital – roads, houses, urban infrastructure, and the like.
44. In retaliation for the bombing of Lübeck and Rostock, German bombers conducted major raids on five historic towns that were featured in the *Baedeker* guidebooks – Bath, Canterbury, Exeter, Norwich, and York. Details are provided in Niall Rothnie, *The Baedeker Blitz: Hitler's Attacks on Britain's Historic Cities* (Shepperton, Surrey: Ian Allan Ltd., 1992).

Thursday, April 30. Two Government candidates defeated in elections, the results of which are declared today. W.J. Brown got in at Rugby by a small majority and Councillor Reakes won Wallasey very easily. I am amused at the various attempts made by the different parties to lose responsibility in this business.[45] Our fighters were out today raiding ports and aerodromes. Last night we raided the Gnome-Rhone engine works just outside Paris. We also bombed Cologne and six aircraft are missing. Norwich got another dose last night and casualties are said to be fairly high. I should imagine the residents of Harrogate and other 'hide-outs' are beginning to get a little nervous. 'R—' was married today, quite a simple wedding, no cake, no strong drinks etc., the sort of thing one would expect of him.

Friday, May 1. J. was married today. She did the deed in white and had a terrific reception afterwards, over 100 guests – quite ostentatious, quite different from 'R—' and I's wedding. I think in these days an affair of this sort is a disgusting waste of food and labour.

Saturday, May 2. Why has Miss R.C. been dismissed from the Ministry of Supply in Eltham? Is it because she has protested vehemently about the waste of time there? She has told many people locally of the way the civil servants there sit around all day long doing nothing, but immediately become very busy when overtime rates are paid. That is to say, they do as much of their work during overtime hours as they can. I wonder if they will able to muzzle R.C. because she is a great believer in free speech and avails herself freely of this privilege, but nevertheless I understand that her case is being investigated by local people.

Sunday, May 3. An eventful day. I drove a van all day on my own. I was a little nervous at first but soon lost that feeling. I had a terrific headache when I finished, the result of intense concentration. We weren't so busy this evening as we now have competition in the form of a Salvation Army canteen which has opened up nearby. It will probably make a big difference to us. R. has to report at Guildford on Friday next. She certainly hasn't had a lot of time to think about herself. She was never interviewed, merely called for an ATS medical, despite the fact that she wanted to go into the WAAF.

[Intervening entries omitted]

Wednesday, May 6. … Miss R.C. has been taken back by the Ministry. I am not sure who is responsible for this. Anyway locally the stir caused by the original dismissal has died down.

---

45. W.J. Brown and George Reakes were Independents who won these by-elections in usual Conservative strongholds. Their victories testified, in part, to public frustration with the course of the war (though support for Churchill remained high).

[Intervening entry omitted]

Friday, May 8. ... Mrs. P. told me tonight of the trouble at D's aerodrome because so many of the air crews write home to their parents and friends giving them information which often results in the death of other airmen. At this 'drome a friend of his was given three months for talking too much in a local pub, and all the mail is opened, both from the camp and into the camp. I know too well that many of these airmen do talk too much. T. is one. He tells us much that he should keep under his hat and he is not exceptional. I hope the RAF authorities do tackle this problem seriously. Went this evening to see *The Watch on the Rhine* [by Lillian Hellman] which I enjoyed very much, but would have enjoyed a great deal more if I had been able to hear more of it. We had a good seat towards the back of the stalls and really I missed quite a bit of what was a very fine play. The broken English accents of most of the cast did not help. I had to agree with Mr. Agate 'that the play is a sermon preached to the converted' but it is a sermon we cannot hear too often.[46]

Saturday, May 9. I took a van out alone again today. I am becoming quite accustomed to the traffic now. Nowadays grumbling by the troops is becoming automatic and when one thinks of what our men in Burma are going through, their attitude seems disgusting. I suppose they are bored, but I wonder some-times – did they live on chocolate before the war? They make such a fuss when we go round without any that you would imagine they were being deprived of a staple food. J. with truth refers to our Army at home as the 'Chocolate Army'.

Sunday, May 10. Churchill's speech tonight contained much that was expected and apart from the warning to Germany about gas warfare contained little fresh news. I wondered at the time whether the Russians had asked for a guarantee of this sort in the hopes that it would deter the Germans from making this step. And perhaps too the Russians are not quite prepared to face this new peril and thought that a Churchill warning might give them more breathing space.[47] Went to see *The Day Will Dawn*. The audience around us was composed almost entirely of noisy Norwegians who became enthusiastic when their

46. James Evershed Agate (b.1877) was the theatre critic for the *Sunday Times*.
47. In this broadcast, the Prime Minister did indeed speak forcefully on this subject. 'There is ... one serious matter which I must mention to you. The Soviet Government have expressed to us the view that the Germans in the desperation of their assault may make use of poison gas against the armies and people of Russia. We are ourselves firmly resolved not to use this odious weapon unless it is used first by the Germans. Knowing our Hun, however, we have not neglected to make preparations on a formidable scale. I wish now to make it plain that we shall treat the unprovoked use of poison gas against our Russian ally exactly as if it were used against ourselves, and if we are satisfied that this new outrage has been committed by Hitler, we shall use our great and growing air superiority in the West to carry gas warfare on the largest possible scale far and wide against military objectives in Germany. It is thus for Hitler to choose whether he wishes to add this additional horror to aerial warfare. ... the British people, who have entered into the full comradeship of war with our Russian ally, will not shrink from any sacrifice or trial which that comradeship may require.' (*Speeches*, VI, pp. 6632–33.)

national anthem was played. I thought the film very good, tracing as it does the war from the beginning of September 1939 to the time of the recent Commando raids on Norway, actual shots of which were included in the final stages of the film. The scenes of the annihilation of Poland, Holland, Belgium, and Norway are imaginative and the evacuation scenes in France were quite realistic, and finally the RAF raid on a U-Boat base is wonderfully vivid and brought forth enthusiastic applause from the audience. Hugh Williams has the role of a horse-racing correspondent turned war reporter and has the largest part. Ralph Richardson plays another war reporter but is killed off half way through the film. I was sorry. He is such a fine actor and we see so little of him these days. Personally, I enjoyed best of all Roland Culver's portrait of a snipe-shooting naval officer. He had some wonderful lines and obtained most of the laughs. The Fleet Street atmosphere, I believe, actually pleased the inhabitants of that much misrepresented neighbourhood. It was quite convincing and Henry Oscar played the editor most gracefully.[48]

Monday, May 11. Gas-mask carrying has not noticeably increased to my casual eye. I expected to see hundreds of them about after yesterday's warning. Listened tonight to the Indian Round Table programme for the first time. The representative of [the] Congress [Party] got a trifle excited and violent as those possessed of a noble cause often are. I find my enthusiasm wanes somewhat when I listen to them.

Tuesday, May 12. It is revealed today that when Italy came into the war there were no planes on Malta, only four Gladiators which were fitted together by the RAF stationed on the island, yet now Malta, despite the fact that she is on Italy's doorstep, is one of the best defended parts of the British Empire as regards aerial defence. P. told us at supper tonight about his cousin who wears 'British Guiana' on his shoulder. He has been staying with them and has a grand time going about without a leave-pass. When stopped by military police he merely mumbles at them with what he imagines sounds like a tribal tongue and has up till now got away with it every time. Another cousin who has been staying with them for his leave – a Canadian – has in that time been to 22 cinema shows and 7 theatres – a record I should think.

[Intervening entry omitted]

Thursday, May 14. Reading *I Lived These Years* [1941] by Eric Baume. I was interested to see references to the *Gneisenau* and *Scharnhost* off Australia during the last war. How different must have been the fighting in the Pacific waters then. The Japanese navy was fighting our enemy too. I met our new manager at the YM this evening. He is middle-aged, active and quite

---

48. *The Day Will Dawn* is set in Norway and follows the adventures of a British journalist before and after the German occupation. The film, in part, paid tribute to the resistance of the Norwegian people.

charming. I hope he will not be 'easy'. Anyway he can't possibly be a bigger failure than his predecessor.

Friday, May 15. Met W. today. They haven't heard from G. in Burma since February. He got out of Rangoon and was seen by some friends in one of the small towns which became British headquarters during the retreat. He was then a Captain in command of an all-Burmese regiment. I personally don't think they will hear again, but naturally they don't think so. W. now is a commissioned officer in the ATS. She is the only girl I know personally who has risen in the services on her own merits, without influence of any sort.

Saturday, May 16. We are very busy today on the van. We now have far more work than we can cope with for the simple reason that we are losing many of our workers. Some are being called up and some leave very quickly when they realise that that the job is hard and tiring, with the result that those workers still remaining are endeavouring to do the work formerly done by twice their number. Met E.; L., her husband, is dangerously ill. He is in the RAF and has just been operated on for mastoids; he is in such a bad state that the service doctors do not think he will get over it.

Sunday, May 17. Answering the Government appeal, I spent today at the canteen minus stockings. Fourteen hours on my feet did not do them a great deal of good. If the Government want us to go without stockings they should see that shoes are made comfortable enough for wearing over bare feet. R. brought in his wife this evening. She is a North-country girl who works in an arms factory and she was telling me about her work. Apparently at her factory they are very busy and she has just been given seven days holiday, the first she has had in a year, and is down in London for the first time. She seemed quite shocked at the bomb damage which we now take for granted.

Monday, May 18. The *Prince Eugen* has been torpedoed and damaged by the RAF at the cost of nine aircraft. Odd isn't it that our ships are always sunk when attacked by enemy planes, yet we can never sink ships in the same way. The *Postscript* tonight was given by Wing-Commander MacLoughlen (I think that is his name), the night-fighter pilot who has an artificial hand. He spoke really well and he sounded a grand person and was amusingly modest. I should think that as a leader he is just about perfect.[49]

Tuesday, May 19. L. died this morning. I am really sorry because E. is my friend, despite the fact that I didn't like him much. The tragedy is that she hasn't even the glamour of being the widow of a man killed in action, if

49. This talk was actually not a *Postscript*, which aired on Sunday evening, but rather a part of the 9 p.m. news on Monday evening. The speaker was Squadron-Leader J.A.F. MacLachlan. (We are indebted for this and other information on wartime radio programmes to Erin O'Neill of the BBC Written Archives Centre, Caversham Park, Reading.)

glamour there is, but I think most people think there is something inevitable about death in action. We must have been raiding on a big scale tonight. I never remember such a noisy night – planes passed over continuously for hours.

Wednesday, May 20. Saw a MOI film this evening called *Free French Navy.* This film really puts the case of Free France very well. I am afraid I have been guilty of a good deal of rather bitter talk about France, what they did to us and what we should do to them after the war. As this film points out there are thousands of Frenchmen serving in the Free French forces, each one of whom has family and friends in occupied territory, and it must be a wrench to give up the chance of going home to be with them, as most of them gave up the chance when France gave in and made their separate peace. However, I think there is a certain amount of risk attached to the showing of this film, if German agents are able to identify any of the men portrayed therein.

Thursday, May 21. This evening I met Mr. Dixon, the headmaster of the school I attended until I was 11. He is an amazing man. Although he has had thousands of children through his hands, he still maintains that he can remember every one by name. Anyway, as I walked up to him he called out 'Hello Kathleen' and asked after Joyce and Philip, recalling every detail of what they are doing now and even their ages. He is one of the very unusual schoolmasters and I think he has influenced many hundreds of boys and girls without any apparent effort, despite the fact that he believed in 'the stick' and used it quite frequently. Although I have forgotten the names of mistresses who taught me only five or so years ago, I still remember odd remarks which Mr. Dixon made to me 16 years ago.

Friday, May 22. Joyce told me this evening about M.'s father. He is Secretary of a company who have premises in the docks. Last night I think it was, he arrived there in order to firewatch when one of their lorries came out. He stopped it and asked the driver what he was doing. The driver claimed that he was acting under instructions from M.'s father, instructions which were given to him the day before. When M's father started to look inside the truck, it lurched forward and made off. Luckily a policeman was nearby and the two of them started after the lorry in his car and although they chased it for about ten miles it got away. Fifteen minutes later the lorry was discovered abandoned with over 100 tyres inside it – in fact the tyres off every lorry in the firm's yard. Actually, from all one hears the motor tyre racket is the latest racket taken up by the black-marketeers. Some people will pay any price in order to get tyres for their cars. Actually, crime in this country is as wicked as anything in America, and it really is a good thing that our police are not armed. I shudder to think what it would be like here if they were.

Saturday, May 23. When I arrived at one of the gun-sites this morning, the troops were marching in to see *Next of Kin.* N., one of the officers there, suggested that I should go in as well because I could do no business until after the show. I wonder what sort of effect the film [which concerns the dangers posed by loose talk] will have on the general public. It made me feel extremely guilty and I made up my mind there and then to be very cautious in future and not to talk unnecessarily even to my friends. The film itself is wonderfully well acted by a first-rate cast. The ending is tragic but for that reason entirely convincing.

Sunday, May 24. My birthday today [her 23rd]. As a birthday treat for Joyce I took her out on the van today. She declared that she wasn't nervous at all – in fact much less so than she is with other drivers. I am not sure whether she is trying to be kind to me, but perhaps she means it. We went out this evening not knowing where to go but met some friends who were off to Trafalgar Square, so joined them. The Square was more crowded than I ever remember it being on other occasions. Mr. [William] Gallacher [the sole Communist MP] was the chief speaker and I heard him for the first time. Actually I thought he was an excellent speaker, despite the fact that I did not agree with much that he said. He made his long speech entirely without notes, which for these times is exceptional. Political meetings are not as interesting as they were a few years ago and my father always says that they have never been interesting since the last war. Heckling seems a thing of the past. The audiences swallow in silence practically everything any speaker puts over. Despite his views I have nothing but admiration for Mr. Gallacher, who stands alone in the House of Commons, the champion of a none too popular cause. The *Postscript* tonight was given by Mr. Duff Cooper [Chancellor of the Duchy of Lancaster] and was quite boring, read as it was with funeral-like tone.

Monday, May 25. We went to Lord's today and as usual it rained almost continuously. It was pleasant to get away from the war atmosphere for a few hours and we met several of our Oval friends there. ...

[Intervening entries omitted]

Friday, May 29. The Germans are now ten miles from Tobruk – only scattered tanks though. However, these infiltrating tanks captured France and we must guard against the same thing happening to us. Spent some time today trying to buy a pair of shoes. There is absolutely no choice these days, and the quality of the shoes must be as low as it can go; they seem to be made of cardboard. If the Government want us to save money and coupons, why don't they see that what we do buy will last. I am sure these shoes I finally bought will not last a year. My Grandmother arrived today – she has to visit to hospital on Monday.

Saturday, May 30. Took a van out alone again today. Now is surely the best time to learn to drive; the roads are comparatively free from traffic and are likely to become even less crowded after Monday. Mrs. R. last week asked me if I would like to help at the New Zealand Club and tonight I went along for the first time. It is terrifically hard work, serving hundreds of suppers to servicemen of every different nationality in the Allied forces, and quite a change from the YM.[50]

Sunday, May 31. Joyce and I are on all day at the canteen. At lunchtime R. told us about last night's enormous raid on Cologne – over 1,000 bombers took part and we lost 44. It is almost impossible to grasp the size of the raid. It must have been hell let loose for 90 minutes – just a sample of the way the RAF are going to treat the Germans and a little revenge for the way London was treated. R. is one of those servicemen for whose benefit *Next of Kin* was made. He tells us much that is highly confidential. His job is very important and very secret, but that doesn't worry him; he just tells us much that he knows. Since his own life depends largely upon the secrecy with which his job is carried out, I don't give much for his chances.

Monday, June 1. The raid is still the main topic of conversation and the news broadcasts to the Empire and Europe are adopting a menacing tone. Actually I think our propaganda in this line is looking up. If I were a German in a big manufacturing town I think I should be getting extremely uncomfortable. In fact I expect many of them would rather be in the Army than down below during a 1,000-plane raid.

Tuesday, June 2. Mr. Churchill announced in the Commons today that we made another 1,000-plane raid last night, this time on Essen. We lost 35 planes. This announcement came as a surprise to most of us as we had been told that it was unlikely that the RAF could carry out more than one of these big raids in seven or eight days. Went to the New Zealand Forces Club again this evening, served in the bar. Many Americans use the Club and in the process of drawing some of them out I discovered that most of them think (or know) that they are disliked here and are resentful of the fact. Several of them told me that they think it is because they are paid much more than our troops, but I don't think this is the real cause, because some of the Dominion troops are paid as well as the Americans. I put down the fact that they are disliked by many people here, because they are so aggressive.

Wednesday, June 3. We had an air raid warning in the early hours. I didn't hear it but heard the all-clear. I gather that many people were caught suddenly and switched their lights on before putting down the blackout. It almost happened to us, but Joyce managed to leap out of bed and pull down the curtain before my Mother pranced in to switch on the light. Perhaps it has done us a lot of good, because now we shall be a little more prepared at night.

50. This was the beginning of Kathleen's long association with the New Zealand Forces Club, 4–6 Charing Cross Road (in 2005 the Charing Cross Library). The Club was opened on 9 August 1940 by Clementine Churchill and was used by members of all the Allied forces. It was a popular meeting place for servicemen on leave and airmen between missions. Documents and photographs concerning the Club are held in the Westminster Archives Centre, Accession no. 2238.

[Intervening entry omitted]

Friday, June 5. Heard from P. today. He had an accident last week. In one of the narrow lanes somewhere in the South of England he hit a Valentine tank with his lorry. Luckily the tank was cruising very slowly or P. and his enormous new lorry would have been crushed beneath. He said that those in the tank were as white as ghosts, as indeed he was, and they all felt that it was fortunate that no-one was hurt. I went again tonight to the New Zealand Club. We were busy and in the hot weather it is very tiring work. The Club was formerly the premises of the British Union of Fascists [in fact, it had been an Italian social club] and the inscriptions on the walls have been covered by Maori words of welcome.

Saturday, June 6. The hottest day we have had this year I think. I drove my little van today and found the traffic lights impossible to see. Recently the attention of magistrates has been drawn to this fact and an investigation is promised, but in the meantime one just has to guess. The sun shines on the thin cross and the colour is obscured.

Sunday, June 7. This afternoon Joyce and I went out to serve a hundred or so boys of the ATC who are being given instruction in gliding. Fields where we played as children have now been levelled for this work. The boys were constructing a road today; in the terrific heat they were working really hard. Once again I envy them. Boys these days have so many chances. The *Post-script* this evening was given by an Australian Squadron-Leader who has recently left the Western Desert and is going back to Australia to fight the Japs. His talk was very descriptive and I got a good impression of what life was like out there, and in future I think we might even give a thought or two to the men in the Desert when we are inclined to grumble at minor discomforts.

[Intervening entries omitted]

Thursday, June 11. It is announced this morning that the King has completed a review of the Home Fleet, including units of the American Navy which have been here for some weeks, a secret which has been well kept, considering the number of people who must have known. Bir Hakeim [in Libya] has fallen, but most of the garrison got away. We can only hope that this is true, because one shudders to think of the treatment which will be given the French prisoners by the Germans out there. Corporal M., one of the WAAF at the camp, told me today that her job is far too big for one person, the girls are now too numerous, and she receives no support from the officers up at the camp, in her welfare work. She told me among other things that many of the girls spend the evening and nights in London at some of the clubs in the West End which in her words are no better than dens. The Anglo-Soviet Pact has been signed in London. I can't enthuse over it until I have had time to consider it and to decide whether it is worth more than the paper on which it is written.[51]

Friday, June 12. The King's horse won the Oaks today as everybody seemed to think it would. The Soviet-British Pact has stolen the headlines today. All things considered M. Molotov's visits were kept wonderfully secret, particularly as, according to some reports today, the Germans had some idea of the visit.

Saturday, June 13. When the result of the Derby was given out on the 6 o'clock news, it is revealed that the King and Queen have been present both days in order to see both the big races. Personally I don't blame him for seeing his own horses running, but was amused at one explanation of his visit to Newmarket – it was felt that if the King did not see the races it would give the impression that he did not approve and support the National Stud! I wonder if anybody swallowed this?

Sunday, June 14. Today is Allied Nations Day. London had a huge parade through the streets and the King and Queen and dozens of Allied royalty took the salute outside Buckingham Palace. I wish I had known; I enjoy watching processions. As it was we were on all day at the canteen. This week, however, for the first time for over 15 months, we were relieved at 6 o'clock and was it a relief! I realise now that our day there from 9 a.m. till 10.30 [p.m.] has been too long and that as long as we were prepared to do it we were imposed upon. Edward Murrow's broadcast this evening was inspiring and I felt less depressed after it,[52] particularly as the news from the Middle East which preceded the *Postscript* was far from good.

[Intervening entry omitted]

Tuesday, June 16. … At the New Zealand Club tonight there were about a dozen South Africans – this despite the fact that the announcer on Sunday (during the broadcast from the Allied procession) said that no South Africans were at the moment in Britain. These men I hear are attached to a medical mission in Britain, and some of them have been escorting prisoners from South Africa.

---

51. This treaty was signed on 26 May but not disclosed to the House of Commons until 11 June. The treaty spoke (among other things) of the urgent need for a second front against German forces in Europe.
52. Murrow presented a fairly sophisticated argument in support of Anglo-American solidarity; he tried to put in perspective issues and attitudes on both sides of the Atlantic that were and had been divisive, and to highlight commonalities. ('Uncle Sam or John Bull?' *Listener*, 18 June 1942, pp. 771–72.)

Wednesday, June 17. Tonight Flight-Lieutenant Gatwood broadcast about his flying visit to Paris. It seems incredible that he was able to fly so low over the city. I expect that many Germans who have been staying in Paris under the impression that they were safe from the RAF will be thinking again after this escape. What a surprise they will get one night. Our own reports of the naval battle in the Mediterranean claim two or three cruisers [and] one destroyer sunk and several ships damaged. American bombers took part in the action. I went to Fulham Hospital with Mother today. She has to go again on Friday for further diagnosis. I expect this means more treatment.

Thursday, June 18. Our troops have been successfully withdrawn from Gazala [in Libya]. Triumph though this is, it seems absurd to boast of it as if it were a great victory, but that is the press and radio all over. The Ministry of Labour have sent a form to my firm asking if they will release me, which, in view of the fact that they gave me permission to volunteer for the WRNS in January, will have to be answered in the affirmative. I discovered by chance today that the WRNS are recruiting again, after more than six months – maddening now that I can't volunteer [she was in a 'reserved' occupation and could not leave it without official approval].

Friday, June 19. Mr. Churchill has again flown to America to confer with President Roosevelt. The news from Libya is not encouraging. Our troops have fallen back on to the Egyptian frontier and half our army is now in Tobruk. The radio today had the audacity to say that we were in a better position today than we were last November, as we are now on the heights at the frontier – then we were in the valley! Do they think we are children? One report says that the troops which evacuated Gazala left their equipment behind; two or three hours later reports say that all equipment was saved and that nothing was left behind – what are we to believe? Not much, in my case. At the New Zealand Club this evening, several men from the Dominions said to me 'What is the good of all this talk about a second front, when on the one front where we are face to face with Germans we are beaten time and time again', and I know this is the opinion of many people in this country. It is my own view and the view of most of my friends. Mother and I went to Fulham Hospital again today. She has to go up in a month's time when they will decide what to do with her neck. She is now under a Czech surgeon. This hospital must have opened its doors to refugee doctors because during the past few years she has been under no less than three Austrians and one Czech.

PART TWO (AUGUST 1942–MARCH 1944)

At this point in the typescript there is a gap in Kathleen's diary, lasting six weeks. During this period she sent no material to Mass-Observation – or, if she did, this writing has not survived. She resumed writing on August 1ˢᵗ and continued until August 28ᵗʰ, at which point an even longer gap appears in the typescript, from August 29ᵗʰ until November 6ᵗʰ (inclusive). Then, on November 7ᵗʰ, she started to produce further daily entries and continued to write regularly up to the first day of January 1943. It is not clear whether these gaps, and later gaps in 1944–45, were because Kathleen wrote no diary during these periods or because what she wrote went missing. Since these gaps are always of a fortnight or a multiple of a fortnight (she was in the habit of posting her diary to Mass-Observation every two weeks, and starting a new instalment on a Saturday), it is possible that during these periods she did produce text but that her submissions to M-O were subsequently lost.

While we lack a continuous daily record of Kathleen's thoughts and activities during these six and a half months, what she did write for M-O was varied in subject matter and often rich in detail, and the editors have therefore presented her writing for this period virtually in its entirety. With one exception only, a passage of some 130 words on 25 August 1942, nothing has been omitted. For these months of 1942, then, all her responses to domestic politics, military events, and reports from abroad are printed in full, along with all the details she provides concerning her family, friends, home life, volunteer work, conversations, movements about London, and opinions on all sorts of public events and policies.

1942

Saturday, August 1 [a Bank Holiday weekend]. The roads today whilst I was out with my van seemed emptier than ever, now that the basic [petrol] ration [for private cars] is abolished. According to newspaper reports the scenes on London railway stations were far worse than peacetime and some of them report fighting at Paddington between people frantically endeavouring to get floor space to stand on. If this is true, the Government are partly to blame; they haven't taken a firm stand. If they had forbidden people to travel all would have been well. As it is, while pleasure travelling is allowed, some people will do as much as they can.

Sunday, August 2. This morning we drove to serve at the glider 'drome and watched the boys going up one at a time. They are having the time of their lives

49

and how I envy them. This evening we came up to see *Eagle Squadron* [a film about an American who joins the RAF]. As we came into Leicester Square, the scene didn't seem to belong to London at all. It resembled a bit of America. There were Americans everywhere – soldiers, Eagles and Canadians of every service – with USA on their shoulders. The audience was predominantly American and they seemed to like the film, although I am sure any Eagle watching it will blush with embarrassment as he listens to Mr. Quentin Reynolds' preface to the picture [he was a strongly pro-British American journalist]. The flying scenes are the best I have seen – quite realistic, as are the air raid scenes. The scene when a Warden calls into the shelter 'Are there any expectant mothers down there?' which is answered 'No, we have only been down here a few minutes', got an immense laugh. I wonder if this is in very good taste.

Monday, August 3. Spent the day at Lord's. The crowd was nearly twenty thousand I think and a very good day it was, with a schoolboy (Dulwich College Captain) stealing the thunder from all the assembled stars, making a most sensational entry into first-class cricket. I left Lords at teatime in order to go to the New Zealand Club and we were pretty busy, but I imagine that most of the Americans and Canadians in London had gone to Wembley as we didn't have many in until quite late.[1] A New Zealand Observer, telling me about a race of natives which preceded the Maoris, by name the Maori-aoris (I think), now extinct, said in a bitter tone 'At the rate we are being killed off, the New Zealand race will be extinct before long'. What can you say in answer to this when the man who says it is risking his life nearly every night bombing enemy territory. I think he is entitled to express his opinion if anyone is.

Tuesday, August 4. Stop-at-home Londoners seem to have had quite a good holiday – [though] the weather was not terribly good for them. I wonder how all those who went off to seaside resorts managed to get home? Apparently in the House today the members were called into secret session. This fact, together with the revelation that Mr. Gandhi has considered approaching the Japanese if and when the British leave India [a 'Quit India' movement was strong], have left our minds buzzing. Certainly we can expect some startling news soon. This period of calm reminds me of the week or so before the fall of Singapore. Then, as now, we got no news at all.

Wednesday, August 5. I have never seen London so packed as it was today. At lunchtime I struggled with thousands of other workers to get something to eat. There were queues everywhere and I am afraid I became rather fed-up. The same thing this evening. It took me 25 minutes to walk from my office to Charing Cross, a journey which can be done in six or seven minutes. I met

---

1. A Canada-US baseball game was played that evening at Wembley Stadium, with Mrs. Churchill in attendance. 'Many first-class players' were available to both sides. Some 10,000 people attended the game, a sum of £950 was raised for the Red Cross, and Canada won 5–3. (*Evening Standard*, 3 and 4 August 1942.)

Eltham/Well Hall Station, 1952. This picture was taken during the last week of the running of the London trams. During the war (especially from 1942) car traffic was very light. Otherwise, this scene is little changed from the early 1940s. Photograph courtesy the Greenwich Heritage Centre in the Royal Arsenal, Woolwich.

Mother and Joyce and we saw *Macbeth*. Quite like a pre-war show – the audience was out to see good acting, not looking for casual amusement, and the theatre was packed. John Gielgud was as good as I have ever seen him in the past and I thought he dominated the play completely. The cast was without exception quite easy to hear, something which is unusual in these days. Some of our actors who have taken to the stage via cinema and radio could well copy them.

Thursday, August 6. Lunchtime placards say that the battle for the oil fields has begun. The news from every front is uniformly bad. I can't see any relief anywhere and the Russian front is changing every day. Parliament broke up for the recess today. I expect they will be called if anything happens. The storm over Lady Astor's speech is still raging and some people are demanding that she makes an apology in public. I don't expect she will because much that she said we know in our hearts to be true.[2]

2. At a United Nations parade in Southport on the Bank Holiday Weekend, American-born Lady Astor, MP, made a speech that denigrated Britain's Russian ally and celebrated the support of the United States. 'I am grateful to the Russians,' she declared, 'but they are not fighting for us; they are fighting for themselves.... To hear people talk, you would think they came to us in our own dire need. Nothing of the kind. It was the United States of America and don't forget it.' (*Southport Guardian*, 5 August 1942, p. 3.) Her reservations about Russia's efforts caused outrage in parts of Britain, and there was much criticism of her views in the press.

Friday, August 7. Went out on a night run this evening to a gun-site in the country. We got back just before dark. This time next week it will be dark before 9, so driving with no lights will not be fun, and our new garages are very difficult to enter in daytime, so what they will be like in darkness I can well imagine. We will have to erect a flare-path or something of the sort!

Saturday, August 8. Had an amusing time today. I had to go round of all the new sites in the district to make arrangements about our visits with the vans. I had quite a job getting inside some of them, despite the van with its bright marking and all my credentials. The more secret the site, however, the easier it was to enter, and I found it far more difficult to get onto a searchlight with a dozen or so men than I did at a secret gun site with several hundred men.

Sunday, August 9. We woke up to the tidings from India that Gandhi, Nehru and many other leaders of Congress had been arrested in the early hours [Britain feared a Japanese attack on India, and possible Indian support for Japan]. From what we are told, it appears that the decision to arrest them was made by the Government of India, consisting mainly of Indians, and that the arrests themselves were carried out in a very dignified and helpful manner (the sort of arrests the Germans or Japanese would have carried out!), but I don't think this decision would have been taken unless the British Government had assured the Indians of their support. Gandhi's followers seem to have forgotten very quickly their leader's ideas of non-resistance. In fact riots have broken out all over India. At the moment the Moslems, appealed to by Mr. Jinnah [leader of the Muslim League], are taking no part in the violence, but probably if they can't get all that they want by this method they will join in with the rioters. Mr. [Leo] Amery [Secretary of State for India], broadcasting this evening, made something of a case for the action taken. Somehow I wish he had been more explanatory for the benefit of his American listeners. I fear they get rather a distorted idea of our doings in India, and a little careful explanation would probably clear up misunderstanding on the point.

Monday, August 10. News from India is increasingly bad. The riots have spread and troops and police have had to fire on the population, resulting in casualties on both sides, some of them fatal. Somehow it seems so dreadful, British troops fighting against Indians (British subjects), but just the sort of thing the Germans would have liked to plan. I wouldn't be surprised if they didn't have something to do with the whole matter, especially in view of the fact that Mr. Gandhi was obviously playing with the idea of appealing to the Japanese. Maybe he even consulted them.

On duty at the New Zealand Club this evening. I met a young American who had just seen the King, Queen and Princesses at Euston. He adores the Queen and said 'We haven't a Queen of our own and she is the only Queen we will ever have. She is really beautiful.' He didn't care for the King – he was an admirer of the Duke of Windsor. In fact he was communistically inclined but he thought Princess Elizabeth 'a honey, with her beautiful hair'. I was amused at these remarks from this tough-looking American, but the more I listen to the men from the USA and Canada, I realise how completely Queen Elizabeth captured the hearts of everyone there during the official visit [in 1939]. Another told me that he had been introduced into the home of a family at Elephant & Castle by a clergyman, and he was full of praise for the hospitality shown him. I think he was a little influenced by the fact that the family contained a marvellous daughter. Anyway I think a lot more of this sort of entertaining could be done and probably the hard-boiled appearance of most of these troops is no guide to their character and maybe many of them would enjoy this sort of hospitality.

Tuesday, August 11. At the New Zealand Club again tonight. An Australian pilot was very talkative. He told me about one of his fellow-pilots, by name S. (an Englishman), who had been on more than 20 operational flights over Germany and a month or so back felt that he couldn't go on any longer. He wouldn't take the responsibility of leading a crew on operations because he didn't feel confident that he could stick it any more. The Australian said in passing that he didn't blame anyone being nervous or cracking up. In fact he said that anyone who says that they are never frightened is just asleep. Anyway the authorities stripped S. of his stripes – they couldn't take his wings or DFM [Distinguished Flying Medal] ribbon – but he gave up wearing them after a time because people made it so unpleasant for him, reminding him of his so-called disgrace. He is now working as ground staff on the planes he used to take over Germany. About a week ago this Australian took S. into the Sergeants' mess for a drink, etc. but after they had been there for a while the Flight Commander (an Englishman) came in and ordered S. outside and the Australian got into serious trouble. He has little opinion of English leaders either in politics or military affairs, and in telling me this story he was pointing out that an Australian officer couldn't have got away with that sort of behaviour. I am afraid this view is shared by most of the men I meet from the dominions. They admire our soldiers but have nothing but contempt for the men who lead them. I feel that we should be doing something about it, but it is not easy to alter a system as old as ours and get rid of the people who are holding up the winning of the war.

Wednesday, August 12. We went this evening to a concert arranged by the RAOC – Artists in Battledress – given by professional performers who are now in the forces. The star was Nat Gonella [a trumpeter and singer]. We arrived just before it started and hoped to slink into the back row, but all the men there are men who have served for years and they insisted on marching down into the front row reserved for the mayor and notables. My enjoyment was somewhat lessened by the fact that Mr. Gonella's trumpet was slightly overpowering at such close quarters. I went expecting an inferior show but came away very pleasantly surprised. The concert, mainly jazz, was really slick, nothing second-rate or vulgar about it.

Thursday, August 13. Mother met Mrs. F., R.'s mother, today. He was killed last week in a plane crash whilst doing work of a very special nature. She is terribly broken up and there is little one can do to help at all. R. was possessed of plenty of courage and initiative despite his many setbacks and the fact that he was disappointed so many times. When he was at Cambridge he caught some complaint two days before his final exams, so he had to come down minus degree, which prevented him from taking up the career of his heart. He then went into the police and in doing so had to suffer much from so-called friends. One would have imagined that he had gone into prison, such a come-down it was said to be. When the war started he was exempt as he was over 25 but he joined up soon after and had been flying in various commands for over 18 months.

Friday, August 14. The Germans are still advancing in the Caucasian mountains – is there no stopping them? We had our first letter from Philip for over a fortnight and it contained a good deal of very interesting matter. At the ATC camp he had two flights and on the last day he went out in a submarine-chaser and they had machine-gun practice, shooting at moving targets, when they joined in a patrol. When he returned to Torquay, he found that his billet had been bombed. On Bank Holiday, apparently, ten planes blitzed the town, dropped their bombs and machine-gunned the town. None of his things were seriously damaged, but as a bomb landed in their back garden the house is in a real mess. The family were unhurt. This was fortunate, as there are three small children in the house. This was not all. Early this week at the agricultural camp, he and some friends were picking broccoli on the side of a hill, [and] two planes appeared overhead. These champion ATC boys identified them as friendly Mustangs, but a second or two later the so-called Mustangs circled round and dived down on them, dropped six bombs and cannon-gunned the gallant harvesters, who hastily dropped prone. Philip says that the cannon shells whistled past them and made a terrible din. The bombs fell about 50 yards off and sunk a launch in the bay. Mother became very indignant about all this. I think she imagines that [Commander-in-Chief of the Luftwaffe Hermann] Göring is after her ewe-lamb only. However he must be quite alright because at the end of the letter he asks us to send him some eatables, preferably something sweet.

Saturday, August 15. We are still getting no full details of the Navy's terrific fight to get through to Malta, and it is not over yet. At the RAOC depot today one of the boys, dashing around on a motor cycle, felt his clutch go and he crashed into my poor little van, behind which I was serving. He didn't hurt himself, but knocked the cycle about a bit and bent my mudguard and scratched the paint badly. This however they quickly remedied. Whilst some were straightening the mudguard others put on a fresh coat of khaki paint and repainted the red and white signs, so that when I got back to our depot G. was none the wiser. The RAOC are always ready to do anything for us, even when they are not responsible, as they were in this instance. Many of the NCOs and officers grumble however at the red tape which cramps their work. If they want a special screw and can't get it from any of their branch workshops, even though they could walk into Woolworth's and buy the thing for 2d, they can't do it because they have such a job to get the money back, so they fill in forms and wait until some high official decides that they can have the screw. This is only an instance. They gave me dozens. Apparently at one time there was some system whereby officers could pay out of a fund for any small article which was urgently needed, but it seems that this privilege was abused and was consequently stopped.

Sunday, August 16. This afternoon Joyce and I went out to the glider-drome to serve the ATC boys. They are so keen and thrilled at the chance of getting into the air and somehow they are keener when they have their own glider. The glider fields have become quite popular, and the British institution, the Sunday evening stroll, is being taken in the direction of the gliders and there are usually several hundred spectators there to watch the fun. This is only another example of the way in which Woolwich is ahead of other boroughs. The council is progressive and sees that those living within its walls shall have the best that can be obtained in these times. The fighting in the Solomons is still going in favour of the Allies and a naval battle is raging in the South Pacific, probably the Japanese trying to get reinforcements through.

Monday, August 17. The Russians announce that they have abandoned Maikop [in the Caucasus] but have removed all oil and destroyed the oil fields there. I shouldn't think such a fighting retreat has ever been known before. Over thousands of years, the Russians fight for every mile of their vast territory. Nonetheless it is rather frightening to look at German conquests in Russia.

Tuesday, August 18. So Mr. Churchill has been to Moscow and has met Stalin – one time when the rumour-mongers were right! He apparently went to the Middle East en route and met General Smuts there. It seems to me with all the alterations in generalship, we could do worse than appoint General Smuts to lead our forces in that theatre. He was one of the few great names of the last war and certainly none of the Generals thrown up by this war seems likely to go down in history as 'Napoleons'. The Prime Minister must have been travelling around for some weeks, as he has not been noticed in public for at least three weeks. I gather from press reports that the two statesmen were firm friends after a very short time, this despite the fact that they were formerly bitter enemies.[3]

Wednesday, August 19. Joyce took Mother to the hospital today. She came home very thrilled with herself because Mr. Joll [her doctor] said that she need not come back until three months have passed. I was awakened early this morning by very low flying aircraft and then heard the announcement on the news that a combined operations was taking place in the Dieppe area. I wonder why they gave this out so quickly? The men were re-embarked nine hours after

3. Field Marshal Jan Christian Smuts (b.1870), Prime Minister of South Africa, was also Commander-in-Chief of his country's armed forces. He strongly supported the defence of Egypt, where South African troops and aircraft were committed. Smuts, who had fought against the British in the Boer War (1899–1902), was much admired by Churchill.

they first landed. Casualties are said to be heavy on both sides. We lost 95 planes of all types, but 30 pilots are said to be safe. We can only pray that results will justify the great loss of life. Presumably this force (obviously not large) was not landed merely to blow up a gun site and radio-location station. I should think there were other targets, which probably will not be made public.[4] Changes in the Middle East commands are announced. Now General [Sir Harold] Alexander is put in charge and we are given details of his very distinguished career, and also given the impressions that our forces there at last have a Wellington to lead them. I wonder? We know too well what happens after these Generals have their first failure. Somehow I can't help thinking that the Germans didn't sack Rommel after his two failures. They left him in charge and he profited by his experience.

Thursday, August 20. The Russians have evacuated the Kuban River area [north-west of the Black Sea]. I expect the troops in Persia are waiting for action at any time, now that the Germans are so near. Commandos are still being landed at South Coast ports. Some of them have been in the water for hours before being picked up. The press was well represented. A whole boat-load of reporters went along. Nobody can say that they have an easy job. Fancy going on a job like that just to write it up. Bob Bowman, the Canadian broadcaster, was talking tonight about his experiences during the raid.

Friday, August 21. Listened to Commander Anthony Kimmins' account of the Malta convoy battle again [*Listener*, 27 August 1942, pp. 261–62 and 276]. It is one of the most moving stories I think I have heard during the war, and he told it so vividly. The strongest impression I was left with was the bravery of the merchant seamen in such dangerous waters, determined to get to Malta, and at what cost – yet they are always ready to go again.

There are some grand stories today from the reporters who were at Dieppe. They are more exciting than any adventure story. From all accounts, it seems to be clear that Lord Lovat and his Commandos made the landing possible. They went in first and did what was necessary. Then the troops landed. Lord Lovat must be an exceptional man, the type that we will need in plenty if we are to build the new world we hear so much about.[5]

Saturday, August 22. I took Joyce out with me on the van today – the last of her holidays. As well as one usual site, we did a site where 700 ATS have just arrived. They seemed everywhere and they certainly were a mixed lot. G. went up to serve the WAAF this morning and said that although the girls behave themselves when Mrs. B. goes up there (she serves them every day and is very good to them), he and the van were almost torn to pieces by the pushing and

---

4. The ill-conceived raid on the coastal town of Dieppe had disastrous consequences for the participants. Canadian troops (almost 5,000) carried out the main attack, over 900 of whom lost their lives; 1,874 were taken prisoner. Little if anything was achieved by the day's action.
5. Lord Lovat (b.1911) was, according to *Oxford Dictionary of National Biography* (2004), 'Athletic, debonair, extremely courageous, and an inspiring leader', and 'also ruthless and intolerant of inefficiency in his army career' (vol. 20, p. 875).

grabbing of the young ladies. Some of the men from one site are going over-seas on draft. They are very pleased because in action most red tape is forgotten – at least they are going off under that impression.

Sunday, August 23. Joyce and I are on all day. Heard about D.'s DFM. His mother came in to tell me; she is terribly bucked. We also heard today that T.C., one of the boys who was at the camp when the canteen first opened, is missing presumed killed in action. He was a very hot-tempered boy, and after some trouble with another fellow in which knives were used, he volunteered as an air-gunner and has been flying for about eight months. He didn't come back from a flight last week. I expect we shall hear details later. Anyhow I felt very bad when I heard, because he seemed such a boy to live. The only thing in his case that can partly make up for his early death is that he had a very good time when he was young. Some 50 Canadians who were killed in Dieppe were buried in England today. This news, as given by the [BBC] news tonight, made us all feel very miserable. I expect many families in Canada are worrying because they think their sons may have been there, but I suppose the nearest relations of those known to have been lost will have been told. Somehow every day the war goes on I realise how huge this war is compared with the Great War, especially now that Brazil and Uruguay are in with us. There are few countries in the world unaffected by the fighting, however remote.

Monday, August 24. Mr. Churchill is back in London tonight. Listened to an amusing tale at the New Zealand Club from a Canadian airman. He was in Lincoln's Inn this morning and sat on a seat beside a boy aged about 14 who was doing algebra. He offered to help the boy and did the work for him, where-upon a man sitting the other side of him asked him what he did before he joined the RAF. He replied 'I was an architect' and it turned out that this man too was an architect and he offered to take the Canadian round Lincoln's Inn. The Canadian said he would like to go and added 'and we can have a bottle of beer together', under the impression that Lincoln's Inn was a beer-house. He soon discovered his mistake and spent a pleasant morning looking around the law courts. He has been here in England with an RAF squadron for more than a year and still cannot decide whether he likes the English. He thinks after careful thought that the Englishman will be friendly with a person if he reasons that it will pay him to be friendly. He also told me that he thinks Londoners are the most helpful people he has come across in this country. If he asks the way of anybody in London they will more often than not walk part if not all the way with him, even if it is out of their way to do it. He contrasted this with the behaviour of a lady in a provincial town the other day when he asked the lady to a certain street. She looked at him and shrunk back with horror when she heard his accent, clutching her little girl to her. To this the Canadian said 'I merely asked you to direct me to ——— Street and since I am only a human being like yourself, perhaps you will do so'. The woman was taken aback and the little girl started giggling, but only then did he get the help he asked for. He says that in most towns outside the capital, people always send him to a policeman; very rarely do they help him themselves. I took this as something of a compliment to London.

This Canadian, together with three Rhodesian members of his crew, were spending their last night in England and were very disappointed because we would not join their all-night party. Mrs. C., who was in charge of the Club tonight, warned us about the Americans who bring their bottles of brandy etc. into the Club and ask for glasses to mix it in. This is now definitely 'verboten'. Also we were told to watch out for a young American who came in a day or so back and parked a case full of Koko-koala (?) behind the bar and came up every now and again to get a bottle. This too is frowned on by the authorities. Personally I was sorry – I wanted to get a glimpse of this young man who had such terrific cheek.

Tuesday, August 25. A New Zealand pilot told me tonight how the other day he was attacked by a coloured American armed with a knife. Apparently this Negro had been called 'dirty nigger' or something similar by a British soldier and in the darkness the infuriated Negro thought that the New Zealander, in the battle dress that some of them wear, was a soldier. It took several men all their time to keep him off. This brought the subject round to the colour question in general. An Australian present said that the same trouble was happening down under. He had heard from his wife that there had been fighting at the 'Waverley' (which I presume is a well-known hotel or something similar in Australia, because all the Australians know it). Then somebody else said that he was stationed near Bath, and the people there were expecting real trouble because the coloured troops take English country girls out and the white Americans won't stand for it. Personally I think this is an attempt by the Americans to introduce the same colour bar here that they have in the States, but despite this thought I can understand something of what they feel. …

Wednesday, August 26. As I woke up this morning, the 7 o'clock news was loud enough for me to hear the obituary for the Duke of Kent who has died in an aeroplane crash. Somehow it never seemed that anything like this could happen to British royalty – the sort of thing that only happened in Europe.[6] In times of peace the court would have gone into mourning and wireless programmes would have been appropriately altered, but today they went on as usual, jazz music following the news bulletin. When the war is over, I wonder how many men will be alive who have flown all through hostilities. Not many I am afraid. Yet some have such a long run of luck, and some go so soon. Saw *Unpublished Story* this evening and thought it quite a good film. I like films with a war background and this [film], despite the rather trite story involving the fifth-column activities of a Peace Society, contained some wonderful blitz scenes and the atmosphere of London at that time was accurately depicted, [and] not over-sentimentalised as Hollywood always presents it.

Thursday, August 27. It seems that there was one survivor from the Duke of Kent's plane. The rear-gunner is seriously injured, but may be able to give

---

6. George, Duke of Kent (b.1902), was the King's younger brother. His plane was en route to inspect RAF installations in Iceland and crashed (probably because of pilot error) in Scotland.

some information about the crash when he recovers. The news from Russia tells of an advance at Rhzev, but the Russians say that this success, however great, does not mean that the situation further south is any more hopeful and they admit that Stalingrad is in grave danger.

Friday, August 28. I think this afternoon it was hotter than at any time this summer – it was almost tropical. Listened this evening to the second in the series *An American in England*, which I think are really interesting. Edward Murrow has something to do with this programme, and he certainly knows how to put a programme over. Mother heard today of R.'s husband who is in the army. He was in the Dieppe raid and has been home ill since; apparently the dive bombers affected his nerves.

   After a gap of ten weeks, Kathleen's diary resumes in early November and continues until the beginning of the New Year.

Saturday, November 7. A most terrible day on the van. I got absolutely soaked, and up in the woods got stuck at one point and had to be pushed out of the mud by some soldiers stationed there. There are rumours coming from German sources that a convoy is on its way to Malta. Mrs. W. says that she heard a German station saying last night that there are hundreds of ships at Gibraltar. Our Air Force has raided Genoa again. Certainly Italy has felt the war this last week or so. Went to see *The Glass Key* tonight – quite a change to see a film quite apart from the war. I believe this picture has been made several times before but the story is quite original, of the gangster variety. We saw, too, the new MOI film about this year's harvest. I had read a good deal about it, and was most impressed with the lovely photography.

Sunday, November 8. What terrific news! Mother really had something to sing about this morning. The Americans have made landings in French North Africa. All the rumours of the past few days were far off the mark, and we can only hope that all will go well. Anyway, it is a beginning, and together with our advance in the desert this should help Russia a little, by occupying the attention of a few divisions of Germans. I went out alone on the van this morning, and everywhere the news was the only topic of conversation, except at the RAOC where the men had to attend Church parade, and they were very bitter about it all. One of the Canadians there, a Sergeant-Major, said to me 'We hear a lot about the forced attendance of the German people, with their controlled cheering and *sieg-heiling* – we are no better here'. I do think the new Arch- bishop of Canterbury would strengthen the position of the Church if he abolished compulsory attendance at Church parades, although I expect the Army chiefs would stop this. Mrs. [Eleanor] Roosevelt gave the *Postscript* tonight and an inspiring talk it was. She has a most attractive voice, with little accent, and she paid great tribute to the people in this country, a tribute that we do not often get and which is long overdue.[7]

7.   The American 'First Lady' was on an official visit to Britain. Her speech was printed in the *Listener*, 12 November 1942, pp. 611–12.

Monday, November 9. Algiers has been occupied by Allied troops and report has it that the French have asked for an armistice. British troops are on their way to join the Americans in action, but many British participated in the various landings which were only made possible by the work of the Royal Navy and the RAF. At the New Zealand Club tonight, naturally, they were all excited by the news, and news bulletins were listened to with more interest than usual. One of the men has brought Mrs. C. a marvellous Max Factor lipstick, a beautiful thing, quite rare these days.

Tuesday, November 10. Saw Mr. and Mrs. Churchill driving to the Mansion House this lunchtime. Mrs. Churchill had a terrifically bright red hat on her head, but looked quite nice. Mr. Churchill's speech was recorded and broadcast tonight and was very witty. He is obviously very glad, at last, to have some good news for us.[8] Taking things by and large, he hasn't had much good fortune. Maybe before long he will have more to tell us. Apparently the lunch was more like old days, with the gold plate etc. brought out for the occasion.

Wednesday, November 11. At 11 o'clock I discovered that I was making a telephone call and I expect other people found themselves doing something similar. It is very difficult to realise that it is Armistice Day, with no two-minutes silence. Parliament opened today and Mr. Churchill made a further speech in which he talked again about the events of the past few days, and in which he said that he would have more to tell us later [*Speeches*, VI, pp. 6696–6709]. It was a triumphant speech, and I see that on Sunday next church bells are to be rung in celebration of the Egyptian victory. I do hope we are not being too violently optimistic, but I am looking forward, more than I can say, to the sound of the church bells again. I hope they ring very loudly. The Germans have landed troops by air in Tunisia. I am very worried about Esperance [a pen pal from schoolgirl days]; she is so pro-British that I expect her sympathies are well known. In any case her letters, which have been coming to me quite frequently this year from Tunis, have been quite definitely in favour of Britain and the British cause. I can only hope that nothing happens to her, although maybe our troops will be in that part of the world before long. It is announced that Admiral [Jean François] Darlan is still in Algiers. I wonder what double-crossing he is up to.

The Germans have been marching into Vichy France today. How ironical that it should happen on Armistice Day, a day on which the last crowd of militant Germans finally gave in. Still, maybe the people of France will be part of an even greater victory, sometime in the future.

Thursday, November 12. The final capture of Oran [in Algeria] is announced. Apparently the force of British Commandos did most of the fighting here, and

8. The wit was mainly in the first two paragraphs, including the observation that 'we have a new experience. We have victory – a remarkable and definite victory.' This is the speech in which he declared that 'Now is not the end. It is not even the beginning of the end. But it is, perhaps, the end of the beginning.' (*Speeches*, VI, p. 6693.)

have suffered heavy casualties. The Admiral Darlan affair is still mystifying. Are we going to trust him or merely to use him?[9] Fighting is going on in the neighbourhood of Tobruk, but whether it is occupied by British troops is still not certain.

Friday, November 13. This evening I saw the newsreels of the desert fighting. They certainly are realistic and give a wonderful picture of what is going on there. Nonetheless it is just a picture. Nobody who hasn't experienced this type of fighting can really imagine accurately what it is really like. It must be [a] worry though for people with relations out there, but quite a thrill if they recognize their son or husband on the screen. I do think cameramen are as brave as any soldiers. They go right up into the thick of the trouble, just to tell us at home what is really happening.

Saturday, November 14. A simply ghastly morning. The fog was really thick, visibility being at most six yards in our district. I drove on an unfamiliar route too, with Mrs. B. as guide and she wasn't much help. We had the windscreen open and I peered out for about three hours into complete blackness. Going into K. Camp, I know the way round the various shops quite well, but found myself hopelessly lost and finally Mrs. B. got out and guided me with a torch. We had two narrow squeaks when other lorries came right at us and we got back to the depot quite exhausted only to discover that the other two drivers had come back after cruising round outside the canteen, considering it to be too dangerous to drive. Actually I found it terribly tiring and had a terrific headache when I got home, but it is quite a test of one's patience and very good practice for a driver. We have all been given Ministry of Labour forms asking for details of hours worked at the canteen etc. I expect they will substitute we voluntary workers for women they want to draft into war work, which seems rather purposeless as they are getting two jobs done in many cases, because many of those at the canteen are doing a full-time job as well.

Sunday, November 15. The bells rang out today for the first time for more than two years. I didn't hear any real bells as I was in the canteen before 9 when they started ringing and once in there the noise drowns anything outside.[10] I listened to the broadcast of *Bells Round Britain*, however, which I enjoyed very much, despite the fact that we were rushing around serving a convoy whilst it was in progress. Most of the men I mentioned the subject to thought the celebrating a little premature. Mr. Morrison gave the *Postscript* tonight and

---

9. The Allied leadership was apparently recognising Admiral Darlan, a prominent member of the Vichy Government, as leader of the French in North Africa. Public opinion had trouble grasping how a collaborator with the enemy could so suddenly become an ally. See also below, 25 December 1942.

10. The *Kentish Mercury*, 20 November 1942, p. 1, reported on the 'Inspiring Service at Lee', near the canteen where Kathleen was working. 'Bells, long silenced, pealed joyously from St. Margaret's Church, Lee, on Sunday, calling parishioners to a special service of thanksgiving for our splendid advances in North Africa.'

talked I believe about civil defence at great length [*Listener*, 19 November 1942, p. 647]. I didn't hear much as we were arguing quite fiercely about Mr. Morrison's character during the talk. Anyway all I wanted to do at 9.30 was wend my way to bed, which I did.

Monday, November 16. The third raid on Italy without loss to our forces. Whilst we go on like this it pays us to bomb them. I expect the Italians by now are fed up with raids. We are very busy again at the New Zealand Club and I was jolly glad to get home. I am always tired when I have had a busy day on Sunday at the YM. Now that Joyce and I are conscripted for firewatching we do it on Monday nights and I hope, since it is my regular evening for the New Zealand Club, that we don't get activity these nights (selfish thought as usual). Out of our entire road [Appleton Road, SE9] only three women have been conscripted and there are at least 70 houses occupied in it. We know that many of the women concerned didn't register at all, not that I expect they will suffer for this. The Government, or local Council, would find it too big a job to tackle.

Tuesday, November 17. As we were having tea today my Father remarked that the table did not look like the table of a country in the fourth year of war, so I noted down what we were having. Spam, cheese, tomatoes, celery, beetroot, pickled onions and two sorts of home-made chutney, Swiss roll and apples. Really we ought never to grumble about the food we get, although everything on our table except the Spam and cheese and Swiss roll came from the garden and in this we are very fortunate.

Wednesday, November 18. Met J. this morning on my way to work. He was just returning from leave and we spent a pleasant journey telling one another just why we thought last night's *Brains Trust* was so much better than most of the present series. The answer is very simple – there were no women and the men there really said just what they thought, without deferring so often to the opinions expressed by the said women guests. Actually the answers given by the Brains to the question about the influence of women in America and England respectively were very amusing just because they were frank. When J. was right through his pilot's course, he was informed that he had failed (I believe because he wears glasses) and now he is in the middle of taking the Observer's course. He was very depressed at one time but has got over this and is still full of beans.

Thursday, November 19. We were very busy at the canteen this evening and had a visit from a boy home on leave from Ireland. He used to be stationed locally and also has his home here, so he dropped into the canteen. Since it was pay-night, most of the RAOC ex-boys were in the 'local' spending all their pay. Some of them came in at odd times but quickly went off to partake of something stronger than tea. G. told me that they were even merrier than usual and were very thrilled because they were spending their whole week's money so quickly. When I read articles in papers about the wonderful effect the Army life has on boys, I smile. I don't really think it is good for them. It teaches them to forget many of the ordinary duties of the citizen. These boys are proud of the fact that they spend their money in one evening, get drunk when they can, then borrow off the married members of their group. It seems such a terrible pity because so many of them could be such useful members of the community if they were living a normal life.

Friday, November 20. Went to the cinema this evening and saw an amusing film called *Between Us Girls* with Diana Barrymore giving a wonderful performance. With it we saw *The Great Mr. Handel* which was a British film in the most exquisite colour that I have ever seen on the screen. Some of the pastel shades were quite breathtaking, particularly one colour, that of a dress worn by Elizabeth Allen. It was the loveliest blue and took one's attention off the story. The music naturally was more important than the story and the scenes showing how vision came to Handel whilst he was composing *Messiah* were most reverently done. Altogether a satisfying film, though perhaps a little slow, but that tempo I think suited the period. Anyway they let themselves go with the final 'Hallelujah Chorus' which was a triumphant finish to the film. The newsreel was lengthy but apparently the new films from the Middle East have not arrived. I suppose they will be included next week.

Saturday, November 21. What a change to drive and be able to see, but the cold was nearly as trying as the fog. I find these days that children are the biggest menace on the roads. Of course, they really aren't to blame. Many of them are too young to have been brought up in the days of traffic-filled roads, and parents seem to think it unnecessary to teach their children to be careful, thinking, I suppose, that the roads are so clear that the chances of the child being involved in an accident are very remote. W. told me today that with the dozens of drivers at their depot, they have as a consequence a good many accidents, and that in the majority of cases young children are involved. I am afraid that after the war there will have to be a terrific campaign in order to reduce the number of accidents on the roads.

Sunday, November 22. Today is the first day I have been able to stay in bed after 7 o'clock for four weeks and I am determined to make the most of it. However I found that I woke up automatically around 7, but I went back to sleep again until 11 o'clock, then got up feeling terrible. The news is still good from Russia [regarding Stalingrad]. I listened to the Empire News and heard our announcer boasting, but he really has something to sing about, for this is quite the best news from Russia for weeks. The Cabinet changes set us all thinking and questions such as 'Why has Stafford gone?' formed at once on our lips. The publishing of letters shows that these automatic questions were anticipated, but do they really explain the move down, for that is what it is? I wonder if it has anything to do with the fact that Sir Stafford has recently taken to speaking on the same platform as the Archbishops of Canterbury and York, and has on these occasions been associated with some rather revolutionary statements?[11] Wireless reports today say that typhus has broken out in a district in Ireland and a death has occurred. I expect the authorities are concerned about this and will have to be very thorough in their examination of people coming from that country over here.

Monday, November 23. At the New Zealand Club this evening I met a young sailor who possessed only what he stood up in. He was one of the force which 'took' Algiers and told me in considerable detail of the whole action. He said that on his ship they carried both Commandos and Americans, many of the latter being soldiers who had not even completed their training in the States. He and his sailor friends could not speak highly enough of their own service and such remarks as 'The Navy never lets you down', 'The Navy always looks after its own and everybody else', came into every other sentence. The ship this boy was on was finally sunk by the French battery in the town, but their casualties were light. However their ship went down quickly, but a destroyer which kept alongside her when she was hit ran her side right up to the sinking ship and most of the crew were able to jump to safety. The battery on shore was finally blown to pieces by the guns of our big ships, much to my friend's delight. He was very thrilled by all he had experienced. Nonetheless it seemed pretty awful that this boy's shipmates were killed by the French, our former allies. The people at the Club were going to see that he got some more clothes. Apparently when a man is shipwrecked, the powers that be provide him with just a uniform and one set of underwear, which means that the said man can never change, and if he has lost everything, he must buy a second set of things in order to be able to wash them. During the evening, I was taken ill, and struggled home, feeling awful, and when I got indoors I felt like dying. I think I must have caught a chill.

Tuesday, November 24. Felt really dead today and spent it in bed with a hot water bottle clasped to my middle. Odd, how when one feels bad, the news seems unimportant. Nothing short of the Armistice could have moved me today.

Wednesday, November 25. Still felt rocky. Got up at lunchtime and read and listened to the wireless this afternoon. I read a book by Evelyn Waugh called *Put Out More Flags* [1942] and was amazed that I managed to struggle through it. I was under the mistaken impression that this type of book had gone out of fashion and imagined that nobody was interested in the doings of the 'smart set' even if they were performing odds and ends of war work. Maybe the only people who read them are people in the same position as I was, stuck at home with nothing else fresh to read. I think the BBC should start a new station and play the record of 'White Christmas' on it all day long. I am sure I heard it at least six

11. Sir Stafford Cripps was dropped from the War Cabinet and became Minister of Aircraft Production. Herbert Morrison, the Home Secretary and Minister of Security, joined the War Cabinet, and Anthony Eden, the Foreign Secretary, replaced Cripps as Leader of the House of Commons. The political circumstances underlying Cripps' demotion are examined in Peter Clarke, *The Cripps Version: The Life of Sir Stafford Cripps 1889–1952* (London: Allen Lane, 2002), especially pp. 354–70.

times today. I am fond of the tune, but really get sick of it in every programme. This is not the only one that is plugged, but it is one of the worst offenders.

Thursday, November 26. Went back to work today and must say I didn't like getting up and going out into the cold again. I envy those who don't have to do it. Didn't go to the canteen tonight. D. deputised for me, although finding deputies these days is becoming increasingly difficult. The news from Russia still continues good. I expect the Germans are getting a trifle worried about the situation.

Friday, November 27. The weather is still bitterly cold. I shouldn't be surprised if we don't get a 'White Christmas'. Tonight listened to Tommy Handley in *It's That Man Again*, a programme I try never to miss. I think it is the best variety programme we get from our studios [it was, indeed, hugely popular].

Saturday, November 28. Took the van out today, but did not do a route. I went to Dartford for the Stores, and quite enjoyed the run down. It seems odd driving right into Dartford when only a little while back it was absolutely forbidden territory to anything but official cars. Listened again this evening to Tommy Handley, this time in a programme which is broadcast regularly to the Middle East and was heard on Forces programme for the first time. He had [the American actor] Edward G. Robinson with him and the programme was quite the best of its kind that I have heard from our studios for a long time – funnier than the Jack Benny or Bob Hope series [both American comedians], and they are really good. Actually I think Tommy Handley is the only broadcasting comedian who compares in any way to these two Americans. I think feeling ill forces one to listen to the radio more often, and I have become quite broadcasting-minded.

Sunday, November 29. Joyce and I were on duty all day at the canteen, and we had a very busy day. Heard the news about the terrible fire in Boston in which hundreds of people were killed. Whilst the announcer was giving details of this catastrophe I watched the faces of three Americans sitting at one of the tables, and was surprised to see that they didn't even appear interested. When one thinks of the state Boston must be in today, with thousands of families affected by the fire, it seems incredible that we English are more concerned than some Americans. When I asked one American what he thought about the fire, he said 'Well I've never been to Boston' as if this excused his lack of interest. Mr. Churchill's speech was not as interesting as some, and he had nothing fresh to tell us, but I imagine he was trying to curb some of the excessive optimism which has swept over many hundreds of people here, who seem to imagine that the war will be over by Christmas.[12]

12. In this 'World Broadcast' from London, Churchill emphasised the hard reality of this fourth year of war. 'I know of nothing that has happened yet which justifies the hope that the war will not be long, or that bitter and bloody years do not lie ahead.' He warned that 'The dawn of 1943 will soon loom real before us, and we must brace ourselves to cope with the tricks and problems of what must be a terrible year.' Changing to a more upbeat tone, he added that 'We do so with the assurance of ever-growing strength, we do so as a nation with a strong will, a bold heart and a good conscience.' (*Speeches*, VI, pp. 6714 and 6715.)

Monday, November 30. Front Line [*1940–41: The Official Story of Civil Defence of Britain*], the government publication dealing with the Blitz period, is published today [by the Ministry of Information] and sales seem to be terrific. It is extremely well got up and some of the pictures are wonderful. Much of the contents is old history, but there is a lot in it which is fresh. Anyway, peculiar though it is, many people here like nothing better than to talk of the Blitz and what happened on this and that night. Somehow the wonderful spirit which seemed everywhere at that time seems to have left us to a great extent, and I feel that many people would like it to return. I don't think it will unless we have another period of communal suffering, as we did then.

Tuesday, December 1. A memorable day – maybe our ancestors will be able to say that, if the proposals contained in Sir William Beveridge's Report are ever carried out. Somehow much of the report seems too practical ever to be carried out, because if the Government will not nowadays raise the old age pension, which almost every thinking person in this country realises to be utterly useless for a man or woman to live on these days, will that Government, in the face of the considerable opposition any new social measure of this nature is bound to inspire, consider these sweeping recommendations of Sir William? I think the only hope we have of seeing this Report turned into action is the power of the people to insist that after this war we do not slip back as they did after the last, and this Report is something solid for the people to hang their own ideas to. Sir William Beveridge has shown us the way, and since we now know that money is no object, judging by the way we can find it nowadays, that cannot be made the stumbling block.[13]

Wednesday, December 2. When I went to my office, just near HM Stationery Office, before 9 o'clock this morning, a queue of some hundreds was lined up waiting to buy Beveridge – the name which is on everybody's lips today. Apparently his proposals have been read with interest in the USA. Bought a watch for my Father today. He has broken the only one he has, which he has used since the last war, and since it is impossible to get them repaired these days, he asked us to get him one for Christmas. It is quite a nice watch. I only hope it is satisfactory because the guarantee given with it is quite useless whilst the war is on.

Thursday, December 3. Joyce and I on at the canteen this evening. We are quite busy too. Mrs. D., the woman we relieve, told me that she spent last weekend in Brighton. She said that there was no shortage of anything in that town, and she was able to buy certain things which we haven't seen in London

13. The Beveridge Report, which was widely praised, laid the main foundations for Britain's welfare state and tried to address concerns about how postwar society could be better – more secure, more equitable, more supportive – than that before the war. Wartime discussions of social security and the pressures for postwar reform are well summarised in 'Beveridge and All That', chapter 6 of Robert MacKay, *Half the Battle: Civilian Morale in Britain During the Second World War* (Manchester: Manchester University Press, 2002).

for months. Food too is plentiful there, and they were able to eat really well all the time they were there.

Friday, December 4. What a rush there is to buy *Front Line*. I have been buying copies for different friends, and quite regularly they are sold out. Of course there is naturally bound to be a great demand for this publication – more probably than for the more technical *Battle of Britain* or *Bomber Command* which naturally had a slightly limited appeal, whereas almost everyone who has heard a siren wailing will be interested in *Front Line*.

Saturday, December 5. I got very cold this morning on the van, and what with the rain, which simply fell from the heavens, I felt far from cheerful. The family had a visit from B. whilst I was out. He is attached to the Commandos and was in the Dieppe raid. Apparently he had bandages on his head and my Father was very sympathetic, but B. explained that he got his injuries in a peculiar manner. Apparently he was with about 20 men, raiding the outskirts of the town. He was being attacked by two Germans and turned to defend himself when he saw a third coming towards him wielding a terrific iron saucepan. He just remembers being hit, and when he woke up he was in hospital in England. Actually I think he was very fortunate to get back. It just shows how brave our men are, to wait until they have picked up their wounded before coming back.

Sunday, December 6. This evening my Father, Joyce and I went to a fire-watchers' film show and demonstration. It was intended that firewatchers in the whole district should attend, but when we got there we found eight other spartans, and when the show started we were about twenty. Actually it was quite interesting and I was glad that I attended, although it was very cold when we came out. We got home in time to hear General Smuts' speech [*Listener*, 10 December 1942, pp. 739–40]. I was glad to hear him, but the speech developed into a eulogy of Mr. Churchill, which from anybody else would have become boring.

Monday, December 7. At the New Zealand Club tonight, M., who is usually on with Eileen and myself, only stayed for a few minutes. She was going out to dinner with V., celebrating before going to the Palace tomorrow to collect his DFC [Distinguished Flying Cross]. We were busy. I felt quite exhausted when I got outside. I am sure the atmosphere of these places is quite unhealthy – so full of smoke.

Tuesday, December 8. We were in the midst of a grand row at home tonight when Philip strolled in unannounced, having travelled up from Bristol without letting us know. He left King's a day early in order to sit for an examination in Kensington tomorrow. He is enjoying life in Bristol although it is very different from that at Torquay.[14] He is really busy, working hard and also doing

14. Philip was now an engineering student at King's College, London, which had been evacuated to Bristol.

strenuous work for the STC [Senior Training Corps] for which they are being experimented on with Commando training. Apparently the Government are watching this experiment with interest, to see if there is any falling-off in examination results because of the amount of time and energy spent on soldiering. Philip prefers the STC to the ATC, although the University Air Squadron members spend their weekends flying all round England with pilots of the ATA [Air Transport Auxiliary].

Wednesday, December 9. Went to dinner tonight with Mrs. F. We were a very jolly party of YMCA people. We gossiped and scandalled all evening and did not drink tea. Actually I can see why there is a shortage of liquor this year, judging by the huge stock of drinks they had in. A huge sideboard absolutely filled with whisky, brandy, port, sherry, champagne, gin, etc. – dozens of bottles. As a matter of fact it looked like the peacetime stock of a club or similar institution, not the stock of a private individual. I have just finished reading *Assignment to Berlin* [1942] by Harry Flannery, and was surprised to find that I enjoyed it quite well. I had been prepared for something very trashy, but although I don't think he writes as well as William Shirer or Howard Smith [author of *Last Train from Berlin*, 1942], nevertheless the matter was interesting, so the style didn't worry me a great deal.

Thursday, December 10. We were busy this evening at the YM – these days we get quite a few Americans in. It is very odd that in the suburbs, like Lee, they seem to be quite apart, and the people do not seem at all willing to try to break down the barriers. The attitude of most of the women who work in the canteen during the daytime is typical. They think that the Americans are all rude, wealthy and do all they can to be as unpleasant as possible. Now I admit that some of them are rude, but so are a great many Englishmen. In fact I think that quite 50% of the men who use our canteen have either forgotten any breeding and good manners they have had, or else have never possessed any. Anyway, I don't find the Americans as rude as some of our men, and have to admit it – not that I blame them being a little annoyed at the patronising tone some people here seem to adopt when addressing them.

Friday, December 11. Went to the cinema with Joyce and Philip tonight, and it was quite like old times. The programme wasn't tiptop, but I enjoyed it, probably because I felt quite good humoured. We saw *Big Shot* with Humphrey Bogart as the inevitable gangster and a new *Dr. Kildare* film with the Dutch actor Philip Dorn in it, which was quite intriguing. We missed Tommy Handley, but they assured us when we got home that it wasn't quite as good as usual. We listened to *Sweeney Todd* [about a nineteenth-century murderer] however – it made me sick.

Saturday, December 12. I did a terrific amount of work on the van today. Several routes had been missed during the week and I was given the job of doing them all, which I did, covering many miles. At some of the sites I was shown toys that men everywhere seem to be turning out this year – tanks, planes, ships, etc., all beautifully turned out. They sell them as soon as they are made, I hear. Actually, where men are hanging about doing nothing, it is quite a good idea for them to put their energy into something of the sort, and remunerative too – they are obtaining five and six shillings for each toy. One of the boys at the Camp has made a marvellous engine which we are going to raffle for charity. It really is super, and so far we have sold about £9 of tickets, and hope to sell quite a few more before Christmas, when it will be drawn.

Sunday, December 13. Joyce and I are on duty all day at the YM. We were quite busy all day. Nowadays we get a sprinkling of Americans in who will insist on having 'toasted spam sandwiches' which consist of two slices of toast with spam between them. We have been amused at this peculiar taste and as far as our canteen goes, most of the spam sent over on Lease-Lend is going back into the stomachs of these Americans. We were very pleased to get a lift home from some of the REME [Royal Electrical and Mechanical Engineers] boys, who came in just before we left. After ten hours on one's feet, it is sometimes almost impossible to stand in a queue for a tram or bus. Tonight we went home in comfort of a sort, despite the fact that A., who was driving, took us along at 75 miles an hour, much to the annoyance of the local police, who, so it seems, can't do a thing about it.

Monday, December 14. At the New Zealand Club this evening, M. was full of her Palace visit – how glamorous the King looked, how he spoke for some minutes to V., and how they had their picture taken by newspaper photographers, only to find later that it did not appear in any London paper. Some terrifically tough-looking Americans tonight told me with considerable eagerness that they were going to a children's party next week and they were wondering what to take along for presents. They have got chocolate, nuts and oranges, so I told them that I thought they would be popular enough without taking anything else. They are really looking forward to this party, but to look at them one would never think they seemed children-lovers.

Tuesday, December 15. Came to work with M. this morning. She has worked locally for the Ministry of Aircraft Production for some time and recently was transferred to the Westminster office of the same department. As she is considered to have been transferred, all her fares are paid and she doesn't have to pay a penny for her season [ticket]. This seems quite wrong, as it is all out of public money. And why should she travel up for nothing when millions of people are coming up daily and having to pay out of their meagre earnings the exorbitant prices charged by the Southern Railway and other companies for their tickets. I must say, R. and I felt rather bitter about this.

Wednesday, December 16. We saw some wonderful newsreels of the Russian fighting tonight. They must have been taken right up in the front lines. The scenes of devastation are ghastly, and when one thinks of the millions of towns and villages all over the world ravaged and torn by the war, one realises how many years it will take even to start rebuilding it all, although as the film commentator said, nature is amazingly swift in covering up these scenes of carnage and destruction. I can remember, too, how quickly the grass and weeds grew over bomb damage in the heart of London, and in the country the process must be much quicker.

Thursday, December 17. At the canteen tonight, we discussed the Christmas party we are giving next Wednesday. I wonder whether it will be anything of a success. Boys with spirit don't seem to care for 'Free do's', and we usually get the scrounger type of person coming along in droves. The 'do' itself is being got up by the 'old women' of the canteen, who have nothing else to do, so we should have plenty of food etc. prepared. All the workers have agreed to make or bring something in the delicacy line – I think I shall make mince-pies or sausage rolls. In these days of tight rationing, it is amazing what we can find for these special occasions. I have recently tried a recipe for sweets, which turn out just like marzipan. Soya flour is the main ingredient, with very little flour. Mrs. T. is going to marzipan and ice the cake with the same mixture. It should be delicious.

Friday, December 18. The news from Egypt is stirring this morning – Rommel's army cut off by the 8th Army. The news makes up for the peculiar weather we are having these days – so mild that one hears cases of spring crops coming up months before their time.

Saturday, December 19. Took Philip out on the van today. He enjoyed himself and the WAAF preferred being served by him. In fact they made up to him all the morning, much to my amusement. We are all very interested in what will happen to Corporal D. who comes into the canteen every day. He was sentenced yesterday to two months imprisonment. Apparently he sold silk stockings to girls at the camp without coupons. This all happened about a year ago, but retribution has overtaken him now. Actually I think he has been unfortunate. At that time thousands of people were involved in this illicit trade, and the police have got hold of a few unlucky persons, to be held up as examples. If he is finally sent to serve his sentence, he will be discharged from the RAF, then automatically called up for the Army when he comes out of prison, and thus a promising career will be ruined.

Sunday, December 20. Spent a riotous day at home, as we had a visit from some small Catholic relations with their parents. The children are three, four and five respectively, and in the past I have always thought it rather unpleasant to have children so rapidly, but watching these three changed my views somewhat. They are such intelligent children, and so full of fun, great company one for the other. Their mother was a children's nurse before she married, and has had less trouble with her brood than some girls I know have had with one. They were all evacuated to Plymouth before the Blitz started, and during the raids on that town she had to trek out into fields and spend the nights there. This happened for several weeks – not that the experiences seem to have had any lasting effect on the children.

Monday, December 21. After we finished our shift at the New Zealand Club this evening a few of us went out to celebrate Christmas – rather a hurried celebration for me, as I use the Southern Railway. This excuse is always enough for knowing people, because my trains are once-hourly or less, and I am always having to rush to catch one of these wretched trains in order to save waiting for an hour at least. Actually I don't think that people who live in districts served by the Tubes appreciate them enough. Some nights when I have been working at the Club, after a busy day at the office, the waiting nearly kills me, as well as wasting so much time.

Tuesday, December 22. At the office today we got our Christmas boxes – this year in cash and not certificates, much to our delight. I think the Christmas box idea is a grand one. One always needs extra money around the festive season, and it always helps me to get out of debt. I made about 60 mince pies this evening for the party at the canteen tomorrow – they are jolly good.

Wednesday, December 23. The party at the YMCA began terribly. When we arrived everybody was quite flat – no pianist, no band and everybody just sitting around the room looking at one another. However the AFS (stationed next door to the canteen) came to our rescue and their band played all evening. The whole of one side of the room was filled with tables laden with good things, and what a show it was, quite like a pre-war party. We had a large Christmas cake iced and marzipaned, jellies, trifles, pastries of all kinds, and lovely sandwiches. The boys enjoyed themselves I think, but it was odd to see how the old-fashioned and childish games went down best of all. Oranges and lemons, and musical chairs, were very popular and helped to get the party going. I do think parties of this sort are a good idea. They spread a spirit that can't be caught by casual kindness.

Thursday, December 24. Christmas Eve and one of the loveliest days we have had this winter. The shining sun was a pleasure to behold. Joyce and I rushed round trying to buy a few last presents this afternoon. We were on duty this evening at the canteen and we were surprised that we sold so much ordinary food. We were much troubled by the presence of the mistletoe from last night. I have often wondered how the custom of kissing under the mistletoe began. It seems so pointless. But how the boys seem to enjoy it. It puts courage into the most timid individuals.

Friday, December 25. Got up at 9 o'clock merely because the radio announcement of Admiral Darlan's death, coming from downstairs, shook me quite successfully from my slumber. What a shock – and are we all pleased about it. The feeling generally seems to be that it is a good thing. I expect [Pierre] Laval will feel a trifle apprehensive when he hears the news. Peculiar, though, that the boy who attempted to shoot Laval was called a hero – by our official circles too – yet this man is called an assassin, and is being tried by court-martial.[15] Listened to the wireless all day and the programmes were very enjoyable. The carols have been really lovely this year.

Saturday, December 26. Joyce and I went out on the van today and what a morning we had. We went to the RAOC depot – got there at 9.30 – and served the few men roaming round the workshops. We gossiped too, and soon the men who had been off on Christmas Day began to arrive back and by 1 minute to 11 o'clock the avalanche descended upon us and we were swamped. Actually we went on serving right in the middle of the parade, but nobody cared about this. We were terribly cold, almost crying in fact, and we had to be really revived before we could leave. The assassin [of Darlan] was executed today. I wonder whether we shall ever hear the real story of these events of the past two days. They will certainly make interesting reading when they are finally published.

Sunday, December 27. Joyce and I completed our 'working holiday' by being on duty at the canteen all day. We were busy too. This year everybody seems hungry despite the fact that there is always more about, even in the Army, at Christmas time. Philip is going back to Bristol tomorrow, so we talked a good deal tonight. He is going to do a fortnight's concentrated Home Guard training. He has got to do this between now and August, and he felt he would rather get it over quickly.

Monday, December 28. Philip went off today and whilst Mother and he were at Paddington six or so German officers were escorted across the platform. Mother said they were exceedingly haughty and perfectly dressed. The amusing part of the whole business was the complete indifference of the citizens of London, who more or less ignored them. I wonder what these Germans thought, when they watched London carrying on so normally. At the New Zealand Club tonight, one of our regular American visitors told me that he had spent a wonderful Christmas with some people in Streatham who gave him a fine time. He was so enthusiastic that he made me feel rather happy about it all. Kindness of this sort will certainly create international friendship that will take a lot of breaking.

Tuesday, December 29. The news today continues to be good, particularly from Russia, in the news bulletins. The Russian news comes first automatically now. The weather here is getting quite wintry. It is snowing a little tonight.

15. Admiral Jean François Darlan, who had been a prominent member of the Nazi-sympathising Vichy Government and Commander-in-Chief of its armed forces, happened to be in Algiers at the time of the Anglo-American landings in French North Africa, and shortly thereafter he performed a remarkable *volte face* and agreed to work for the Allies. He was assassinated on Christmas Eve by a young French royalist.

Wednesday, December 30. Finished reading *Crisis in Zanat* [1942, a novel] by G. M. Thomson, one of the books I had for Christmas. I enjoyed it immensely. It was something of a relief after reading so many books of the *Berlin Diary* variety. Many of the characters and events can be compared with actual persons and events, which is one of the reasons why I found it so amusing. I am now going to begin my other present, *A Word in Your Ear* [1942] by Ivor Brown, which should be interesting.[16]

Thursday, December 31. The radio reports a naval battle in the North Sea. It is still going on, so we must wait. But how terrible it must be up near the Arctic Circle, when it is so cold down here. It is New Year's Eve, and we decided to celebrate at home because it is so cold and miserable these nights. At the canteen tonight all the customers were off to celebrate somewhere or other, and usually wanted us to go along too.

Friday, January 1, 1943. I wonder what this year will bring. To Joyce it has brought an abscess, which is causing her face to assume terrific proportions. We dashed round to the doctor tonight, but she can do nothing for it until the dentist has seen it. Meanwhile Joyce will have to hibernate.

*   *   *   *   *   *   *

 The year 1943 in fact brought serious tribulations to Kathleen Tipper's family. On the night of January 17/18, the Tippers were bombed out of their house on Appleton Road. Kathleen recalled some of the details of this painful experience over 60 years later, in July 2004. 'We went to our shelter [that night] for the first time for weeks, urged on by Joyce who must have had second sight. Many houses were destroyed by incendiary and HE [high explosive] bombs, several neighbours killed, including a great friend. When the All Clear sounded we gathered in a neighbour's house and then went to a local school for the night. Our parents stayed there for three nights whilst Joyce and I stayed with an "honorary" aunt and uncle until we went to Strathaven Road, a requisitioned house.' The family lost all their possessions, and thus were entitled to get new provisions. 'As we had only what we stood up in,' Kathleen wrote in 2004, 'we were provided with four camp beds (canvas stretched over wooden slats), dark grey blankets, minimum sheets, etc. In those days people were not insured as they are now. So we received the maximum government entitlement, £300 for our parents and £50 each for Joyce and myself. I remember the official who interviewed us looking at my long typed list of house contents and possessions being very upset that the maximum grant was so low. We were then able to buy "utility" furniture, i.e., a table and chairs, sideboard, wardrobes, etc.'

 The other major worry for the family in 1943 was the health of Kathleen's mother, Alice Mary Tipper. She had been diagnosed with cancer in 1938. Four

---

16. This book concerns selected words which, according to the author, 'caught my fancy during my casual war-time reading' (p. 5).

years later she seemed in good health. But then, shortly after the shock of losing her house and all that the family possessed, the cancer, as Kathleen recalled, 'flared up again and despite further surgery there was no chance. She travelled to and from Fulham to the Cancer Hospital (now the Royal Marsden) for awful treatment and was bed bound for some months before she died in hospital.' Alice Tipper died on 2 November 1943 and was buried in New Eltham Cemetery in Falconwood, where a white marble stone marks her grave.

Given these losses, it is hardly surprising that Kathleen was disinclined to keep a diary for many months. She had pressing matters to think about and contend with, and diary-keeping must have become a rather low priority in her life. She only resumed writing for Mass-Observation on 8 January 1944, and from then she continued to write every day, without interruption, and often in considerable detail, until 31 March 1944. This portion of her diary, which coincided from January 21 with what came to be known as the 'Little Blitz', is again reproduced in full.[17]

1944

Saturday, January 8. This afternoon went to see *The Demi-Paradise* [an uplifting fantasy concerning Anglo-Russian relations], ranked by some critics with the 'best 10 films of 1943' and by others as one of the worst ever made in Britain. I thought the whole idea of the film rather trifling and insulting, and didn't think it showed the people of Britain in a good light, even during the blitz. Laurence Olivier gave a wonderful performance in the leading role [as Ivan Kouznetsoff, a Russian engineer], a performance which ranked, in my opinion, with Roger Livesey's in *Colonel Blimp*, although I expect these actors are unknown in America. I wonder what the Russians think of this film. I expect it would make them laugh (the film stresses the wonderful sense of humour possessed by the Russians). I wonder if films like this do more harm than good?

Sunday, January 9. Quite a rush round this morning, as Joyce and I are at the canteen this afternoon. My father was working today – this seems quite a regular thing now, they are so busy – so we left Philip working this afternoon when we went off. Now we are so busy, we all find that the weeks simply fly. It seems incredible to me that I ever found the days dragging, and the weeks too long.

Monday, January 10. A filthy day today, terribly wet underfoot, especially in town. I know the farmers want rain, but it is most unpleasant in towns when it comes in torrents. Went to the New Zealand Club as usual this evening. We weren't so busy as we often are. I talked to some RNAF [Royal Naval Air

---

17. A major reference source for the damage done to London during the war by German air attacks is *The London County Council Bomb Damage Maps 1939–1945*, edited by Ann Saunders and introduced by Robin Woolven (London Topographical Society, publication no. 164, 2005).

Force] officers about clothing coupons and the black market generally and was horrified to hear that they quite openly admitted buying things in the black market. One said to me 'When I was a Sergeant and Flight-Sergeant I couldn't get pyjamas or shirts from an ordinary shop, so I naturally went to the black market, where they charged me 28s for a shirt which cost 17s 6d before the war'. He offered to get us anything from the black market in the way of stockings, etc., but we refused, M. rather reluctantly I know, but she couldn't face our disapproval. A naval officer with the party said he and his friends had an effective way of dealing with the black market. They agree to buy something from an agent, and when they get the article refuse to pay for it, knowing that men dealing in black market goods wouldn't dare to go to the police. I think these fellows just do these things for the sake of breaking laws, and going against authority.

Tuesday, January 11. This evening I had a visit from our insurance collector, accompanied by a young man who obviously 'owned' the book, and was on leave or something similar. He came to persuade Joyce and myself to increase our policies. We pay 1s a week for 15 years and after that time get about £36. We know now that this is a racket, but these insurance people are so persistent, and my Mother was persuaded to take them out for us a few years ago, so we carried on with them. Anyway I told him that far from increasing our contributions, we had talked of redeeming the policies, and he seemed so taken aback at this attack that he retreated. There is something sinister about these people. They are relentless, particularly if you look 'soft'.

Wednesday, January 12. The Germans this morning are claiming 123 American bombers from yesterday's big raids by Fortresses and Liberators. It is obvious that losses are big, because they haven't announced them yet, and the radio is preparing us for big losses, in both bombers and fighters. Wednesday evening is ironing evening for us – a job I hate, but it must be done.

Thursday, January 13. The Americans lost 59 bombers and 5 fighters yesterday, and shot down over 100 German fighter planes. I am afraid we expected to hear of many more German losses, because reports said earlier that the Germans lost four to every one of ours. What a terrific number of men to lose though, because most of the American planes hold a dozen men. Whilst we were at the canteen this evening the warning sounded, but we only heard a couple of bursts of gunfire.

Friday, January 14. The papers this morning say that Americans are now on ack-ack guns in London – in other words defending us! I don't know that this is a comforting thought, but I expect it merely means that one or two Americans have been attached to each battery. To judge by some of the articles appearing in our press it would appear that our army, navy and air force could well be demobilised – it seems superfluous. The Americans are ready and able to do all that is necessary as regards 2nd front, ack-ack etc. Some of this is a little ill-timed I think, but I suppose it is put in as a sop for American troops and public.

Saturday, January 15. Terribly foggy all day. I was meeting Joyce at Charing Cross this afternoon to go to see *While the Sun Shines* [by Terence Rattigan] and I had a job to get there as no buses or trams were running and I had to walk most of the way to the station. Fog is a terrible thing. It does so much harm, and must affect the war effort. We enjoyed the play, although it was merely a trifle, but the dialogue was witty and the acting pretty good. We didn't like Jane Baxter a bit; we thought her silly and affected. Hugh McDermott ran off with the show. He plays an American air force officer, and to my mind, with a slight knowledge of Americans, he typified them, in a very nice way I admit, but it was either a pleasant performance of his own character, or a very clever piece of acting. The audience came in quite late – the fog delayed them I suppose. Philip didn't go rowing today. They got lost on the river last time there was a thick fog. Pop took hours to get home from work this evening. Uncle Len came to see us this afternoon and stayed the night. The cinema hit last night was at Croydon – a most peculiar business. The warning sounded this evening, and the firing was quite heavy for a little [while]. Heaven knows what they were firing at – the fog was like a blanket.

Sunday, January 16. Very foggy this morning, but quite suddenly it cleared and the sun shone. I went over to the cemetery this afternoon and whilst waiting for a bus the fog came up quite suddenly again. The thick blanket of fog just rolled towards me and enveloped me in a moment. I had a job to get home. The bus kept hitting the curb, and in the 100 yards or so from bus to house I went wrong twice. My father took three hours to get home from work tonight, because all transport stopped again, and he flopped into a chair utterly exhausted and filthy dirty. This fog is no joke. It must damage the war effort in no uncertain manner, because nothing can move quickly. Mr. Churchill has fully recovered. I expect he is home by now. They certainly wouldn't have announced that he was convalescing in Morocco if he were still there. The Soviet National Anthem was played for the first time in great style this evening, and the whole business seems farcical. When the Russians came into the war they wouldn't allow the 'Internationale' to be played, so this does seem absurd now.

Monday, January 17. Everyone has their tale of the fog this morning, and they all seem remarkably similar. There was a bad train smash at Ilford Station yesterday afternoon. Several persons were killed and many injured; some of both sorts of casualties were Americans. Very unlucky to be killed in an accident of this sort after coming all the way from America to kill Germans. We have so few train smashes in this country that they seem very terrible when they happen. What a good thing Win didn't go home this weekend because the express is the train she always comes back by. Went to the New Zealand Club this evening and spent a busy five hours. Two very burned pilots came in. I have often noticed that these men go about in pairs. I expect it helps. As a matter of fact I have seen them before and they are much improved, but these terrible face wounds take years to heal, and I think they are very brave to go about at all because some people are rather unfeeling and rude to them.

Tuesday, January 18. The Polish-Russian dispute seems no nearer solution, and I expect the Poles will have to give in, but it seems to be causing a good deal of uneasiness here, and people I have spoken to about it seem to have violent feelings one way or the other. I went to see *Acacia Avenue* [by Mabel and Denis Constanduros] today and enjoyed it immensely. The humour was innocent and not of the slick variety but was better because of that I think. Some of the actors and actresses were very poor, but the show as a whole was good. The *Brains Trust* was rather dull this evening. I suppose the BBC are ensuring a quiet atmosphere at least for a while until the Hogg business becomes forgotten.[18]

Wednesday, January 19. Spent an enjoyable evening at the cinema. Saw *Now, Voyager* – a sentimental and pretty impossible Bette Davis epic – she turns anything into a first-rate film. I think she is far above any other woman on the screen, and I know many people share my view. Gladys Cooper gave a fine performance in the film. I wonder what it feels like to take parts like this, middle-aged or elderly parts, when she was once considered the most beautiful woman on the English stage? We saw the film of the repatriated prisoners, which is being shown as part of a Red Cross appeal in all cinemas this week. It is most moving, unbearably so some of it, but it does seem disgraceful that these men have to appeal to charity. The Government should provide adequately for every man injured in the service of his country. The newsreel contained some grim pictures of the 14th Army in Burma – the most amazing battle pictures I have ever seen containing shots of men hit by snipers, and some most grim shots of dead Japs. This is surely one of the most ghastly battlefronts in the world?

Thursday, January 20. A short warning this evening whilst we are at the canteen, but it didn't last for more than ten minutes I am glad to say. Odd how they are usually on Thursday.

Friday, January 21. Heard from my grandmother today. She is hoping to take her first walk soon, accompanied of course, but what progress she has made. The warning sounded before 9 this evening, and when the guns started we found that Mrs. L. and Pauline, who share our shelter, had been in it since 8.15, when apparently one siren had sounded. Mr. L. is deputy ARP [Air Raid

18. Quintin Hogg (b.1907), Conservative MP for Oxford City, had been recruited to be a member of the *Brains Trust*. In a recent instalment of this popular programme he had attacked Professor C.E.M. Joad, a long-established 'brain' and member of the 'trust', in rather fiery and intemperate language. The episode is recounted in Geoffrey Lewis, *Lord Hailsham: A Life* (London: Jonathan Cape, 1997), pp. 101–02. The producers of the *Brains Trust* strove to avoid political controversy.

Precautions] for the Borough and is on duty every night, so they like company, and even if we don't go in the shelter one of us go out and talk to them. The firing was terrific. For one period of about half an hour they didn't stop, and the shrapnel was coming down like rain. Some phosphorous bombs dropped near – a few streets away. We recognised them by the bright white light, something I couldn't be wrong about, and we heard several lots of bombs come down in the vicinity. Several fires were burning all around, and the wind didn't help matters. We realised as we came in that we had missed Charlie McCarthy [with his ventriloquist, Edgar Bergen], the first time for ages. I hope this is all for the night.

Saturday, January 22. A second warning early this morning. The firing was almost as intense as it was last night. One of our large front windows smashed – a large piece of shrapnel went through the window, showering powdered glass everywhere, tearing and lodging in the curtain. It makes such a mess. When we have had smashed windows before – at the other house it was quite a common occurrence when raids were bad – we always went off to work and when we got home Mother had cleaned up, but this time I had the job and the glass seemed everywhere. Popped in to see *Flesh and Fantasy* as I was on my own this afternoon – quite an unusual film, and as such deserved support I think. There was little humour in it, and the audience sat in almost complete silence during the showing of the film – rather unusual I think. A terrific night – the wind roared – in all a 'Wuthering Heights' sort of night. British and Americans have made a landing on the coast near Rome. When I heard this news I expected news of the second front, because I was upstairs and didn't hear 'Rome' at the end of the sentence.

Sunday, January 23. Twelve planes shot down on Friday night now. The number is increasing little by little. Our troops are doing well in Italy, and apparently meeting little opposition as yet. Joyce and I on duty this afternoon, which meant a rush around, but as my father was working, there were only three to consider, which helps. Quite busy this afternoon. The time soon passes.

Monday, January 24. Joyce in bed today. She feels dreadful and looks very ill. No fun being ill in an empty house, so we realise that she must feel bad. Went to the New Zealand Club tonight and we were very busy. Talked to several sailors who had been shipwrecked recently. They were full of stories. M. in a dither tonight because she doesn't wear her engagement ring when her fiancé is not with her, and his best friend turned up, so she had to rush out and put it on. Then a New Zealand pilot who has been staying with her this past week came in eager to entertain her, but she had to keep him away from fiancé's friend. And two other men came in – both of them had taken her out and were obviously more than casual friends. We have always told her that she is dishonest, but she managed to keep all these men apart and attracted. Her fiancé must be a fool because he knows that she goes out nearly every night with someone or other and must realise that they don't just take her out – looking at some of them it is obvious. It merely confirms my opinion that men are rather stupid where the female sex is concerned. When too I think of women I know who are working very hard, perhaps have [a] husband overseas or a prisoner, with sons away too, they can't have much fun, yet this utterly worthless girl has all she wants in the way of food, clothes and fun, and deserves so little of it. She told me the other day that she never has margarine – she has butter on everything, even toast. I realise that she doesn't do this on two ounces of butter, but this is merely one example of what is going on all over the country.

Tuesday, January 25. Joyce still in bed. She has received a notice from the Labour Exchange calling her for an interview on Friday, which hasn't cheered her up. She certainly couldn't work longer hours – she does 8.30 till 6 – but I expect she will be sent somewhere like Birmingham [where labour needs were greater]. I think I will go mad if I am left on my own to run the house. It is so much easier with two. Even so it is a lot of work to tackle in the evenings and at weekends.

Wednesday, January 26. Joyce went back to the office today, called in at the doctor's on her way home, and was sent back to bed. She shouldn't have gone back but I think the call-up worried her and she wanted to discuss it with her boss. Tonight was ironing night. Mrs. L., our neighbour, told us about her brother's experiences on Saturday (or was it Friday?) night whilst the raid was on. He works in the Arsenal, is a shop foreman, and had a shift of girls fresh from Manchester on with him. They were thrilled when the siren sounded, quite excited to be in a blitz, but when the guns got up they were frightened and screamed, etc. He got most of them down to the shelter in the second raid but some were still there (in the shop) when the incendiaries came through the roof, and he said he thought they would go mad. It seems so crazy. These girls are billeted in Woolwich and Plumstead in houses where accommodation is only available because the girl of the house has been called up from the Arsenal (or similar factory) in Woolwich, and sent North to work. People in our part of the world get very bitter about it.

Thursday, January 27. Joyce had to return to bed today. She is much worse than she was on Tuesday and has suffered from her rash excursion yesterday. I had a very busy day at the office, rushed home with Joyce's medicine, then back to the canteen, which I did on my own tonight, and was quite busy. One of the RAF boys was telling me that he is going to get to Australia after the war if he can. He is tired of England and its ways. I had quite an interesting talk with him. His ideas are similar to the thoughts running through many fellows' minds. I wonder how many of them will be able to carry out their desires. Mr. W., Joyce's boss, said he would postpone her interview. Sixteen planes shot down last Friday night – over 17%, which is marvellous we all think.

Friday, January 28. Berlin raided last night. Over 1,500 tons – 35 planes lost. We always pray that damage done justifies these losses. The powers that be in the RAF assure us that the losses are not too great, but somehow persons in authority seem to talk very glibly, avoiding the personal side of the question. Losses are mounting, and many homes in Britain are now feeling these losses. Mr. Eden made a serious speech in the Commons today, giving details of the Jap atrocities. Reading it makes one feel very ill, but it merely bears out all that we have heard from various sources, some good, some just rumours. I don't know whether I think it is a good thing to make this public, because many thousands of people will be made very unhappy by it. But I suppose they think it is necessary that a statement should be made.[19]

Saturday, January 29. Went to see *An Ideal Husband* [by Oscar Wilde] – my idea of a good play. The settings and dresses were lovely – so rich and colourful they took the breath away, particularly our 'utility minded' breath. A noisy raid this evening, obviously retaliation for last night's heavy Berlin raid. Hundreds of flares were dropped and we heard several high explosives come down, some fires burning nearby too – the wind seemed to fan the flames. One of the fires is a gas-main Pop says, a nasty target.

Sunday, January 30. There were several incidents in Eltham last night. The damage looked quite severe as we passed by in the bus this afternoon. When we got to the cemetery, it looked a mess. About 70 or 80 incendiaries fell over the ground and it looks to be covered with holes and the white powder they leave behind them. One fell just between Mother's and the next grave, and another on the grave the other side – it looks most unpleasant. I hated to look at it. Pop says the damage at Peckham is quite bad – the shelters were hit there. My mood of depression was increased by listening to [Henrik Ibsen's] *An Enemy of the People*, which is so true to life. Shaw, Ibsen and Chekhov are all so modern. The ideas and the dialogue always seem so topical. Roger Livesey is excellent. His voice has such character. He seems to be in the room with the listener.

Monday, January 31. Dorothy went to a lecture by John Morris, author of *Traveller from Tokyo* [1943], during the weekend, and had some interesting bits of information to pass on to us. Mr. Morris said that the Japs would never give in. They will have to be completely beaten. He also had some strong words to say about the American raid on Tokyo, which he said made little impression on the city. He was there at the time and didn't know a raid was on. He was merely illustrating the wrong impression the press (particularly the American press) give of this raid. Crowds of Australians in the New Zealand Club this evening. Many of them were very drunk too.

Tuesday, February 1. Had an interesting talk with the manageress of a book department in the Strand. I am trying to buy some [John] Galsworthy with some money given me at Christmas, but it is unobtainable, and I have tried

---

19. In this speech, the Foreign Secretary reported on the poor conditions in Japanese POW camps and the abusive treatment of Allied prisoners. 'I have said sufficient to show the barbarous nature of our Japanese enemy.' (*Commons Debates*, 5th series, vol. 396, cols. 1029–35.)

dozens of shops. I think, and she agreed, that it is disgraceful to allow printers to waste their allocation of paper on the trashy books that are coming out in their thousands, whereas good books, classics and decent modern books, are never to be had. She said they are offered this trash, much of it very expensive, or the alternative of having their shelves empty. It seems amazing that I cannot buy the works of one of our greatest British writers, yet could buy any amount of modern filth, or cheap American literature. The *Brains Trust* tonight was not amusing. Lord Darling [Sir William Darling, Lord Provost of Edinburgh] infuriates me. He is so intolerant, and they are all so obsequious with him. I was glad that [the writer] Louis Golding stood up for his rights, and seemed to get the better of the battle of words.

Wednesday, February 2. The doctor wouldn't let Joyce go back to work today. She said she might let her go back Monday. This is the longest period she has ever had away from work and is obviously very run-down. J., our former office boy, who is now a budding officer in the Merchant Navy, came in today, having travelled all over the Middle East since he last saw us. He has had an interesting time, but apparently conditions in Spain have made most impression on him. He told us that the Spaniards are starving and quoted as an example [that] one of their crew threw a crust of bread over the side of the ship whilst they were in port, and about 15 men fought to get it. It seems so awful. I remembered vividly Christmas 1937 when we collected tins of food for [the Republican] Government [of] Spain. Then conditions were bad enough, but Franco has caused them to become much, much worse.

Thursday, February 3. Fort[resse]s raided Wilhelmshaven today, and according to first reports have done a great amount of damage. An American member of our staff over here in the American Army called in today complete with a girl he had picked up. He was a friendly young man, quite a good officer rank, but his girl looked a real 'pick-up'. I suppose they don't mind who the girls are as along as they are girls. I was on duty at the canteen tonight alone, as Joyce didn't venture out, and was alone when the siren sounded. I didn't like it much when the guns started up but soon became too busy to notice it. Still I was glad to hear the all-clear.

Friday, February 4. Another raid early this morning – this time quite a severe one, hundreds of incendiaries, and flares. Trains were awful this morning. I was very late and we had to fight to get in a train. I joined forces with a WAAF who is often on the same train. She is a Yorkshire girl billeted with her mother-in-law in Catford. She is very lonely and doesn't like London a bit – this travelling doesn't help either. Rene had casualties at her First-aid post this morning, mostly burns from the incendiaries. The Americans only lost four Fortresses yesterday, which is good news. Queued up for ballet tickets today for Dorothy, but didn't get them. In the queue talked to a very intelligent woman who was trying to get them in order to take an American girl friend of hers. In the course of the conversation she told me that she knows the pilot who occasionally takes the Premier on his journeys, and he was in [the] USA on

November 6 of last year (1942) when the landings in North Africa were made, and until he got back to England a few days later he had no idea that a single British soldier had landed in North Africa – the American press made no reference to this fact. I expect they are the same now about the fighting in Italy. I think we should launch something of a campaign to educate the Americans with regard to what we have done and are doing in the war, or they are going to get something of a surprise when we and the Russians start to take a lead in the peace negotiations, as they probably think that as they have done all the fighting, they should run the peace.

Saturday, February 5. Hundreds of planes going out all the morning in the direction of the coast. Fortresses and Lightnings made a wonderful picture in the sky. It is announced later that they raided aerodromes in France, some in the Paris area. Losses are small. The bomb we heard whiz past our heads on Friday morning was a container with 500 incendiaries of all types inside, which didn't open. It fell in the meadow near our houses and another bomb which fell at the same time and at the same place caused all these bombs to explode, which caused the fire and smoke. What a piece of luck that they didn't fall all over our estate, or there might have been fires and much damage. Went shopping this afternoon – found it very difficult to use up my remaining points. Philip was utterly exhausted this evening when he came home. STC in the morning and rowing in the afternoon take it out of him. He is training very industriously for the race on February 19th against Bristol and Reading Universities.

Sunday, February 6. A warning early this morning, this time at 6 a.m. Gunfire was quite heavy for five minutes, but after that we didn't hear a thing. Joyce and I at the canteen this afternoon, the first time Joyce has been there for some time. Mrs. K., one of the paid staff (she cleans urns, etc.), an Irishwoman, is in trouble because her two youngest boys about 10 and 11 have been summoned to the Juvenile Court, together with 15 other boys, for stealing from an Army dump over 13,000 rounds of ammunition and mills bombs, and model aeroplanes. They all went along to the police station on Friday, the 17 boys and all the parents. She said they were like the 'Dead End Kids'. The parents were much more worried than the children, who were informed by one of the boys (son of a wealthy family in Blackheath), who had spent a week in a Remand Home, that they would have a lovely time if they were sent there – plenty of food, oranges, apples, etc. And Mrs. K. said the boys were all looking forward to a stay in the Home. I don't think her boys will be punished because they did not steal anything themselves. They were merely given two planes by one of the others who said that his uncle had made them, but she is very worried nonetheless. This is merely one instance of the sort of thing that is becoming quite common these days. The children are left to their own resources, with fathers in the forces and mothers at work, and this is the natural result. Philip is 19 years old today. He spent it working [most of the faculties of King's College had returned from Bristol to London for the 1943–44 academic year].

Monday, February 7. After a busy day at the office had a busy evening at the New Zealand Club. A naval officer promised to bring us some silk stockings one Monday evening. He told us that he had got rid of 20 pairs this morning, and we made him promise to remember us next time he comes back from a trip with such precious cargo. I read in the paper this evening that my great hero James Stewart is in London. I have been an enthusiastic 'fan' of his for about ten years and have had to suffer a good deal of teasing from the rest of the family as a result. But they became his fans themselves after a time. He certainly was an accomplished actor, and has been in the Air Force for years, which is more than can be said of many of our young actors.

Tuesday, February 8. Listened today to a broadcast by Anthony Kimmins from an American base on the landing on the Marshall Islands [*Listener*, 24 February 1944, pp. 212–13]. I am always struck by the generous way our press and radio treat an American action – over-emphasizing the glory of each action it seems to me. I suppose this is part of our national character, to praise everyone else, but I compare it with the way in which the Americans treat our activities. I notice that when things were going well in Italy the emphasis was on the American troops and Air Force. Now that things seem serious, we see many references in American broadcasts and extracts from American papers to the British Fifth Army, Navy, etc. etc.

Wednesday, February 9. An interesting article in today's *[Daily] Herald* – one of the weekly articles written by Sumner Welles, in which he discusses the Russian problem, so called.[20] It appears that many Americans are worried by this recent Soviet action of making independent all the various 'States' of the Union. They think that at the Peace conference the Russians will be in the majority, that is, if they send a delegate from each of these independent states. It seems to me early days to worry about such matters, but I know only too well that these same thoughts will probably be filling the minds of many of the prominent members of our own Government, who have no love for Russia, despite their public utterances. Now that the news is serious from Italy, the Russians are again taking the headlines in press and radio.

Thursday, February 10. Mrs. K's boys got off I hear tonight, although several of the other lads were sent to Remand Homes for a week. This seems rather stupid to me. What good can a week in a Home be. It would save the country money if these short stays were abolished. These are the thoughts of one who knows very little about such matters, but I feel that no good or evil can come out of a week in a Remand Home. But presumably the powers that be are of a different opinion. We were very busy at the canteen this evening. Joyce was welcomed back by one and all, and as a result I was less rushed. Bright moonlight as we walked home – too bright for the Germans I think. In the news

20. Sumner Welles (b.1892) was an American diplomat and writer on international affairs. In this essay, 'We Must Grasp this Polish Nettle!', he discusses the future of Poland as a strong and independent nation, probably within revised borders.

tonight it said that Flying Fortresses and other heavy bombers had been sent to help the men on the beach-head – not too soon it seems to me.

Friday, February 11. Called in for my shopping this evening. Was rather amused to see tucked away in a brown paper parcel a packet of custard powder and a tin of floor polish, the first of either I have been able to get since July, when I took over the housekeeping, and I know there is plenty about – if you know the way to get in with the shopkeepers. Quite a noisy alert this evening. The gunfire was pretty violent. We heard two come down; one absolutely rocked the earth – something rather special I should think. A beastly night to be homeless, so cold and dark. We always say that when the all-clear sounds, knowing what someone is going through somewhere.

Saturday, February 12. Apparently the object which caused our shelter to shake was a bomb which fell in North Woolwich. It must have been something rather large because windows this side of the river were broken, and the explosion was felt over a tremendous area. Pop overslept this morning – didn't wake up till 8.30, the time at which Joyce should be at the office. Both Joyce and Philip (who was due on parade at 9.30) were out of the house before 9, but Pop, who usually leaves the house at 7, didn't go, as he is working seven days a week now, could do with the rest. Went to see *Wuthering Heights* this afternoon. It is four years since I saw it before, and it doesn't seem possible that this film was made all that time ago. It wears so well. Maybe it is because the acting was so good, and the atmosphere of the book captured so accurately. An alert this evening, with a little gunfire. The wireless went off over half an hour before the siren sounded, so perhaps there were planes around.

Sunday, February 13. Spent our usual violent Sunday, rushing around and doing jobs left undone all the week. We find so much to do that we never get a chance to sit down. This morning while we worked, Philip played his new symphony, Brahms' *Piano Concerto No. 2 in B flat*, which he bought with money given to him for his birthday and Christmas. It cost £2 19s 6d, as each of the six records cost 9s 11d, a great amount of money, but I really think the enjoyment repays the cost. A very noisy raid this evening. The gunfire was very heavy – lots of new-sounding guns. There were several fires around during the raid.

Monday, February 14. Bomb stories are again popular. I think people are getting very tired of the raids now. It is not surprising, because the number of people who are affected by raids is definitely limited. Some parts of England (many towns and villages) have never had raids and certainly don't realise the strain they impose on those who live through them. I don't think they compare in the remotest degree with the dangers experienced by our soldiers, sailors and airmen, but it is a definite fact that only a small proportion of the population are suffering in this way, and the rest don't appreciate that fact sufficiently. All my friends tell of their relations and acquaintances, living in various parts of Britain, who are not interested [in] or pooh-pooh raids, etc. Most of my relations write to us and tell us of the terrible times they are having, when none of them have heard a bomb drop, and certainly the barrage doesn't worry them. Yet they have the cheek to write to us, who have experienced everything there is to experience in this line, and make these comments. Joyce tells me that several of the married women at her firm have evacuated themselves. A friend of D.'s goes off to Chislehurst [Kent] caves every night, leaving husband to fend for himself. I was at the New Zealand Club tonight. Rumour has it that the King and Queen are going there this week, so there is much polishing and cleaning going on. I wonder if the King and Queen would get a shock if someone one day received them naturally – without all this cleaning, etc. They must think everything is very good in England. They only see that which is clean, attractive and happy. This is rather cynical, because neither of them seem to lack intelligence, merely the opportunity to find out the truth.

Tuesday, February 15. A WAAF has been murdered in Well Hall and the whole district is buzzing with it. Last night when I got home from the Club I found my father dressed ready to come to meet me, but I had left earlier than usual, so he hadn't started out. He is naturally worried, and I don't really care for walking about alone in the blackout.[21] A friend of D.'s had a talk with a returned Eighth Army man this weekend. He is one of the men whose experiences have caused him to refuse to sleep in a bed, and behave generally in a way to cause worry to his relatives. He did tell her some interesting facts though, particularly with regard to atrocities committed by the Germans in Italy. He said that it was fairly common to find a child with a hand cut off, and he is fairly itching to get at the Germans in the 2nd front. Joyce is firewatching tonight. I hope it is quiet.

Wednesday, February 16. Berlin got the heaviest raid ever on an enemy target during the night, over 2,500 tons in 20 minutes. We have lost 43 planes, which the Air Ministry take great care to say is not excessive out of over 1,000 planes. Nevertheless it means that over 300 airmen are lost, no small number. The search for the murderer goes on, and there is something like a minor panic, and there are dozens of husbands, fathers and boyfriends queued up at Well Hall station every night, ready to escort their women-folk home.

Thursday, February 17. Another girl has been attacked locally, so Philip came to meet us from the canteen this evening. I must say that I had never imagined that mass-emotion could be roused so quickly. Even Mr. R., the manager of the YMCA, admitted that he is rather nervous, although I can't imagine that any man would mistake him for a female. The King and Queen went to the Club today, I notice, so their cleaning and polishing wasn't in vain.[22] The

21. The partly naked body of Iris Miriam Deeley, a 21-year old WAAF stationed at Kidbrooke Camp, was discovered near Well Hall station on the morning of 14 February. She had been strangled during the previous night. Ernest James Harman Kemp, a gunner in his early twenties in the Royal Artillery stationed at Woolwich, was later arrested (on 22 February) and tried for and found guilty (on 18 April) of her murder.
22. This royal visit was reported, rather briefly, in the *New Zealand Herald*, 19 February 1944, p. 6.

Government's plans for a national health plan are announced today – takes the sting out of the Beveridge plan, and is certainly a clever move by the Tories, with a view to the next election coming soon, I suppose.

Friday, February 18. An American troopship has been lost with over 1,000 casualties – quite the most serious loss of this nature we have suffered. The West Derby election result was announced today. Alderman [Charles] White, the Independent Labour candidate, has won the seat. What a jolt this must have given the Government. No doubt they will put their backs into winning Bury St. Edmunds.[23] The Tory machine is quite cunning as we well know when it really tries.

Saturday, February 19. A raid in the early hours of the morning – quite a severe one, with many planes around, and many fires burning when the all-clear sounded. Heard four bombs come down, which was not much I suppose. The barrage consisted almost entirely of rocket guns and quick firing guns, which don't fire to a great height, and no wonder because the planes seemed to be flying very low. The damage seems to be widespread, as in the Blitz, and many parts of London have had a share. Went this afternoon to see Orson Wells' latest picture, *Journey into Fear*, with Joseph Cotton, which although disappointing was at least a real account of how a person would behave under similar circumstances, I feel. I get a little tired of the spy story, with the very handsome hero, outwitting everyone else in the story, whereas in this film the young man in question behaved in rather an ordinary and somewhat cowardly manner. This evening we thought we were going to hear *Pink String and Sealing Wax*, but instead they broadcast *The Poetical Gentleman* by Eden Phillpotts. Quite the most sinister play I have heard for ages, but although some of it repelled me, I was obliged to sit through to the end. One thing I do hand it to the BBC for, and that is their plays. They put them over so well. And wireless seems to add to the atmosphere of many.

Sunday, February 20. The RAF lost 79 planes over Leipzig. The city was attacked by American planes today. Over 1,000 planes used in last night's raid, say the reports, and over 2,000 in the Yank raid today, so the people in the city must be out of their minds. A nasty raid tonight. The gunfire was heavy again, and the fires were burning all around when the all-clear sounded. The wind, which was high, seemed to be fanning the fires up. A basket of incendiaries fell in the streets around us and the men enjoyed themselves putting them out.

---

23. The Government suffered numerous defeats in by-elections, though it was to be successful in the one forthcoming in Bury St. Edmunds. In its comments on the West Derby results, the *Daily Herald*, 19 February 1944, p. 2, editorialised that while the conduct of the war was satisfactory, 'there is throughout the nation a suspicion, which is deepening into alarm, that the National Government's preparations for the post-war years lack urgency and decision; that they are flagging for want of unity of purpose.' This by-election defeat was seen as a protest against privilege and backward-looking attitudes, and a vote in favour of planning for a better future.

Some fell on a house already bombed in an earlier raid, and the rest were put out before they did much damage.

Monday, February 21. My throat which was pretty thick yesterday is very sore this morning, so I decided not to risk the wind. I woke up at 4.45 this afternoon, so had to rush downstairs to get some tea ready for those brave enough to go out. Felt pretty dreadful. Hope there is no raid tonight. Hear that Willesden had it pretty badly at the weekend, so was worried about Dorothy, who has never had a really bad raid there.

Tuesday, February 22. Heard from Dorothy this morning. She did have a bad weekend, which apparently everyone else shared in a lesser or greater degree. I slept till 3 today, then got up and prepared some pancakes for the family. Mr. Churchill has made a speech in the House in which he called for unity once more, a hint I feel to the electors of Bury St. Edmunds, as he was rather bitter about the citizens of West Derby and the man of their choice.[24]

Wednesday, February 23. Another bad raid tonight. We are getting rather to expect them. The fires burn very brightly all around, and the firing was absolutely terrific – [it] nearly deafens us. Pauline is still very good whilst the raids are on, and is not frightened. Joyce brought me three lemons today. Dorrie sent them for my cold, and I was glad to see them. I do love them, but what a terrific amount of sugar they need. I had forgotten how sharp a lemon is.

Thursday, February 24. The papers are still full of bad blitz stories, and it is obvious that the casualties are quite high. Went out for the first time this week, and had a hearty lunch, the first day I had really fancied food. Rang the office. They are all very weary and rather tired of the raids. Of course we, in the South of London, have rather got used to this barrage, because most of the raids for the last few weeks have been as loud, but some of them at the office, living in other parts of London, haven't heard a sound until these past few days. A very noisy night tonight. The gunfire seemed even louder than ever.

Friday, February 25. Last night 13 [German] planes were shot down, quite a good number really, although the searchlights get dozens in the beams, but the ack-ack seems miles off the target. I suppose the difficulties are immense, but somehow it does seem awful, when we can see the plane, for the gunners to

---

24. Churchill's appeal for unity was placed in the second last paragraph of his speech on 'The Progress of the War'. 'My hope is that generous instincts of unity will not depart from us in these times of tremendous exertions and grievous sacrifices, and that we shall not fall apart, abroad or at home, so as to become the prey of the little folk who exist in every country and who frolic alongside the Juggernaut car of war, to see what fun or notoriety they can extract from the proceedings.' At the start of this paragraph he had spoken against the zealous criticism of his Government – 'I find that hard to bear with Christian patience'. (*Speeches*, VII, p. 6894.)

miss shooting it down. I went out again today. It was bitterly cold, and my joints still ache through and through. Our planes seemed to be over all evening.

Saturday, February 26. Got up early this morning in order to go along to the chiropodist. Did quite a bit of work this morning. It has been neglected these past few days. Then as I was on my own I ventured to a tiny cinema near us and saw an excellent programme, *The Scarlet Pimpernel*, one of Leslie Howard's best films in my opinion, and a Charlie Chaplin selection, which did amuse me. The quiet night last night was welcome, but no-one expects another.

Sunday, February 27. Another quiet night. What a thrill to sleep the night through. I went over to the cemetery today. It is bitterly cold, and I was on my own in the cemetery. Dorrie came to tea, and we talked about her experiences in the NFS [National Fire Service], and she gave us some very amusing tales of what 'goes on' at her station; and Philip played the gramophone the while, which made the time pass rather pleasantly. She left soon after 8 as she has to go to Plumstead, and that is rather an unpleasant journey to make in a raid. We are still expecting a raid every night. The General Forces programme made its bow today, and we were soon very tired of it. The voices of the women announcers may charm the men in Malta and elsewhere, but they grate on my poor nerves, and the scripts they read seem to [be] futile. Still no doubt this programme will be hailed with joy by press and public.[25]

Monday, February 28. Went to the office today. Didn't like getting up early, and I felt miserable when I got out into the 'bitter'. After an hour or so I felt better. The company cheered me up. We exchanged bomb stories, like old times, and all felt pleased that we had had a quiet night or two. Called in at the New Zealand Club. Saw Eileen, who told me that they were very worried when I didn't turn up last week, thinking me a mangled corpse. B. (Air New Zealand pilot) was in, and he told us that he was rather nervous of spending the night in London because of the raids, and made us laugh when he said that the other day there was a hit and run raid on Brighton where he is stationed, and when the bombs fell and the glass tinkled down there was a terrible rush for the exits of the hotel. He said that the beds were emptied in a flash and that the stampede was awful. I asked him what they were running for, and he answered 'a safe place in the shelter', and he was absolutely serious. I was amused, but remembered all I have heard and seen of the behaviour of other pilots and air crews, and it seems to be a general fact that they are all very nervous in air raids.

Tuesday, February 29. Another quiet night – one which I really enjoyed. It is pretty certain now that the Russians and the Finns are negotiating some sort of peace, although how it will be enforced I can't see. Whatever happens Finland will still be in the war, because one can't imagine all the German troops in

25. The purpose of this new programming was to strengthen the bonds felt by the men fighting abroad with their families and friends at home by broadcasting details of everyday life on the home front, such as popular songs, sports news, and vignettes of local life.

Finland will just lay down their arms without a fight. They will have to be forced to. Finland has certainly paid a terrible price for her part in the war. The warning sounded this evening and there was a little gunfire, nothing terribly serious.

Wednesday, March 1. I made some lemon curd this evening, with a recipe given me by a girl at the Club, who runs a cake shop. It is absolutely lovely, just like the pre-war variety, although made with dried eggs and custard powder. I always feel that much of the jam, etc. we had before the war was made with substitutes just as much as it is now. Anyway we are going to enjoy this curd, which only used three lemons, and will make a change for the family meals, which give me headaches. Got to bed early tonight in order to get some sleep in before the siren sounds.

Thursday, March 2. The siren woke us around 2.45, and the gunfire sounded almost at once. Our shelter nearly shook down when a stick of six bombs fell nearby, and then the incendiaries came down. One fell on the bombed house next door (I nearly passed out for a moment because it looked as if it was on our house). Then a house opposite caught alight, and another in the road [Strathaven Road, SE12], and soon there were about a dozen houses blazing in the small area around us. Philip rushed upstairs in the burning house because neighbours thought the people were in bed, but they weren't. Then the trailer-pump team (my father and three other neighbours) arrived, and contrary to all instructions, they set about the biggest fire and had it out very quickly. About five of the houses in our little district are quite burned out, and others half burned. Everyone helped to put out other incendiaries that fell in gardens, with pumps and buckets of water, and as a result our hall (and all the others in the road) was a terrible mess, what with soot, ceiling plaster and water. The whole district is ringed with fires, and when we were bathing an hour or so later small ammunition which was obviously hit early in the raid was still going off. Our church in Well Hall was a terrific landmark and is completely gutted – we could see every window and rafter burning quite clearly. There is much damage in Well Hall and the victims are mostly people we have known all our lives. Joyce came home this evening with news of the fires in Siemens, Charlton, Woolwich, [and] also with information about several DAs [delayed-action bombs] which are within 50 yards of our house. In all a wretched night. Joyce and I had been talking yesterday about what we would do if we lost our home again, and tonight I thought it had really come to pass. It is impossible to pack everything we value, although now I have no possessions worth anything, but my clothes took such a lot of getting that I would die if I lost them.

Friday, March 3. We are hearing more about the damage in Well Hall, and Joyce went round this evening with a man in her office who has lost his home. She says it is absolutely ghastly. About 40 or so houses laid completely flat, and hundreds damaged terribly – all from one bomb. It seems incredible. Apparently as the 'all-clear' sounded, they used a mobile searchlight to flood-light the area, and this enabled rescue work to be carried on more easily. A couple we know – garage proprietors – were left in their night clothes only, and there are dozens of cases where families were in their houses and the shelters were smashed, and dozens of examples of the opposite, families in shelters and houses down to the ground. Mrs. L. and Pauline next door are going away on Monday for a fortnight, as Mr. L., when he saw little children being brought out of the wreckage with legs and arms smashed and all manner of dreadful injuries, said that Pauline should be out of it. I think this is alright for them, but there are thousands of people in London who can't go back and forth as the raids get bad.

Saturday, March 4. The American father of the Quads has given an interview to the press. He is, as most people guessed, a married man, which makes the whole affair rather sordid. Philip tells me that I would not be able to listen without blushing to the jokes, etc. that have been going around the University these past few days, and I believe him because I have heard quite decent people making rather risqué remarks on the subject.[26] This afternoon we went to Greenwich Granada to see *So Ends Our Night* [1941], a film about the refugee problem, which I missed some years ago, and which I always looked about for. We enjoyed it very much, although some years have passed since it was made, and my opinions on the subject have changed somewhat, and the war has made some of the ideas seem rather ancient. Nevertheless, it was one of Hollywood's best I think. The audience was composed almost entirely of children from this dock-side part of the world, and we were most amused by their behaviour. During the newsreel they deafened us by their cheering, and the roof almost came off when General Montgomery or Joseph Stalin appeared – we could not hear a word the commentator was saying. I was reminded of the days when I used to go to see serials on Saturday afternoon in a local 'bug-hutch' for the price of 2d! On the way home we passed the damage in Well Hall, and walked by the shattered homes of many of our friends. The local authorities are overwhelmed by this latest disaster, and can't find accommodation for the 500 people who are absolutely homeless as there is no more room in the borough. We heard today that 900 houses are damaged, and this is obviously a conservative estimate because houses a half mile away have been damaged. It is rather ironical that the Government have today given details of the new 12,000 pound bomb the RAF are using. The locals think that this bomb in Well Hall must have been almost as large, although Philip assures me that it couldn't possibly be so.

Sunday, March 5. Berlin was bombed in daylight yesterday by the Americans, and today's papers are full of it, as we knew they would be. We had a visit this morning from Dol [wife of her Mother's step-brother] with David and Jill on their way home from Mass – they called to see if we were still in the land of the living. We heard today that the Fenns (who occupied Mrs. L's house next

---

26. Staff Sergeant William Thompson, 26, from Pittsburgh, Pennsylvania, admitted to being the father of Norah Carpenter's quadruplets (one of whom had just died), known as 'the Heanor quads' after the location of the nursing home where they were born. He was accompanied at his press conference by a US Army officer.

door when we first moved in), who were bombed out early in the Blitz, losing their mother at the same time as Lily lost her leg, were bombed in a nearby road on Wednesday night, and have gone to the country to recover. Amazing how bad luck follows them around. Joyce and I at the canteen this afternoon were terribly busy. We gave some addresses to an American who wanted accommodation, and we hoped afterwards that he would be all right, as he wasn't one of our Ally's most attractive subjects. Joyce, who always supports the Americans when Philip and I attack them, wasn't very pleased with my suggestion that she should entertain this one.

Monday, March 6. The news this morning was all Russian, as it is when we have none from the other battle fronts. Went to the Club tonight and was pretty busy. Had an amusing talk with a couple of pilots, during which they told me that they go down into the tube during raids as they don't like to be out or in a building when a raid is in progress. The Americans have bombed Berlin again today, and obviously in greater number than their first raid. It is said that the biggest air battles of the war were fought over the German capital – rather like the Battle of Britain in reverse. These quiet nights are enabling us to make up some sleep, but they make me dread the raids all the more I think.

Tuesday, March 7. The Americans lost 68 bombers and 11 fighters yesterday, but shot down 176 German planes. All this proves to me anyway that invasion can't take place yet, until most of the German fighters have been shot down, and these raids are certainly helping to do this, but the cost in men is rather high. Mr. Churchill has refused to do anything more about Service pay, despite the row in the House last week. It seems rather petty when one considers the amount of money the war is costing – everyone practically benefitting except the men fighting the enemy. I happened to listen to one of the news bulletins to the General Forces programme and was rather surprised at the tone of the report on the strikes in Wales – definitely spoken with the intention of encouraging resentment by the Forces against the miners. I suppose this is Government instruction!!

Wednesday, March 8. The first day I have felt comfortable – really spring-like, apart from the heavy frost this morning. Berlin was raided in daylight today. We are becoming quite used to these raids now, and take them as a matter of course. The siren sounded tonight – it had to be when we were in the cinema. The place emptied very quickly and as we had seen the programme, we walked home. We saw *Lost Angel* with the child actress Margaret O'Brien. I marvel at her. She is as assured as any adult, and brings out all her lines as if she understands them.

Thursday, March 9. Over 90,000 miners are now on strike and the position is very serious. I am afraid the miners haven't many friends now. I have heard bitter comments everywhere, many from people I know who are earning many times the amount a miner earns, doing some sit-down job, which isn't as arduous or as dangerous as the miner's. I feel drawn two ways. I don't approve of strikes in wartime, but I feel that people forget the awful deal the miners had between the wars and I also think £5 much too little for the work they do. When I paid out 4s 8d a hundredweight for coal that formerly cost 2s 1d, I feel that I wouldn't begrudge it so much if the increase went to the men who dig it instead of into the coal-owners' pocket. I am told by those who know that the miners don't get any bonus on the small coal which is mostly what is sold to householders. My father too heard from several ex-miners who work for his firm, and they say that the coal-owners are keeping the good seams till after the war, making the miners dig the poor seams, which produces this small coal. Still the whole problem is very difficult. The fact that it is so serious may cause something to be done, but I am certain the Government won't forget this.[27]

Friday, March 10. Full moon tonight. Most people are taking their last evening outing tonight, expecting the raids to start again any time now. I went to the hairdresser's tonight, and she was full of her experiences in last week's raid.

Saturday, March 11. The Government have cut down the coal allowance in South Wales, mainly the districts affected by the strikes. I know the allowance is still enough, but I am sure this will cause dreadful bad feeling, and justifiably so I think. The Irish Government have refused the request of the USA Government to turn out the German and Japanese consuls, etc., and all are waiting to see what steps the British Government take to support the American demands.

Sunday, March 12. Went to tea this afternoon with our small cousins, and they amused us immensely. They are really intelligent children, considering they go to a Catholic school which has a poor reputation. David told Dol (his mother) during the week that she should send Paul (age three) to school so that she could go out to work, earn some money, and buy him a piano-accordion. Odd thoughts for a child of five. I shouldn't have thought he knew what a piano-accordion was. It is odd how some women bring their children up so well even in these days, so that the children have nice manners and nice habits, yet other children are so badly brought up. I suppose it will always be [so] whilst slatternly women are allowed to bring their children up in their own filthy ways. The siren sounded around 9.45 this evening, and the children were brought downstairs. They were very sleepy, except Paul, who went to bed before 6, and he was ready for a romp. It is a shame to have to get them up, but with three it is difficult to wait until things are happening.

Monday, March 13. The Home Secretary has banned travel between Eire, Northern Ireland and England, as a result of the Irish reply to the American

---

27. Kathleen's mixed feelings towards the miners are understandable. The complicated background to and broader context of their grievances are discussed in Barry Supple, *The History of the British Coal Industry, Volume 4, 1913–1946: The Political Economy of Decline* (Oxford: Clarendon Press, 1987), pp. 567–81. He speaks of these disputes as 'the severest crisis of industrial relations of the War' (p. 571).

note. Things are becoming serious, and I feel that even people who were beginning to get tired of the Irish question will feel bitter again. I was at the Club tonight, and Eileen, who is half Irish, says that she has had many arguments today on the subject. She agreed with me though that if Eire really wants to be disinterested and neutral, she should leave the Commonwealth. I am sure she would be worse off, but maybe the problem would be somewhat solved. The only snag, Eileen pointed out, is that Northern Ireland probably wouldn't agree, considering themselves to be part of Ireland, even if disagreeing with the policy of Eire.

Tuesday, March 14. Air raid casualties for February announced today – 961 killed, and 1,712 injured, the heaviest since 1941. Much more air activity during the day. We hear the drone almost all day long up in London, and this is unusual. Didn't hear the warning which apparently sounded during the night, and mighty glad that I didn't. The siren sounded this evening about 10.30, just as I was nicely tucked down in my bed. It was a noisy raid, and several bombs made us duck, three landing quite near. It was obviously another fire raid, as at one time there were about 20 fires burning all around, some very large. My father went yesterday to interview the local council, as our old house is to be rebuilt shortly, and they wanted us to go back. We don't want to return as the house will probably look somewhat the same, but with our bits and pieces of furniture it will make us miserable to be there. Anyway, my father has signed the lease of the present house – a wartime measure – and we are safe until the present owners wish to return, so really our best plan will be to look around for something before that eventuality arises. This will be a dreadful task, but we must do our best.

Wednesday, March 15. At 8 o'clock they announced that nine planes were shot down last night. At 1 p.m. it had gone up to 13, so it was obviously a fairly heavy raid. A short warning this evening, a little gunfire, then all quiet – the sort of raid we can stand easily. The Americans were out again today in force. I wonder what the people of occupied Europe think now when they hear planes going over towards Germany night and day. It must be comforting, and surprising for them really, after so many years.

Thursday, March 16. Only two planes over last night, which accounts for the lack of noise. Joyce and I on duty this evening. The warning sounded soon after 6.30, and the all-clear went at 7. It was an unusual event, a daylight warning, and on the news bulletin at 7 on the General Forces programme they announced that a warning had just been sounded. We had no disturbances during the evening but were glad nevertheless to get home. I hate being too near the rockets during a raid.

Friday, March 17. This morning at the office we listened to a broadcast about my boss's father, and all had to attend. One of the staff brought a portable wireless to the office, and we sat round and listened. As a matter of fact the broadcast was very good,[28] but it is always difficult to listen under these circumstances. A warning this evening, noisy for ten minutes or so. We said during the raid that we wouldn't like to have to endure RAF raids, as we make enough fuss now at these two or three plane raids. But I think we are making more fuss now because we are in the fifth year of war and are all very tired.

Saturday, March 18. Two tiles off after last night's raid. I hope it doesn't rain hard before they are put back, as I don't relish clearing up rainwater. Mrs. L. and Pauline have returned after their fortnight in the country, having had a very quiet time. I wondered whether they would stay there, but apparently they are going to risk it for a time. Some grisly accounts of the local murder in our local rag this week.[29] How local papers enjoy anything of this nature. They write in a most sensational manner. 'Lady Bountiful' has been given six years for her enormous swindles. I wonder if she had been a working class woman whether six years would have been the sentence?[30] I was on my own this afternoon, all the rest of the family being at work, so I went to see *The Nelson Touch*, one of the best films of the sea I have seen. I feel that I know all there is to be known about corvettes now!!

Sunday, March 19. The papers today carry stories of the evacuation of parts of Rumania. Our papers tell us that Rumanians are hurriedly leaving those parts of their country nearest the Russian advancing armies. This latest advance of the Russians must be giving the Germans some headaches, as they are only 30 or so miles from the Rumanian border, which isn't far for the Russians. Actually it will be interesting to see how the advance proceeds once the Russians get on to German-occupied territory – by that I mean non-Russian territory. Pauline is going to be vaccinated on Tuesday. Her parents, like many others in London, are worried about this smallpox scare. I have seen quite a few red bands around, on adults too. Mrs. L. entertained pilots from a nearby aerodrome, whilst away, and talked to one who had the previous day taken 12,000 pound bombs to Germany. He said he hated doing it, but he made himself think that it was just a job of work. The Germans would never give us credit for such thoughts. In fact they would probably consider it weakness. One doesn't imagine that German pilots feel sorry for the suffering they are dropping on Britain when they come over in their bombers.

28. This broadcast, between 11.20 and 11.40 a.m., was on the Home Service (Schools) and intended for children; it was part of a 'Useful Citizens' series. The subject, Charles Booth (1840–1916), was a successful businessman, student of urban poverty, and author of the multi-volume *Life and Labour of the People in London*, the first volume of which was published in 1882. The broadcast was structured as an 'imaginary interview' between an actual 1944 radio personality, Freddie Grisewood, and Charles Booth in his London home in 1900. The script included some topical references, such as Grisewood's remark upon entering Booth's study, 'No difficulty about coal supplies in 1900, of course'. A text of this broadcast is held in the BBC Written Archives Centre, Caversham Park, Reading.
29. She was referring to the murder of a young woman in the WAAF on 14 February, see p. 85. The 'local rag' was the *Kentish Independent*, which was published in Woolwich.
30. Miss Dorothy Elliott, 47, had embezzled some £91,000 from two colliery companies of which she was secretary. She was also a JP in the West Riding of Yorkshire. Since she apparently gave much of this money away, the word 'bountiful' was applied to her criminal behaviour.

Monday, March 20. The last two nights have been a surprise, but much appreciated by Londoners I know. At the New Zealand Club we talked to pilots who had been on several of the recent raids on Berlin. When we asked them what Berlin was really like, one of them said, 'Berlin is a large place – bombing it hasn't destroyed it by any means'. This merely bears out what others have told me at odd times, that bombing alone won't win the war, although they are having a good try. Heard some grim tales from some New Zealand Eighth Army men of their experiences in Africa and Italy – an unusual thing to get them talking about them. These men who have done so much are usually rather reticent. D. told us about the son of a friend of hers, writing home from Italy, [who] said that he hadn't been able to do more than wash his face in a frying-pan for a month. He said that he was 'lousy', in the same condition as everyone else. Another tale to add to those we know of the conditions under which our men are fighting. The men in Burma must be experiencing even worse times because the country out there is so dreadful.

Tuesday, March 21. King Peter of Yugoslavia was married yesterday, and one feels rather sorry for him. What sort of a chance will he have of living long? Joyce has heard that the application by her firm [the Royal Arsenal Co-operative Society] for her deferment has been turned down by the Manpower Board. We are wondering what will happen to her [see below, March 28]. A girl in her office went to an interview yesterday and was told she must become a porter on Camden Town railway station. The girl refused saying that she wasn't strong enough to do that, and the young woman interviewing her said, 'That is for the Railway Company to determine'. Anyway Joyce's colleague persisted in her refusal, so the Labour Exchange people said that as a special favour they would try to get her into a Government training centre for her to be trained for munition work – preferable to the portering job I should say.

Wednesday, March 22. The siren sounded just before 1 this morning, and we had a very noisy and frightening hour. At one time planes seemed to be diving and dropping high explosives and incendiary bombs continuously for 20 minutes or so. I was very frightened at one time. The fires were very bright, and one large one seemed to be an ammunition store of some kind, because ammunition was going off for hours after the all-clear sounded. I expect when we get to work all the others living in North London will be bored to hear our tales. They seem to be so lucky.

Thursday, March 23. Have just finished reading *Death and To-Morrow* [1942] by Peter de Polnay, which throws a new light, for me, on the events which preceded and followed the invasion of France [it is a memoir of the fall and occupation of France]. I am never tired of reading about 'occupied Europe', as so many people are, and certainly it gives one a little idea of what is going on there, even allowing for some of the facts to be untrue or exaggerated. Joyce and I were very busy this evening at the canteen, after we had inspected the holes caused by incendiary bombs through the roof. We nearly lost the canteen for a second time. It was practically burned out early in 1941 and had to be rebuilt.

Friday, March 24. A warning this morning – a little heavy gunfire then nothing much afterwards. Our planes seemed to be going out all the while. It must have been difficult to distinguish the Germans amongst the planes in the sky at the time. The Americans sent out another 1,000 planes yesterday. Hamm [near Essen] was attacked. We now take these 1,000 plane raids for granted it seems, so rare is the comment one hears. The siren sounded this evening around 11.30 and the barrage was as heavy as I have ever heard it. We had an accident during the raid. Philip was in the garden, and hearing a couple of 'whistlers' he dived for the shelter, knocked his tin-hat off and caught his head on one of the iron ridges on the shelter, cutting his head quite badly. No-one nearby seemed to know what we did for medical attention. The wardens couldn't help, the first-aiders seemed reluctant to do anything, so Philip and I set off, with my father in attendance, after first bathing the wound, and finally knocked up a doctor living a half mile or so away. He was Scotch, and terribly rude and bad-tempered to start with. However, he soon saw that the wound was quite bad, and when I skillfully (I thought) brought the conversation round to rowing, he became quite human, and in fact we thought him rather pleasant when we left him. He put three stitches in the cut, and Philip didn't bat an eyelid the while. I felt most ill. When we got home Mrs. L. had made a cup of tea for us, and sent it in on a tray, so we had that, and got to bed around 3 o'clock.

Saturday, March 25. Philip felt fairly well this morning, and went round to see the doctor who said that he could row today. His crew were taking part in the [annual] Head of the River races [from Mortlake to Putney], and hoped to put up a good show. When he came in we knew something had happened, and it seems that their cox didn't turn up till five minutes after the race was due to start. He is a slack youth, and as a result they were not able to take part. Philip is most upset because it is the only Head of the River he will ever be able to take part in. He says that London was packed today for the opening of 'Salute the Soldier'.

Sunday, March 26. Our young cousins came to see us today. We had a real spread for them, and they soon became friendly with Pauline next door, and in no time were in her garden playing on her swing. The house was like bedlam for the few hours of their stay, and we were all dragged into violent games, so that I was exhausted when they left. David was rather nervous during Friday's raid they say, which is unusual, but I am not surprised because the noise was deafening. Listened to some of Churchill's speech ['The Hour of our Greatest Effort is Approaching', on the BBC: *Speeches*, VII, pp. 6907–16], but as he had nothing much to say, and what he did say was in a most monotonous tone, I went off to bed in the middle of it.

Monday, March 27. Yesterday's summer weather has continued, and at lunch-time I was in the Strand as some sort of procession passed [part of 'Salute the Soldier' week]. Hundreds of soldiers were the most important part of it, and I was struck by the 'tough' appearance of them all. I have often read of the fierce appearance of the German troops, but I think the people of France and Belgium would get a surprise if they could see these present-day British soldiers. They are certainly a different lot from those we sent out to France in 1939. Many of the soldiers in the procession were Grenadier, Irish, Scotch and Life Guards, and they seemed to tower over the spectators. Certainly an impressive array of might. But I thought whilst watching them – I wonder how many of them will come through the invasion of Europe? Saw rather a nice gesture in the Strand. I walked behind two Indian pilot officers, one with a blue silk turban on his head, and every British airman who came towards them saluted them in a most friendly way. I wondered what the Americans watching thought about it?

Tuesday, March 28. A warning last night before 12 o'clock. Quite a bit of gunfire but I think it was confined to the SE area. This morning the Germans claim Bristol as their target. At the Club last evening I talked to two Canadians, who were discussing the fact that over here people don't care for the Americans, and are not really fond of the Canadians. One of them told me that early in the war when the first lot of the RAF went over to Canada he lived in a town just near their base. He said that his town was one of the most English towns in Canada, having 'bobbys' and many other English customs kept up. Anyway after these Englishmen had been there two or three days no one would have one of them inside his house. They broke up the town and were pretty rough. His excuse was that these RAF men were mostly regulars, and subsequent shipments of cadets have changed the opinion completely. All the boys I know who have been to Canada have been welcomed everywhere, and have nothing but praise for the Canadian people. The Government was beaten by one vote in the Commons today on an amendment to one of the clauses of the Education Bill – something of a problem for Mr. C.? Joyce went along to the Labour Exchange for her interview, and gave the girl there particulars of her work, education, Matriculation with distinctions etc., and in fact all her business. This female told Joyce that she would have to go away and would not be able to do shorthand typing, as there was no demand for shorthand typists. Joyce is going to try to stay in London, or near enough to help me run the house, because we want to keep it on if we can.[31] One interesting fact was that the interviewer, when asking for details of my age etc., said 'I presume your sister stays at home doing housework etc.', which amused us because we are both out at full-time work, and give up as much of our spare time as we can for voluntary work. I didn't know that there was any chance of a girl of 25 being able to stay at home and do the housework!!

Wednesday, March 29. Nikoliev [Nikolayev] captured by the Russians. I am now adopting my own spelling for these Russian towns, as it is impossible for

31. Since 1938 Joyce had held a secretarial position in central Woolwich with the Royal Arsenal Co-operative Society and travelled there from Well Hall by tram. (The fare had once been so cheap – twopence – that she often came home for lunch when her mother was still alive.) At its peak the RACS had some 170 shops and employed around 9,000 staff in south-east England. The Tippers did their shopping at a branch of the RACS at 158 to 172 Well Hall Road. Despite being fully employed, Joyce was liable, as a single woman in her twenties, to be moved to another part of the country where her labour might be used in ways deemed more valuable to the war effort.

me to memorise the spelling of them all. At the office we enjoy ourselves teasing the 'monied' of our staff, i.e., those with good jobs, and die-hard ideas, about the possibility of the Russians continuing their advance and including England amongst the liberated lands!! I am afraid these people, so secure in themselves, frightened to give up one of their privileges for the betterment of mankind, are terrified of the thought.

Thursday, March 30. I have a filthy cold coming on. This weather is so treacherous and I left my scarf off one day, so am paying for it now. I think the food must be the reason that I catch cold so easily now. At one time I thought I was tough. We were busy at the canteen tonight. One of our soldier friends told me how they got up a delayed-action bomb weighing 2,250 pounds today. He said it was 18 feet long and 2 feet across. It fell through the roof of a house belonging to some acquaintances of ours. They were under the stairs and were dug out of the rubble about an hour later. But what a miracle that it didn't go off!!

Friday, March 31. Finished reading *I Sit and I Think and I Wonder* [1943] by Sidney Dark, which I have enjoyed as much as anything I have read recently. He writes so well, and with such authority. But I can't think that a man with such enlightened ideas will ever be able to have much influence in our Britain. I feel though that he does express the thoughts of many modern Christians, perhaps thoughts that others cannot put into words. Nuremberg raided last night, 96 bombers missing, the highest total we have lost so far, and we all pray that it will never get to this huge figure again. One pictures the hundreds of homes receiving the dreadful telegrams today, and it makes me very miserable. A raid here early this morning, a bit of gunfire early on, but silence afterwards, although planes around all the time. One plane dropped five bombs in Well Hall before the warning sounded. Fortunately none of them have gone off yet. At the hairdresser's this evening, the young assistant (my former Sunday school pupil) told me that her brother, aged 18 (or 19 – I forget which), has been sent to prison for six weeks for refusing to go into the mines. I feel for the boy, because the court case occurred on the same day as her grandmother's funeral, and as a consequence none of the family were present in the court, and the boy was taken straight off to prison without being able to say good-bye to his family. This whole affair is dreadful. I do feel so sorry for these boys being sent to this most unpleasant of jobs.[32] I called in at the doctor's for some more gargle for my throat, which is like a rasp, and to ask for some advice about the pain I get in my 'gammy arm'. Anyway she would not do anything about the latter until I have been up to the Orthopedic Hospital to have it X-rayed. She thinks something might be able to be done for it. Anyway I must go sometime next week.

32. This teenager was a so-called 'Bevin Boy'. Bevin Boys were men aged 18 to 25 who were chosen by ballot to work as coalminers rather than serve in the armed forces. The scheme, a specialised aspect of conscription, was introduced at the end of 1943 because the mining industry was short of labour. The name 'Bevin Boys' derived – by popular usage, not official authorisation – from that of the Minister of Labour, Ernest Bevin.

PART THREE (JULY 1944–MAY 1945)

After a silence of more than three months – and let us assume that she did not write during this period – Kathleen returned to keeping her diary on 8 July 1944, and she was to continue with it, with only brief interruptions, until well after the end of the war (her last entry is for 1 February 1947). This final and longest part offers selections from the diary for the months from when she resumed writing in July 1944 until her 26th birthday in the following year, on May 24th, shortly after the war in Europe had ended. As in Part One, these selections highlight her experiences and activities in London and leave out many passages in which Kathleen was responding to and, as a rule, mostly summarising the published news of the day, usually news on domestic politics and news from the Continent, where Anglo-American forces, after their June landings in Normandy, were pressing eastwards towards the heart of Nazi power. London was still very much under attack from German air power, which since mid-June had been lethally displayed in the form of 'flying bombs' – that is, the V1s, sometimes referred to as 'doodlebugs' or 'buzz-bombs' or 'pilotless planes'. Later, from September 8, ballistic missiles (V2 rockets) started to land in London; they would continue to threaten its inhabitants until late March 1945. The dangers from these German innovations in military technology figured prominently in the life of London for most of the last eleven months of the war – and in Kathleen Tipper's life as well.

The first fortnight of the diary for July is reproduced in full.

1944

Saturday, July 8. Fairly quiet during the day, for which I was thankful as I went to the dentist at lunchtime and loathe being in his chair when anything happens, as the whole side of the room is thick glass. I have finished with him for the time being now, though I expect I shall be visiting him before long. Joyce was telling me about Winnie's brother who is a Sergeant in the Home Guard and was sent in charge of a squad of men to protect some property in Plumstead, as looters were out. During the night someone caught sight of intruders armed with torches and the Home Guard ran after them, during which time Winnie's brother fell over a collapsing wall and broke his leg in three places. Here is this man, in hospital and out of action for some months, all because other so-called citizens of London are behaving like vultures where any bomb-trouble has occurred. I see that the Home Guard have the power to shoot them, but the trouble is that they never get the real thieves. If the police catch a looter it is usually some innocent man who has dug up a carnation plant from a neglected garden, or something equally inoffensive. Some peculiar pilotless planes over this evening. They seemed all alight and made no sound whatever.

99

Sunday, July 9. The result of the Rushholme bye-election caused us some surprise, for although the Government candidate won, the Common Wealth man polled over 6,000 voters, which at this stage of the war is certainly amazing. I expect Mr. Churchill is pretty annoyed, because that means that at least 6,000 voters are not quite satisfied with the Government's policy at the moment, and voted against the Government despite the acid words of the Prime Minister the last time an election went against the Government.[1] Caen has been captured at last – the announcement has come officially from SHAEF [Supreme Headquarters, Allied Expeditionary Force]. Tony T., who used to drive a van for the YMCA, and who is now an officer in the Navy, told us an interesting tale today. He has been over to France quite a few times since D-Day and with regard to snipers, etc. said that on his last visit he saw a 17-year old French girl hanged (she had already been hung). She was a sniper apparently and the Americans had caught and hung her. He wasn't at all shocked. He thought it quite the best system, and said that he considered British troops who 'capture' these people were fools.

Monday, July 10. We were much busier at the Club – absolutely full of sailors, all very noisy and 'matey'. One American sailor down in London on sick leave told me that he has spent his nights in the air-raid shelter of whatever place he is staying in. Last night he was at the Union Jack Club [91 Waterloo Road, SE1] and when he went into the shelter it was quite empty, so he made himself comfortable and went to sleep. When he awoke the place was absolutely packed and he had someone sleeping right close beside him on both sides. A New Zealand sailor with him said that he was thoroughly scared of them, although I should imagine that torpedoes are more terrifying than pilotless planes. The roads around our former house have been very badly damaged again by a flying bomb which fell this morning at about 10 a.m. Joyce went round this evening this evening to see how Mrs. R. was, and found her in a bad way. She has been very ill, and just before the bomb fell she had received a telegram from the War Office to say that K. was wounded and back in England from Normandy. Joyce did what she could for them, and she will try to find somewhere for Mrs. R. to stay near K. when they get definite news of his whereabouts. Auntie Lila and Uncle Arthur have been blasted by this bomb and when Joyce got there they were quite unworried by it all, and they are both 79. Uncle was fixing window frames and doors as if it was the most usual thing in the world for him to do. I think some of these old people are absolutely marvellous, but they are a bit of a responsibility for others I think.

Tuesday, July 11. Aunt Win [a nurse] is in Plymouth now. She has moved from Sherborne and is in charge of the officers' block there. She seems to be

1. The major political parties had agreed since 1940 not to contest by-elections against the party previously holding the vacant seat, and thus the new Common Wealth Party, founded in 1942, which expressed socialist values, became the main institutional voice of opposition to Churchill's coalition. In this by-election in the Rusholme Division of Manchester, the Conservative candidate got 8,430 votes as against 6,670 for the Common Wealth candidate in a light poll.

pleasantly impressed by everything at Plymouth. Apparently there is much more luxury than there was at Sherborne, which was a hurriedly built place, rather like a prison in appearance. Sylvia [a cousin, suffering with diabetes] is apparently in hospital again, and Win says that she must be in a bad way judging by the amount of insulin she is being given. No doubt being away from these raids will be a little beneficial. This evening we did our usual run on the van and did good trade. An additional lot of men made us sell out of almost everything. The C.O. (the only officer on the site) came out and obviously expected us to sit with him for a bit, but we got away because we had much to do at home. I feel very sorry for these officers who are on their own, because they are pretty much cut off from congenial society, because however friendly they are with their men they can't spend the evenings with them, and also keep discipline. There were several alerts this evening but I didn't hear anything, although several times as we were driving along the sight of people staring into the sky just over our head made my heart beat a little faster.

Wednesday, July 12. Rene had a bad night at the FAP [First Aid Post]. One crashed nearby and they had casualties in, some of them quite serious. We had a quiet night afterwards though. Mr. Roosevelt has said that he will serve a fourth term if elected. Somehow it doesn't seem possible to me that any other man could be President of America, but Mr. [Thomas] Dewey [Republican candidate for President] has much support, and some of the papers here aren't exactly antagonistic!! General [Sir Bernard] Montgomery has been in Caen – this despite the rumour we heard that he had been captured by the Germans. This worried me I must confess, but I wonder who invents these tales in the first place? Quite a nasty day. Several fairly unpleasant incidents reported. Dorothy came back to London today after a few days away, and a very unpleasant time to come back – it was raining and a raid on.

Thursday, July 13. Some bad bomb incidents today after another raid-free night. Pop saw a couple of near ones this afternoon, and we had quite a few 'dangers' at the office. This evening soon after I arrived at the canteen there was a terrific explosion. We thought we had been hit, but we discovered it was way up the road, near home. Joyce went off to investigate and discovered Pop trying to push in doors which wouldn't shut, and clear up glass, etc. He has boarded up the French doors and windows as they are all loose and blow off each time there is an explosion in the neighbourhood. Several other noises in the evening – something in Woolwich we hear. We have been looking up trains for our holiday next week, and heard from Miss Hendry today giving us details of getting to Kirn. Apparently there is only one train to Glasgow each evening, the 9.15, so it will be packed I expect. Somehow it seems silly to plan too much though. Anything may happen to alter them.

Friday, July 14. Philip arrived home from camp today with a shocking cold, caught when the place was flooded, causing all their bed-clothes to become damp. He says that it was a complete waste of time. They did little training and were fed rather badly I gather. A pilotless plane glided over the house as we

101

were talking and we did a quick run to the shelter, listening to the whistle as we did so, a most uncanny few minutes. Decided to try to sleep in bed tonight, as Joyce is firewatching, and I can jump out as soon as the warning goes. I get rather cramped in the [Anderson] shelter and long for a good stretch. Got some blackcurrants ready for jelly making this evening. It took me hours to press the mixture through a sieve we have been able to borrow.

Saturday, July 15. At last a night in bed. How I enjoyed it – although about 5 I awoke at the sound of an explosion. I saw smoke coming from a field nearby, but didn't hear another sound, so returned to my bed quite happily. I know it is a risk, but I shan't mind going to shelter if an alert sounds, even if I have only an hour in bed. A very busy day for me – cooking, housework, and jelly-making, which took me hours. I tried out a fancy cake recipe, and it was a failure I thought, but Philip enjoyed it alright. This afternoon Joyce and Philip went to Lewisham, and during one alert saw a pilotless plane diving towards them, so they ran away from its path and lay flat on the ground, as did hundreds of people in the street. It fell about 50 yards away and made a terrific noise they said. Philip said everyone moved quite as quickly as the pilotless plane.

Sunday, July 16. What a day of rest, doing jobs right until 11 this evening, and still a lot more to do. Although we are making no plans for our holiday, we must do a little preparing, so today we washed clothes. I washed my two precious summer dresses, and wretchedly enough the weather has changed now so I will swelter all the week, not daring to wear my clean dresses. Joyce did most of the other washing, and I then spent hours mending the garments of one or other members of the family.

Monday, July 17. Dorothy back at the office today for the first time since they were blasted. Their house is in an awful state, with every fresh bomb bringing more of it down. That is the trouble with bombed houses. If they are lucky enough to be left standing, they are most likely to be made uninhabitable by further bombing, so there is no end to it. Quite a long break this afternoon and evening without alerts – quite welcome. We were quite busy at the Club this evening, short-handed too. Lots of girls just don't turn up these days. Some soldiers returned from Italy for an OCTU [Officer Cadet Training Unit] course told us quite a story of their experiences in Africa, Tunisia, Sicily and then Italy, which country they left just before the entry into Cassino, they were glad to say. When they have finished their course they will rejoin the division in Italy (or in Europe if it is that far advanced). Some New Zealand airmen were abusing the Americans and one of them told me that the one thing wrong with them was that they were

> Over paid
> Over dressed
> Over sexed, and
> Over here.

To which many who overheard echoed 'hear hear'. A Canadian friend of ours who serves with the New Zealand squadron hates Americans, whom he refers to as 'a great plague of syphilis'. He also says that if he had charge of the invasion for one day, he would send every American in this country to it. I am afraid these sentiments are often held by the nicest of men, and they are difficult to argue with, particularly as all they say about the Americans is fairly true.

Tuesday, July 18. Slightly better night and not so many warnings today as we had some days last week. Towards evening the siren started up again and we had several this evening. We were very busy at our gun-site, but were in a hurry because we wanted to get to see our dress-maker, who called us for a fitting. We stayed with her talking until about 10 p.m., far too late for two girls who are going away on Friday and have prepared nothing so far. The siren went again soon after 10 and up till midnight there was plenty of activity, more than any night for a week or so.

Wednesday, July 19. Last night seems to have been the worst for ages everywhere. Everyone at work had something near them, and this is quite unusual. We are still very busy at the office, and the danger warnings interrupt us quite a bit. Several up in the City today – one by Cannon Street, and another by the Bank apparently. This evening's paper says that these latest pilotless planes are coming from bases 100 miles inland, and I wouldn't be surprised. They seem to come in many different ways now. This evening we packed our cases. Haven't yet decided which class to travel up to Scotland. We hear so many different tales about the travelling. It appears that all the 1st class accommodation on these Scottish trains are taken (reserved) by American troops and officers, so we feel that we would be furious if we paid 1st class [and] then had to stand in the corridor. I shall be very glad to get away for a bit by Friday.

Thursday, July 20. Another noisy night – at least near us it was noisy – and this morning we had a couple of nasty 'near-ones' just as I was going to work. The new offensive in Normandy is going well according to General Montgomery, who should know, although they don't tell us much about it at this stage. The news from Japan is making people laugh, but I think still that the Japanese are far from falling to pieces and feel sure that a great many lives will have to be sacrificed before we have them conquered. Have prepared everything I can for Pop and Philip to exist with next fortnight. They are sure they can manage, because they won't be in very much. I expect they will enjoy themselves messing around on their own, although I shall worry about them all the time. Despite the fact that they assure us they will write very often, I know them.

Friday, July 21. The plot to murder Hitler is front page news today. To me it seems to be another 'Reichstag fire' episode [27 February 1933] and an excuse to get rid of a few men unpopular with the Nazis in a strictly 'legal way'. A dreadful day for me. I was trying to shop and clear everything up, leaving all jobs for next week, clearly labelled Pop and Philip. Also I was trying to have a bath, but the doodles seemed to be coming over continuously. Finally I ran the water at 12 o'clock and determined to bathe whatever happened, but things got too hot [so] that I didn't dare [go] upstairs until 1.30, and when almost through, the doors were blown in on me and there was a most terrific explosion, and one had fallen a few hundred yards away. Did I get out quickly! This afternoon too they came over continuously and I thought that fate was determined I shouldn't get away. Joyce went from the office and Philip went up at about the same time with her luggage. I left home around 5.30 and got up there at 6.30, and my father came up later with my luggage. We decided to travel 1st class in the hope of procuring a seat, but what a scramble it was, with dozens of porters with cases fighting passengers to get inside the train first – before it stopped too. Joyce said that people were giving porters tips of 10s and £1 and they were taking them as if the sum was a usual one. We were lucky enough to get seats and then Philip and Pop packed our luggage in and departed. Several bombs landed near enough to hear whilst we were sitting in the train, but I noticed that no one moved. Our companions were an odious fat man, richly dressed, who wore ladies' silk stockings and was obviously on the black market or some-thing, and three other women – very dull they were, but I suppose they were 'war weary'. We went to sleep around 10.15.

Saturday, July 22. Woke up around 5.45. It was light and we were almost to the end of our journey. The train arrived in Glasgow at 6.45 and we caught the 7.03 to Gourock, and from there travelled by steamer to Kirn. The steamer went all over the place and at one time we were certain we were on our way back to Gourock, but at 10 o'clock we got onto the pier at Kirn and Miss Hendry was there waiting for us. We inspected her house – a large house divided into two flats standing on a hill overlooking the Clyde, with a magnif-icent view of the river and miles in all directions. She has hens, twelve of them, all named, and seven chicks, which she hatched about six weeks ago, all of which wander around her large garden and the gardens of her neighbours. We breakfasted on boiled eggs, buttered toast and oatcakes, which we enjoyed more than any breakfast we have had for months. This afternoon took bicy-cles, which we have been loaned by the next door folk, and went off to Glen Masson to have our tea. This is called the 'wild glen' and the noise of the waterfalls is at all times practically deafening, but a most beautiful sight it is, and we sat on the rocks and dangled our feet in the water, so attractive did it look. Miss Hendry is terribly interested in flying bombs and is surprised when we told her about the numbers coming over and the damage they do. She is fond of London, and spends about four months every year in London, going to the Oval, proms, etc. among other things. Met Ada, an Englishwoman who was companion to Miss Hendry's uncle for many years and now is companion to Mrs. F., who has the flat underneath. She is a grand person, efficient and a terrific worker, and we liked her on the spot. She too is very interested [in] and naturally sympathetically inclined to London and the South at this time. We were very glad to get into bed tonight. I haven't slept in such a comfortable bed since we were bombed.

During their holiday in Scotland, Kathleen and Joyce were warmly treated, had time to relax, and kept busy with various recreations. On the 23rd 'Ada and various other people around brought books, etc. for us to read – I can see that we are going to be well looked after.' They walked and cycled in the countryside. They enjoyed watching the ships on the Clyde – 'I have never seen so many in my life' (July 23). On July 25 she saw the great ocean-liner 'the Queen Elizabeth pass our window today. She is a wonderful sight. All the other ships look like toys beside her.' (This image remained vividly in her mind 60 years later – and she recalled that the huge ship was packed with troops.) 'The submarines passing our window thrill me,' Kathleen wrote on the 27th; 'they move through the water so easily.' Kathleen and Joyce picked berries in Miss Hendry's allotment and viewed some noteworthy gardens. As in London, they came across Americans in uniform. 'On the steamer back [from Kilkreggan on July 31st] an awful little man scrounged some cigarettes etc. from some Yank officers. I felt so ashamed that I was glad he wasn't English. There are crowds of American sailors on the steamers, and some are always on the wrong one and have to be sent back by another. I pity them. The accents are so strong up there that they have no chance of understanding where the steamers are going or when.' On August 2nd Kathleen and Joyce went to Loch Lomond, on the afternoon of the 5th they sunbathed, and on the 6th at Dunoon they 'took out a rowing boat, and rowed around in the bright sun.' On two or three days they cycled at least 30 miles.

London, unsurprisingly, was not forgotten by the Tipper sisters, notably its constant alerts and alarms, and on one occasion (July 24th) Kathleen remarked on the very different mood in the town of Dunoon, where they 'queued up to get our emergency ration cards .... The whole place seems so remote from war and most thinking people up here agree that the war makes no difference to their way of life. The people here too still talk of "the blitz", meaning the raid they had one night when a few houses lost windows, and seem to think that raids on London are of a similar character! I suppose one can't blame them. But it doesn't need a great stretch of imagination for people in London to know what people in France are going through.' Air raids were rare in this part of Scotland, and there was little of that unrelenting sense of danger that weighed so heavily on most of the residents of south-east London. At a gathering on the 28th 'most of those present wanted to hear about flying bombs, having no idea of what London is like now.' There were occasional reminders of the continuing battleground of London. On July 31st Kathleen 'heard from home' about a bomb that fell in the market at Lewisham on July 28th. 'It is obviously dreadful, and to happen with no warning sounded awful too, because it is such a crowded place. No one would stand a chance with no warning.' (In fact, some 59 people were killed and 124 seriously injured.) Living in London continued to be impressively perilous. After listening on August 2nd to a speech by Churchill, Kathleen observed that the 'words about rockets are not comforting. I dread the thought of what that will mean. People up here all suggest that we don't return. How tempting their words are.'

Of course, they did return home. On August 7th, after a long wait in Glasgow for a train with room for them, they found space on the one at 5.40 p.m. 'and we set off chock a block on a train which goes half over England before it gets to London. We felt very miserable as we travelled down through

105

Scotland, and as it was light and sunny until a very late hour, all the country-side looked very lovely and remote from the war. Tried to get to sleep, but it was very different from our journey up when we were so tired through loss of sleep that we slept the entire journey. This time we were very wide awake, and couldn't drop off in an uncomfortable position.'

Tuesday, August 8. Woke this morning around 5 and it was just getting light. The train had travelled the whole way with lights blazing and no blackout up. I suppose they are not so careful now. The warning sounded when we went through Reading, which implied that we were near civilization again! Arrived at Euston at 6.40, luckily got a taxi, which we shared with a sailor, and so by 7.30 we were home, very dirty and cold. I washed and ate and then went off to work, which I reached at 9.10 – not bad going. Philip and Pop seem well and have done some frantic housework this last day or so, after leaving it for a fort-night. Gossiped at the office. Heard all about the latest bomb news, etc. Didn't go out on the van this evening as we had so much to do. Unpacked and inspected the house, doled out presents etc., and talked and talked. The siren went around 10.30 – didn't hear anything. The weather seems to have changed down here. It has been lovely today – unbroken sunshine. The war news is good. Everyone up here seems to expect it over in a week or so. I am not so sure.

Wednesday, August 9. Siren this morning early. Heard about four drop. Another lovely day – too nice to be in the office. I would rather be in Scotland. The Canadians have advanced ten miles on their front, and the fine weather has meant that the air war has been increased terrifically. Met Eileen this evening and we talked a great deal – also ate. Did more odd jobs this evening – much to make up.

Thursday, August 10. A lovely night. Only one hour of warning and very little doing then. My shelter bunk doesn't seem so hard now. I have slept like a log since my return. This evening we went to the canteen and inspected the damage. It is quite badly blasted, with all the windows and roofs gone, although no one was hurt when it happened. It would have happened on our night, Thursday, if we hadn't been away – so we were lucky to have missed this particular incident. Lots of stuff was damaged. The glass got into it and it was condemned by the Ministry of Food. Once again the policy of hoarding things, i.e. chocolate, sweets and biscuits, has not been sensible. The last time the canteen was bombed, February 1941, loads of chocolate, cigarettes and sweets were destroyed. I should have thought they would have profited by experience. We were fairly busy, and gossiped with a Scotchman who knows the part we have visited. Didn't seem too far away then.

Friday, August 11. The Americans are now about 65 miles from Paris. It doesn't seem possible, after all the bad news we have had since we were last in Paris. It seems to me that Stalin had better get a move on if he hopes to be in Berlin first!! At lunchtime another scare at the office – a doodle stopped it seemed right overhead and burst not far away. This was 2.15, only five minutes after the time of the last Kingsway incident. When I collected my shopping I looked at the bomb damage in Well Hall. The bomb by some miracle landed in the Plesaunce [a park near the train station], and consequently did little damage as these things go. The local people must have been thankful that it landed there, because the damage is mostly confined to windows. It might have been so much worse.[2]

Saturday, August 12. Pop's birthday – we almost forgot it. Luckily remembered during the morning, so were able to get a card, etc. for him. It is disgusting how easily I forget birthdays and anniversaries nowadays, even of those nearest to me. I suppose it is because we have so much to occupy our minds now. A nasty night last night. Several landed too near to be comfortable – even shook us in the shelter. General Montgomery has issued an order to his officers and men and indirectly to those back at home, and it was broadcast this evening in the news. He seems to think things are going very well – rather different from the last time he was in France.[3] Mr. Churchill is in Italy. The war is certainly being run the Churchill way. Heard from Miss Hendry today. I had forgotten my Identity Card, which she returned. I think she has really missed our company. She said the place seemed very much quieter than it had been for a fortnight. Heard from Win today. She gave us news of an Aunt of mine who has just lost her house in Teddington, but a relative of ours who lives with her and is over 100 years old survived the bombing.

Sunday, August 13. A lovely sunny day. It really became too hot this afternoon. Did cooking this morning. It was a hot job, and I did a good deal trying out some recipes I brought down from Scotland. This afternoon Joyce and I went to the [New Eltham] cemetery [in Falconwood], which looked very lovely despite a flying bomb which landed on the chapel a week or so back. I am always surprised when I go there that from week to week it seems to fill up enormously. I realise now why cemeteries are causing a grave problem, because they are full in such a comparatively short time. Grandma called this afternoon. Her old house which was damaged during the Blitz was hit by a flying bomb just three weeks after she had vacated it. Sat in the garden this

2. People's knowledge of bomb damage came mainly from personal observation and the reports of family and friends. As the London correspondent for the *New Yorker* reported on August 13, 'Until the casualty and damage figures were given out by Churchill, no one really had much idea what mischief the bombs were doing outside his own neighbourhood. The censorship is still strict and usually it is only from chance conversations, or from glimpses through a train or bus window of that familiar rash of green tarpaulins spread over the roofs of blasted houses, that you learn that a place has been having a bad time.' (Mollie Panter-Downes, *London War Notes 1939–1945*, ed. William Shawn [New York: Farrar, Straus and Giroux, 1971], p. 338.)
3. Montgomery's inspirational message to his troops was printed in the press and included a reference to the Home Front. 'Across the water in England, the starting point for this great adventure, our families and friends are playing their part and they are bearing up well to this flying-bomb nuisance and other troubles. We are all in this together.' (*Manchester Guardian*, 12 August 1944, p.5.)

evening trying to make up three weeks arrears in darning. Our men folk seem to tear their clothes to pieces.

Monday, August 14. North London seems to have had a bad night. I must admit that I didn't hear much, and what I did hear went on a long way [away]. General Eisenhower has told his troops that they are in sight of a great victory. Things do seem to be going well in France at the moment, and the Air Forces are giving the Riviera a terrible pounding, preparatory to landing some people [I] think, particularly as Churchill is out there. At the Club this evening I was on my own as Eileen has to be ordered to give it up for some time, and I missed her company. We had crowds of airmen in, all of whom are taking part in the battle of France, and all said without exception that they are taking terrible toll of the Germans, whose Air Force seems to have vanished. Several airmen said that they thought the Germans were keeping planes back for the battle of Germany, and I shouldn't wonder if this isn't true. A Canadian in this evening, who went to Normandy on D-Day, has been wounded and is off to France again in a day or so. London is full of Americans again. They seem to outnumber the British.

Tuesday, August 15. Invasion No. 2 announced at lunchtime – this time in the south of France. So far there seems to be little opposition, and the landings have taken place on a 100 mile front. This invasion is apparently greater than the Normandy affair, which seemed to be the biggest in history when it happened. Last night I met an airman who was on the fourth floor of a five-story building when he saw a flying bomb coming towards it. He lay on the floor and escaped with no injury, although his tin helmet was damaged by the falling bricks. He and another fellow removed all documents from the building just before it collapsed, and for this they have been granted a month's leave, which has pleased him very much.

The Allies were, by this time, clearly and successfully on the offensive and the Axis powers on the defensive. Anglo-American forces were advancing east and north on the continent, and Soviet forces were moving toward the west. There seemed to be little doubt that, in due course – but who knew when this might be? – Nazi Germany would have to accept defeat. In her diary Kathleen wrote a lot about major items of news from various war fronts, and while she sometimes offered comments on these reports, or linked them to broader inter- pretations of current history or perhaps to conversations she had had with others, often her words are largely summaries of what she had read in the press or heard on the radio. Many of these summary statements – especially the longer ones – are not reproduced below. This war news represents the bulk of the diary material that is omitted. The selections presented focus on what Kathleen reported of her own experiences in London; what she witnessed; what she heard or overheard from others; and what worried or angered or enlivened her as she and other Londoners lived through the last eight months of the war – along with her thoughts on the violence of the war's concluding months and her reflections on the peace to come.

[Intervening entries omitted]

Saturday, August 19. A flying bomb this morning narrowly missed the War Memorial Hospital [on Shooters Hill Road] and fell on a putting green nearby, causing only windows to be damaged – a lucky miss. The weather continues foul, as apparently it is in France at this time. The Germans are retreating fast in front of our armies towards Rouen, which makes me wonder whether they will retreat from Holland and Belgium first or wait for us to drive them out. Anyway this amazing advance brings many possibilities forward, and we should be surprised at nothing. This evening we went to see *Fanny by Gaslight*, quite a good British film. I should think this is the type of British film which would go down rather well in America. On the news we saw the rocket Typhoons shooting up planes and trains in France – most amazing pictures of an amazing plane. The days of Dunkirk and the great German Air Force seem as remote as Waterloo.

Sunday, August 20. A torrential downpour this morning caused water to leak through our shelter where the earth had dried and left big cracks. Pop had a terrible job to build it up again and make it completely waterproof, but he finished it this afternoon. General de Gaulle has arrived in France, presumably to take over the country as it is freed. The Allies are now near Paris but news is still vague. The Russians are still attacking Warsaw and fighting is going on in the city, but it hasn't fallen yet. Sir Henry Wood has died in hospital, and tonight Sir Adrian Boult paid a fine tribute to him. He was obviously one of the greatest figures in British music, and I am sorry I never managed to see him conduct.[4] Reports coming in say that the Maquis [members of the French Resistance] have captured Vichy, but so far these are not confirmed. I expect the so-called French Government have gone off to Germany, although they will meet the same fate if taken later on I hope.

Monday, August 21. … Met Eileen for lunch today. She had found her office bombed this morning, and the Civil Service sent them home for the day, so she lunched with me. At the Club this evening I had some assistance – a young Jewish girl helped me, and amused me too. She was quite young and gave me details of her many amorous experiences, which for one so young were plentiful. I am afraid this young lady will land herself in trouble one day. Recently she has been up in London as late as 3 o'clock in the morning with no transport home, etc. I gave her some good advice, which she took quite well, no doubt thinking me something of a Grandmother. Each of her escorts who kept her up so late suggested that she join him in a room at the Strand Palace [Hotel], which is the usual line. I am always amazed at the conceit of the men. They seem to imagine that any girl they take out is just dying to leap into bed with them at the Strand Palace, Regent Palace, etc.

---

4. Sir Henry Wood (b.1869) had been principal conductor of the annual and very popular Promenade Concerts in London. Sir Adrian Boult (b.1889) was the permanent conductor of the BBC Symphony Orchestra.

[Intervening entry omitted]

Wednesday, August 23. Paris has fallen. Somehow I never thought I could feel so moved by anything like this, but tonight, listening to the broadcasts from France, and listening to the commentaries about the marvellous deeds of the French people inside the city, I felt I was glad to have lived to see this day. No better way of liberating the city could have been imagined, and certainly we who had given up all hope of the French ever rising again will have to think again. The 'Marseillaise' has been playing on and off all evening. We heard it five times and we were in bed by 11. B. called this evening to tell us that K. has gone back to France, and they are naturally very worried again since it seems unlikely that his wounds have so quickly healed.

Thursday, August 24. Fighting is apparently going on in Paris suburbs, but one is not able to get a clear picture exactly from the vague reports in the papers and on the wireless. A terrible day here. It rained heavily and this evening the flying bombs were a curse. Between 6 and 9 we heard more than 50. They seemed to be overhead all the time and we heard a good many explode near enough to shake us. We were at the canteen and had quite a dozen danger whistles, whereupon we retired to a so-called safe spot in a passage. The canteen is in a bad way. It was practically under water, the rain pouring through the roof from which the tarpaulin had slipped and through the windows from which the covers had blown – in all a miserable show. We said several times that a night like this must be the very worst on which to be bombed. Every time fresh men came in they told us where different bombs had fallen. They seem fairly widespread. One fellow telephoned his wife in Bolton, and she said that the sun was shining brightly up there, and that she was sunbathing. I felt once or twice this evening that people from the provinces ought to go through a few nights like tonight. Then they might have a little sympathy for the evacuees, and bombed-out folk.

[Intervening entry omitted]

Saturday, August 26. Details of the latest British flame-throwers are announced today. They have exciting names such as 'crocodile', etc. It certainly is a terrible weapon, but one I would prefer to use if I had to take up arms against the enemy. No raids today and it was lovely in all ways. The sun shone and I got on with my housework and cooking with a glad heart. This afternoon went to see *This Happy Breed*, which I thought an excellent British film. The colour is lovely. In some ways I liked it more than the play [by Noel Coward], because naturally more of the happenings of the period 1919/39 could be presented on the screen, and some of them, i.e. the first talking film, the Charleston, etc., made me feel quite elderly. Some of the characterization in the film was not as true to life as that of the play I felt, particularly the younger generation in the film. They seemed to remain young all the time, whereas in the stage version they certainly aged. I missed Mr. Coward's performance. He was a more convincing 'middle classer' than Mr. [Robert] Newton, although he probably had his tongue in his cheek the while. I do feel that Noel Coward is one of our greater playwrights now, but he succeeds in depressing me exceedingly by the brilliance of perception.

Sunday, August 27. Amazing broadcasts from Paris. They seemed like a drama broadcast. The attempt on General de Gaulle's life was obviously a bloody business, and it seemed unbelievable that fighting was going on actually in Notre Dame. Of course in Paris the people can't know who is fighting for which side, and must be expecting shots from every window and corner. I know there is much that can be said against de Gaulle, but I feel that he is one man who can help unite France at the present time, and later on the French people can always turn him out if they want to (if they can in view of the peculiarities of French politics). A report has come in that Maurice Chevalier has been shot by the Maquis – and we were wondering what to do with collaborators!![5] Here, even with a few flying bombs this morning, the war seemed very remote. What with the ban on [travel to] the coast lifted, and bright sunshine, it seemed much like a pre-war summer day.

Monday August 28. A dreadful plane crash in Scotland today – an American [mail] plane on houses near Prestwick, killing 26 people in all. This is the third crash in a week – first the school, and then over the weekend another crashed in Hitchin, and now this one. Certainly the people who foresee planes falling out of the sky all day long after the war have something to use as an argument. We were busy at the Club this evening. Met B., a full-blown Chinese who is a pilot (officer) in the Australian Air Force. He is of Chinese parents, but an Australian by birth, and it was queer to hear such a broad Australian accent coming from about 4 feet 6 inches of Chinaman. His friends, mostly New Zealanders, told me afterwards that he is a marvellous fellow – non-smoker, no drinks – and in all a wonderful character, which I could see by his expression. Later Dan came in on leave before going to his battle course in Wales, and with him was a fellow OCTU, a Canadian, who was a full-blooded Red Indian. He amused me immensely. He was so excitable and earnest, and had definite ideas about the soldiers who were winning all the battles – the Canadians of course. At one point in the conversation he told me quite seriously that the English 'had been browbeaten for so long that they were quite used to it', which amused me somewhat. A naval officer in [tonight] distributed chocolate and cigarettes ad lib to all those in the Club – hundreds of good class cigarettes and dozens of bars of chocolate. I am glad to say he remembered the lady helpers.

5. Maurice Chevalier (b.1888) was a famous French music-hall singer and comedian. He was accused by many during the war of being a collaborator because he performed before audiences made up largely of Nazi officers and their companions and gave radio broadcasts that were of propaganda value to the Germans. He was later officially cleared of collaboration.

111

Tuesday, August 29. The Pope's message is still causing me great indignation, and judging by the correspondence in some of the papers, other citizens feel the same. It seems peculiar morals to expect the Londoners to forgive and forget, yet I never remember hearing his Holiness tell the Italians not to use gas on the Abyssinians nor rebuke the Germans for their cruelty in Europe. Only the British are silly enough to listen to such a message![6] A good many warnings today. The klaxons aren't very effective inside a building. We can't hear a thing when we are all working, and the building system of bells is non-existent again. Joyce phoned me this afternoon and told me that a flying bomb fell at Eltham Church at lunchtime, and we are both worried because Philip lunches there every day at the time it fell. However when I got home I discovered that he missed it by five minutes, because he stayed and listened to Bing Crosby[7] and didn't start out for Eltham till 2 o'clock, a remarkably late hour to lunch. The place is in a terrible mess, and obviously a good number of people were injured because it fell at a busy corner. Another plane crash – this time a British courier plane has crashed in Sweden.

Wednesday, August 30. Rouen has been abandoned by the Germans, and the Allies are now 35 miles from the Belgian frontier. The fly-bomb bases in France are now within grasp of our troops, and they have been told in a special order from Monty that they now have a special interest in advancing in this area because their advance will help directly their wives and families at home in England. I am glad British troops have been given this job. I am sure they will fight the Germans with more feeling than any other soldiers could possibly have. Mr. Churchill has arrived back in London. Lots of stories are passing around about General Montgomery, whether [US] General [Omar] Bradley is his equal, etc. etc.

Thursday, August 31. ... Joyce had a bad day at the office, with two or three flying bombs landing within shaking distance. One which landed in Charlton they all thought was making straight for them. At the canteen this evening we were very busy, and talked quite a bit to Mr. Watson, who is running the canteen for a fortnight. He is the official YMCA artist and goes round to various gun sites, etc. painting murals on the walls of the YM huts in the camps. He has such good ideas, and some of the huts he has painted he described to us, and they sounded lovely. It is a fact, he says, that soldiers and

---

6. In his message to the people of London, the Pope, Pius XII, had said: 'We exhort you to bear your trials with Christian resignation and fortitude, and also with Christian sentiments of forgiveness, charity and mercy, so that God will reward in you what the world will admire in you—an example of magnanimity inspired by the spirit of Christ's Gospel, and thus the present severe trials will bring forth for you and your fellow-sufferers fruits of expiation and amendment, of spiritual elevation and eternal life.' (*The Times*, 28 August 1944, p. 2.)

7. The American singer, Bing Crosby, was in England at this time, recording tracks to be broadcast at various times. On Sunday, 27 August he had recorded the *Variety Bandbox* with Tommy Handley, which was broadcast on 29 August at 1.15 on the Forces programme – and captured Philip's attention. The previous day, the 28th, the famous singer had participated in a live broadcast for the armed forces. (Malcolm Macfarlane, *Bing Crosby: Day by Day* [Lanham, Maryland and London: The Scarecrow Press, 2001], pp. 279–80.)

the ATS take much more care of a place painted for them personally than they do a drab hut which is not very attractive.[8] J. came in this evening. I haven't seen him for ages. He told us that his brother now has the DFM, DFC and DSO [Distinguished Service Order] and is a Squadron-Leader, which makes him rather proud I think. He gave us news of many of our old friends, some of whom have been killed or injured in Italy or France. It is nice to meet an old friend again, and get news of people we have almost forgotten.

[Intervening entries omitted]

Sunday, September 3. Our thoughts have been going back a long way today, and although it is such a long time since September 3rd, 1939, I can remember very clearly what we did on that hot day, and I still remember running down the garden to our shelter when the siren went, clutching a chair to sit on. These years have passed very quickly, but nonetheless they have been a fifth of my life and of course for many of my friends a larger proportion than that. I couldn't help thinking too of what the boys out in Japanese prison camps are thinking today – wondering no doubt how we have managed to stick out these years, because things were in a bad way when they left, and when I think seriously about it I often wonder <u>why</u> we have managed to stay the course, because on September 7th, 1940 I really thought the war would be over the following day, so little faith had I in the power of the people to 'take it'. This evening the news says that British and American troops are well inside Belgium, and the French say that the Yanks are in Namur [south of Brussels]. During the day great explosions have been observed over the Channel, and we are wondering if the Germans are blowing up some of their bomb sites or even more horrible sites they have on the coast. This evening I heard what I consider to be one of the best tales in a *War Commentary*. It was included in the account of the re-entry of the 51st Division into St. Valery. The commentator said that he met a young officer who was with the 51st before Dunkirk [in May 1940], and this young man buried all his possessions beneath an apple tree in an orchard in the town, including a gold cigarette case and quite a bit of money. He thought he had identified the tree, had dug about a bit with no success, but when the broadcaster left the young man had a mine-detector at work on the whole orchard. How like a Scot!!

8. We have been unable to identify Mr. Watson or locate any of his work. In a diary entry after the war (20 December 1945), Kathleen reported that 'he goes in for views and flowers and natural things generally. He had decorated the hall [of the canteen] today, and it certainly looks completely stylish, as opposed to the sort of mucky effect most decorations assume. He had made some artificial hydrangeas and rhododendrums which he had attached very cleverly to sprays of laurel which deceived nearly everyone who came in, and all the touches were definitely professional.' The decoration of YMCA huts and canteens was, for the organization, a matter of national policy. 'A Scheme for the Use of Artists in the decoration of YMCA Centres for HM Forces' was outlined in early 1942 (typescript attached to the Minutes of the National Emergency War Committee, 19 February 1942); and a report to this Committee on 25 June 1942 noted that 'Special attention has been given of late to the general appearance of our huts and centres ... [and] art students, troops and artists have been used in a number of places to execute special designs.' (These sources are held in the Special Collections Department, University Library, University of Birmingham.)

[Intervening entry omitted]

Tuesday, September 5. There were flying bombs over early this morning apparently, but we didn't have a warning at home. We heard a rumour this afternoon from a man from New Zealand who called into the office, who said that he saw on the 'Stop Press' of a paper that the German army had given in. When I went out to get the papers, dozens of people had also heard the rumour, which was denied in the first paper I read. The rumour apparently came from Brussels and had got everywhere. Joyce heard it in Woolwich and in some offices I hear there were scenes, girls crying and wanting to go home, etc. We were a bit doubtful at our office. We expected more noise and pandemonium in the streets. …

Wednesday, September 6. … Home Guard duties have been made less arduous, as a result I think of the railway strike, which was caused by the men having to do long duties, then drive trains, which wasn't a good idea for the men or passengers. This sort of overworking has been happening in all walks of life, and particularly in London and the South of England the men in the force have been terribly hard-worked this last year or so. Mr. H., one of Joyce's fellow workers, an officer in the Home Guard, told her what the Home Guard can do with his uniform, etc. He has been doing night duty on a London gun site for years, three or four times a week, and as a result is quite fed up with it. This evening we went to see [G.B. Shaw's] *Arms and the Man* at the New [Theatre]. One of the most enjoyable evenings I have spent at the theatre since the war started. The audience was enthusiastic and received the wit with much pleasure. The subject is so topical, and the jokes about Bulgaria and the Balkans would please any Russian!! Laurence Olivier ran away with the show with a wonderful comedy performance which kept the audience rocking, with his heel-clicking and fondling of moustaches!! The cast glittered, and Ralph Richardson, Sybil Thorndike and Nicholas Hannen were all fine. With a company like this they are sure of packed houses. It is ironical though that a year or so back *Johnson over Jordan* failed, although it was an intelligent play, with a good cast, but I am sure that if [the playwright] Mr. [J.B.] Priestley put it on now with Ralph Richardson he would fill the theatre every night. The same can be said of Laurence Olivier. When he appeared in *Queen of Scots* [by Gordon Daviot][9] that play too came off, because in those days only John Gielgud could carry a play like this, and Robert Donat too had mostly failures. But the three of them took to the films, and now they can make anything pay, whatever the play. John Clements too kept *They Came to a City* [by J.B. Priestley] running. I think it was too deep for casual theatre-goers. It is obvious nowadays that in order to be a success on the stage it is necessary to appear in films, get your audience, then put on your plays.

9. Gordon Daviot was a pseudonym used by the Scottish novelist and playwright, Elizabeth MacIntosh (b. 1896), who also wrote as Josephine Tey.

Thursday, September 7. The Americans have made patrols into Germany itself, so the battle of the Siegfried Line [German fortifications opposite the French Maginot Line] is on. Today is an anniversary we shan't forget in a hurry, the day on which in 1940 I thought the war would be over in a few weeks. To my mind that Saturday when the Blitz started will always rank as the day of this war. I suppose it is because we were so near the docks and in the middle of the chaos of the Blitz, and although we have had many raids as bad, none seem to me as memorable as that first one. At lunchtime today a van caught alight in Piccadilly Circus, and as I passed a crowd had gathered around to watch a young American airman putting it out very coolly with his gloves. The blackout has been modified as from the 18th, a very welcome piece of news. Also Civil Defence, etc. has been made less arduous, in all places but London and the South of England, which is still within range of Hitler's rage.

Friday, September 8. The British are now 30 miles from Germany as well as the Americans, so all the armies are getting ready for a final push over the frontier. General Montgomery has been in Brussels, and was given a wonderful reception it seems. Odd how he has not yet been to Paris. There has been an awful mutiny in Australia in a Japanese prison camp, which apparently resulted in about 200 Japs getting killed and some Australians. Somehow these tales of the Japs who kill themselves and their fellows so easily seem horrible. They are a peculiar race, with no regard for the sanctity of human life. I wish for our sakes that they will start a national hari-kari. It would save us much bloodshed. Philip met one of his friends from college today. This fellow passed his degree at the same time and is due to go into the Ministry of Supply on research, but so far has heard nothing from them. I do think it is a disgrace that these boys have been left for months with no indication of what is going to happen to them. It is the same whether they are going into Army, Navy, Air Force or industry. They are mostly still waiting for news. This has been one of the worst weeks for weather this summer. It has rained practically continuously, and this afternoon we had another dreadful thunderstorm. I am afraid Mr. Berry mustn't raise his lamentations for saving water just yet awhile or he will receive insults from the population generally I think.[10] When I was in the Co-op this evening picking up my shopping I was most amused and disgusted at the words of an old woman (50 or more, but looks about 70) who was at the counter. She was it seems intending to evacuate but had waited till this week for her dividend. She said however that her chances of a 'free holiday' were receding as the war got better, etc. etc. Mrs. R. to whom I was talking said that lots of women she knows have the same idea. They make the most of each evacuation scheme to get a free holiday.

---

10. Henry Berry (b.1883) was Chairman of the Metropolitan Water Board. He was a prominent local Labour politician and member of the London County Council, and had been Mayor of Woolwich, 1935–36. He lived in Eltham, SE9, not far from Kathleen's previous home on Appleton Road (though in a more affluent neighbourhood – and he had a telephone).

Saturday, September 9. A <u>lovely</u> day for a change. Heard from Mrs. L. She is thinking of returning soon, and I shall be glad to have a neighbour again. The details about the flying bombs, [and] the damage and casualties caused by individual ones, are interesting and we are making it our business to distribute some of these details to the provinces. This may seem petty, but we know that many people haven't much idea of the damage, etc. one of these things was able to do. I notice that I am using the past tense, which shows how happily we have assumed that they are a thing of the past. This afternoon I was on my own. Pop went out to a greyhound racing meeting, Joyce had a date in town, Philip was working on something, so I departed to the pictures, and enjoyed myself alone. I suppose in days gone by I should have devoted myself to an afternoon of sewing or a little cooking, of which I have plenty to do, but I felt bored with both jobs so went off to the cinema, and felt quite ready to do mending when I came out.

Sunday, September 10. The British are through the Albert Canal [east of Antwerp] and on for another ten miles. Holland is becoming increasingly menaced now, and I wonder whether the story that some of the airmen told me ages ago, that the Germans would clear out and leave Holland, will prove to be true. Joyce went last night to see *The Banbury Nose* [a play by Peter Ustinov] with some friends and enjoyed it immensely. Some of the performances she thought were wonderful, particularly that of Hugh Burdon, an actor of whom I never have had a great opinion, but maybe he has improved. Princess Juliana [of the Netherlands] has returned to London [from Canada], looking much slimmer according to our well-bred press. London is rapidly filling up with royalty waiting to go back to long-suffering Europe.

Monday, September 11. Mr. Churchill is in Canada for more talks with President Roosevelt. Philip got his papers from the Admiralty this morning. He has to report at Portsmouth on Sunday afternoon and begins his service on Monday [he had graduated from King's College, London in June with an engineering degree]. I didn't imagine he would get such generous warning, but it is fortunate as he has a great amount of kit to collect. We were very busy at the Club this evening, particularly as Eileen is on holiday and Mac and I were alone. Had quite an interesting talk with an Australian from 'records office', and he told me about the extremely delicate work they do. He deals with articles, large and small, left behind by Australian airmen when they are posted missing or killed. Small articles are sent home, but large things like bicycles, cars, motorbikes or wireless sets are either auctioned here and the money sent back home or with permission of next of kin are given to some friend or relation here. He said that this part of their work has caused a great amount of good-will towards their department. Also he traces property. That is, some people wrote to him saying that an Australian airman who used to visit them said he was going to have his photo taken just before he was killed. They wonder if he did have it taken, and if so, whether they could have a copy. My friend said that they go to endless trouble with cases like this, first trying to find out about the photograph from the fellow's squadron, [and] failing that they get in touch with photographers in London, etc. etc. I think it is all a very good sort of job, but must require a good deal of tact and heart. The only thing I didn't like about this officer was that he told us the usual 'line' married Australians take nowadays, i.e., that his wife had run off with an American, and that he was going to divorce her as soon as he gets back. I am sure I have heard this line at least six times this year.

Tuesday, September 12. Le Havre has been captured at last, and the British have advanced into Holland. Dover is getting rather bad shelling now. I suppose the Calais and Cap Gris Nez garrisons are going to use up all their shells before giving in. Met Philip at lunchtime. He has been to Moss Bros. for his uniform. They will have it ready by Thursday, and apparently he is quite pleased with its appearance. We popped into shops and got a few odds and ends which he will require.

Wednesday, September 13. The Americans are now into Germany in two places, and the Germans will now have to suffer some of the consequences of this war, which they can't appreciate until they have armies fighting on their territory, in the same way that the French, Belgians and Russians have [had] time and time again. The Warsaw squabble continues [Stalin refused to send support to the Polish rising against German occupation], but the commander of the garrison there has had the grace to thank the RAF for its latest help. The 'rocket' tales continue to go around, but the Government is obviously saying nothing this time, and very good too, although the population is seething with talk about it.[11] Met Mr. L. tonight and he told me that in our borough the orders for reducing full-time Civil Defence personnel and shutting posts in daytime had today been countermanded, owing to this latest aerial menace [from V2s]! We all feel that they can't last for long, and the fact that we can discuss them amongst ourselves helps to use up some of our violence. Philip is still shopping. We do miss all the odds and ends – i.e., suitcases, toilets bags, shaving cases, etc. – which we had before [being bombed out of their house in January 1943], and which naturally we haven't got now. I am afraid Philip will have to buy a case or something, because we just haven't a large one now, and he ruined Joyce's Utility weekend case at cadet camp, and mine has been ruined in the shelter.

Thursday, September 14. This morning there were two explosions – 'more faulty gas mains' Joyce calls them – and the second at 7.20 was like an earthquake, which seemed quite near. We all rushed out and the tremor was echoing around for many seconds. Later Joyce rang me and told me whereabouts in Eltham it fell – unfortunately on or near a house belonging to a school friend of ours. Her parents and sister are buried, Joyce tells me. Later she told me that Mr. W., the father, was upstairs when it happened and he came down on the debris and was unhurt, but Mrs. W. and the youngest daughter at home were

---

11. The first V2 rocket fell on London on September 8. Initially the authorities did not acknowledge the V2 attacks and spoke publicly (if they spoke at all) of exploding gas mains.

killed. The damage is quite bad I understand, but naturally nothing was announced about it. Another fell in Walthamstow, a workman in our office told us – he lives there. How the RAF and American Air Force are pounding Germany. I think all Londoners are enjoying it at last. Nothing is falling on the territory of 'our friends'. This evening just as I was off to the canteen a low-flying Dakota gave me a start. We all thought it was a pick-a-back plane or something equally sinister!! Mr. Heath Robinson, the artist [cartoonist and illustrator], has died, and I was interested to read the universally kind obituary notices. They seem genuine, I feel. He certainly did quite a bit to make this world a happier place, and caused people many laughs in the last decade or so. Philip went to see *Richard III* this afternoon, and came home very enthusiastic about it. He thought Laurence Olivier was wonderful, and he is encouraging us to see it as soon as possible. This we will do if we can get seats at that terrible theatre [the Old Vic].

Friday, September 15. The Americans are now well into Aachen, which must be a much battered city now. I read somewhere that the Americans aren't sparing German villages as they tried to spare the French. They just leave them burning, and one reporter gave a grim picture of the scene he had just watched of farmers standing in the fields watching their farms burning, and of German people in small towns looking at the scene of desolation around them. Although I suppose it is wicked to say it, most people here are glad to read this. Certainly this is the greatest vengeance the world has ever known. The Russians have captured ('liberated' I believe is the term Stalin's announce-ment made) [the] Praga district of Warsaw, so perhaps that unlucky and suffering city may in the near future see an end to her trouble. Mr. Eden has arrived in Quebec [where Churchill and Roosevelt were meeting]. Some folk here think he had such important news for Mr. Churchill that he had to take it for secrecy's sake. We spent this evening marking the rest of Philip's garments. He got shirts, socks, gloves, etc. today, and this evening he met me in his uniform, of which he is very proud, and in which he looks very smart. A couple more 'defective gas mains' today.

Saturday, September 16. Another two explosions this morning. One didn't sound far away, but the peculiar thing about these latest horrors [the V2 rockets] is that people ten or twelve miles away from the incident hear the explosion very clearly. I suppose coming from such a great height they make a greater explosion. An alert in the early hours this morning. We saw one flying bomb come over. It exploded in the direction of the river. Philip did his final shopping today, and we packed his kit in the bag he got from Moss [Bros.] – not bad for a wartime article. I am annoyed that he has got to take sheets, pillow cases and towels from my small stock, but nevertheless we can't do anything about it. We felt better tonight when the clock went back and our bedtime was only 10.15 instead of 11.15, an extra hour much appre-ciated by us all, although people on night work or night duty must curse their luck at being on duty the night the clocks go back. Philip is disappointed that he won't be in London for the dim-out, but I don't think there will be a great deal of difference for a time. I think the order was somewhat premature, in view of the latest raids, etc.[12]

Sunday, September 17. We rose early, and had dinner at 11 o'clock. Philip asked Joyce and me to go up to Waterloo with him, so we did and got there around 12.30. Soon he located a couple of King's fellows off to Portsmouth too, so he soon ditched us, and we went off to town intending to cheer ourselves up with a visit to the pictures. I think Philip felt much more brave at the thought of arriving with some of his friends. These two boys looked very young I thought, especially as boys of 18 or so these days usually pass for 20 or so. We went to see *Double Indemnity*, an unusual thriller, which we enjoyed, as something different in Hollywood entertainment. With it we saw one of my favourite British pictures, *Quiet Wedding*, which seemed to amuse the audience, which was almost entirely American. London was seething with them, with their girls in tow. I wonder what these girls will do when the Americans go home and the British soldiers come home battle-weary and hard up. I am afraid they won't get taken about in such style then, to all the best hotels, cinemas and theatres. Actually it is really a serious problem. Whilst we were in the queue a taxi drew up beside us and two girls aged about 15 got out. They were obviously of very low mental state .... However one said to the other, 'We'll wait here, then we can pick up two Yank officers' – and they did!! When we got home we found that a rocket had fallen in Brockley or nearby and had shaken everyone up quite a bit. The 1st Airborne Division have made a landing in Holland at an unnamed place, and all is apparently going well at the moment, although the news of it is scarce. Some of our neighbours seem to have taken Mr. Sandys' speech, together with Mr. Morrison's words [concerning a 'dim-out'], to heart and seem to have no blackout at all at their windows.[13] Most, like us, have kept normal blackout up – actually our curtains are not able to cover the windows completely, so are no good. The siren sounded, however, around 8.50, so blackout had to go up anyhow.

Monday, September 18. I wonder how Acting Temporary-Probationary Midshipman P.R. Tipper, RNVR [Royal Naval Volunteer Reserve], is getting along today. We will probably hear from him tomorrow – that is if he bothers to write. Some wonderful pictures of yesterday's airborne landing appear in

12. As the *Kentish Mercury*, 8 September 1944, reported, 'On September 17, when double summer time ends, window black-out will be replaced by "half-lighting" over the whole country except in a few special coastal areas. Windows other than skylights will need only to be curtained sufficiently to prevent objects inside the building being distinguishable from the outside. This will enable ordinary peace-time curtains or blinds, except the flimsiest kind, to be used, and a diffused light will be visible in the streets. On an air-raid warning complete obscuration will be required, either by drawing black-out curtains or putting out the lights.' Shop display lighting was still not allowed. 'The police will exercise discretion in deciding when an unreasonable amount of light is shown.'
13. Earlier this month Duncan Sandys, MP, the Chairman of the Flying Bombs Counter-measures Committee, had asserted that, 'Except possibly for a few last parting shots, what has come to be known as the Battle for London is over.' (*Evening Standard*, 7 September 1944.) In fact, German aerial attacks on London continued until late March 1945.

today's papers. They are the best of their kind I have seen during the war. The British troops seem to be nearing the airborne troops and are expected to join up any time now. We were busy for an hour or so at the Club – then we sold out. Several of the airmen in are on leave preparatory to going home to New Zealand. Odd now that some of them aren't at all keen to go, and for years they have been telling us how they disliked England, etc., yet when the test comes they can't loathe us as much as they thought. Studied the blackout on my way home, and although in London itself I didn't notice much if any difference, in Lewisham whilst I waited for my tram the public houses had quite a pre-war look. They certainly have taken Mr. Morrison seriously and had only flimsy curtains up. The cinema too seemed quite bright and cheerful. In the streets nearby some of the houses look pretty bright, but as so many windows near us are permanently blacked out, there isn't a great deal of light. Eileen said that Dan was quite thrilled on Sunday evening to see the bright windows, something he hadn't hoped to see in England.

While Kathleen continued to produce daily entries in her diary, some of them long and detailed, during the fortnight after September 18th she wrote much less about life in London and her own experiences at home or in public places. She talked a lot about the progress – or setbacks – of the Allied troops. She was alarmed and dispirited by the extent of the casualties – and the prospect of a further slaughter of young men. The anticipated victory over the Axis powers was, apparently, to be depressingly costly. From early October she came, once again, to speak more of domestic matters.

Tuesday, October 3. Warsaw has stopped fighting. The Poles asked for an armistice and the Germans accepted, and now we can expect some pretty nasty reprisals by the Germans for this uprising. The Dutch people living on the islands in the River Scheldt have been warned by the Allies that they will be very heavily bombed in the near future, and they have been advised to leave the area, or at least get away from targets. Joyce has an awful cold caused by firewatching last night. They are a fire party of 15, and owing to many of the blankets having been stolen recently they only had two apiece. As a result they shivered all night long and the draughty shelter will probably result in 15 very bad colds, and some absence from work later on. Philip and I were up at crack of dawn this morning, getting him off to Colchester, and he hoped to catch the 8.12 train from Liverpool Street. He hadn't come in this evening by the time we went to sleep, but the trains these days are rather irregular, and I don't think he will stay the night there as they are not supposed to sleep away from home on this leave. Around 11 this evening there was a terrific explosion which seemed very near. Everyone came out into the road in pyjamas and various other nightwear, but we couldn't see an atom of smoke or fire, so it was probably much farther away than we at first thought.

Wednesday, October 4. We decided not to go and see *Richard III* as we both have bad colds and wouldn't enjoy it very much. Dorothy saw *Arms and the Man* last night. Mr. and Mrs. Churchill were there. She thought Mr. C. looked very old – much older in fact than his newspaper buildup would give one to understand. Philip had a good day yesterday and came home with a carriage-full of American Fortress officers stationed somewhere near C[olchester]. They told him quite a bit of news and told him of their experiences with the German jet-propelled plane which apparently can climb vertically at the same speed that a Spitfire flies horizontally!! Let us hope that the Germans have a limited number of these planes. These fellows gave Philip some figures of losses incurred through meeting the jets, and they certainly give one food for thought!! The Americans are through the Siegfried Line in places, but the Germans seem to be putting up terrific resistance. The trains are now running over the hole of Hungerford Bridge. I think this is wonderful but it gives me a peculiar feeling to look out of the window and see river both sides. They have repaired the one line on the extreme side of the hole.

Thursday, October 5. Apparently Mr. and Mrs. Churchill were at the New Theatre again tonight, so we missed them. Sergeant came back at lunchtime with two bits of news: (a) the British have landed in Greece with little opposi-tion, and (b) the heating is to be put on next Sunday – pieces of news which assumed equal importance to we freezing mortals in London offices. A warning tonight whilst we were at the canteen, and a couple of danger warn-ings from the [nearby] fire station. Three came over pretty low, causing us all to duck, and our new manager seemed somewhat scared. He has had little experience of them, and the noise was worse than he had anticipated.

[Intervening entry omitted]

Saturday, October 7. Waiting for Pop to return from Colchester with Philip's laundry, which they are doing for him there. I can't manage white shirts as we have no boiler or wringer, and no facilities for doing important washing. He turned up around 7 having travelled up with an American who had intended to be a minister – in fact was at theological college there – but his experiences in England had changed his mind, and he is going back [a] rabid Communist he told Pop. He was shocked at all the bomb damage all round Liverpool Street – if I remember rightly it is rather nasty for a little bit of the line outside Liver-pool Street itself. I find myself once again marking and mending for Philip. Heaven knows how fellows who are on their own manage? A siren again tonight, but didn't hear anything at all, although Pop saw one explode in mid-air he thought. The BBC can't make up their mind whether 3,000 or 5,000 planes have been out to Germany during the last 24 hours. Either figure will make a good deal of an impression in Germany I think, although naturally we hope the second number is the correct one.

Sunday, October 8. Up at the crack of dawn this morning getting Philip off. It was foggy and we couldn't hear any trams, so wondered if he would have to hike. Pop went with him and they did it in about 1½ hours, then got into a half empty train, the 10 a.m. No others from Portsmouth were on the train, so Philip will be pottering about Greenock [his new posting] in the dark hours tonight, trying to find someone who knows something about him. The reports about yesterday's bombing appear to confirm the 5,000 figure. Of these 3,000 were bombers and 2,000 fighters – a mighty figure. Joyce and I went to tea with Em this afternoon, walked part of the way through Plumstead, [and] passed some of the worst bomb damage in Woolwich. We were much amused at the large boards up on some of the houses saying that ———— of Cardiff was doing the repairs, and judging by the work being performed by the workmen it will be 1950 before any repairs are made. They were all sitting about, drinking tea, etc. Not one did we see doing a spot of work, but we heard plenty of talk by fruity Welsh accents. Wendell Willkie has died in New York, aged only 52, a fact that will make many people here upset, for I feel that he was a great friend of Britain, after he had come to see, although still a critic of us.[14] Em with whom we had tea was married about 34 years ago to a German, who was killed in 1917 in the British Army, so she has been a widow for 27 years. Next door to her is a family with an Italian name, although they have always lived in Britain. The father works in the Arsenal, and one son was killed when a plane crashed at Leytonstone recently. They laugh sometimes and say that in one house there is someone with a German name, next door people with Italian names – quite a fifth column!!

[Intervening entry omitted]

Tuesday, October 10. I only knew this morning that Mr. Churchill and Mr. Eden are in Moscow. They didn't tell me last night. This habit of Mr. C's of going to theatres, etc. just before he leaves on a trip will soon be changed, I feel, as everyone will now look for it. Mr. Eden was in England on Saturday, so they must have made a very quick trip – not via the Middle East as they have in the past. Have just finished reading *C/O Postmaster* [1943] by Thomas R. St.George, recommended to me by Dorothy, and recommended by me to everyone interested in Americans and their habits or lovers of Damon Runyon,[15] whose style St. George resembles. I enjoyed this book immensely and found myself chuckling heartily in trams, trains and restaurants, and noticed people surreptitiously trying to read the title, so they might also laugh. The author has a tremendous sense of fun and an ability to 'see himself as others see him', something we can't always do, yet beneath all the humour I feel that he shows very plainly just how the Yanks feel abroad just now – also how they are sponged on by the 'soft and slow' British, whether they be in Australia, India or England.

[Intervening entry omitted]

14. Wendell Willkie, though a Republican – he was his party's presidential candidate in 1940—supported many of Roosevelt's foreign policies, including Lend-Lease, and espoused an internationalist rather than an isolationist perspective. He was author of the best-selling *One World* (1943).
15. Damon Runyon (b. 1884) was an American journalist and writer of colourful and comic short stories, rooted in New York City, including *Guys and Dolls* (1932).

Thursday, October 12. The Japs are going to let every prisoner send home a short cable (ten words) in the near future, the expense to be borne by the Red Cross. This simple announcement will stir up hope in many a heart in England and Canada and many other countries in the world, and will cause some rather peculiar situations similar to one Pop told me about today. One of his colleagues has a friend whose husband has been posted as missing since Singapore fell. She is now married to a Canadian soldier (grand fellow apparently) and has a child, and a few days ago got a card from her husband to say that he is a prisoner of war in the Far East. Actually the date of his capture was one year after Singapore fell, so probably he has been wandering around all that time. Yet what a dreadful situation, and it cannot be an isolated case. In my opinion no woman should consider marrying again until she has absolute proof that her husband is dead. You can never be sure about men who were out there – not until the war with Japan is over – and I think the Government should forbid people to marry again, at least until after the war.

Friday, October 13. … At the canteen last night several airmen asked us if we could help find them new billets as they are so unhappy and uncomfortable in their present one. It seems that they are mostly away at the weekend, yet their landlady never offers them food to take home, and seems to be using these men as an excuse to fill her pockets. I know many of them are uncomfortable in their billets, but I am afraid I think it is an unsuitable way for the Army or any service to go on. Private billeting is rarely as successful as barracks, because there they mostly get the same service whereas private places are liable to vary very considerably.

No diary survives for – or perhaps was written during – the following fortnight, 14–27 October.

Saturday, October 28. A rocket this morning nearly shook the senses from me. I seemed to be the only inhabitant in our neighbourhood. Later we heard where it was, and Joyce said that it gave them a dreadful bump at the office. I think the unpleasant part of this attack is the suddenness of the explosion, with no warning or whistle or preparation of any sort. Another couple fell this evening whilst we were in the cinema watching *Rebecca* and everyone stirred but no one left. Actually there is no point in altering one's life because there is just nothing one can do about these things but forget them. Together with *Rebecca* we saw a documentary film (the title of which I have forgotten) about disablement, and the various methods adopted by the Ministry of Pensions organisations to enable disabled people to fit themselves for carrying on with their old jobs. It was most interesting, and apart from showing the great courage of various war victims, it showed just how the limbs are made and fitted so that they are almost as good as the old limb. The sailor who had lost two legs and was shown dancing, playing tennis, etc. was so cheerful [that] he made one feel thoroughly ashamed of oneself. I feel though that recovery after losing a limb is really a matter of temperament, because L. (our neighbour when we came to this house), although she lost her leg at the beginning of the Blitz, just hasn't been able to get on with her new one and is obviously going to find it difficult to continue her ordinary life. But there again as the years pass science will be making more discoveries, and will perhaps enable people like her to wear artificial limbs with ease.

[Intervening entries omitted]

Tuesday, October 31. ... Quite a busy morning for rockets and even three warnings, with flying bombs over. I am afraid the sirens got me in a whirl. Mr. Churchill's speech today will depress many people, I am afraid, with his forecast of the war lasting till early summer – then the Jap war going on 18 months after that [*Speeches*, VII, pp. 7020 and 7022]. Wishful thinking on his part I am inclined to think. Perhaps he enjoys the war!! Mrs. Arnot Robertson in the *Brains Trust* this evening expressed the views of every woman in this country when she mentioned 'corsets'. I believe the quotation she produced from Shakespeare called them 'stays', but no matter, it put our case rather well. A great pity Dr. Summerskill doesn't do something about this problem. It could come under the heading of 'public health' I think.[16]

Wednesday, November 1. Joyce rang me this morning to tell me that the rocket at 2 a.m. fell at Plumstead on the garden of the house my Grandmother sleeps in. It is owned by a doctor, whom she assists in his dispensary during the evening, and always stays the night there as company for his wife in case he is called out. This is the second narrow escape they have had in about five weeks, as the house was severely damaged by a flying bomb recently, and was only patched up to give them one room to live in and one for the surgery. Another

16. E. Arnot Robertson (b. 1903), a novelist, journalist, and broadcaster, was a guest on this instalment of the *Brains Trust*. Edith Summerskill (b. 1901), a Labour MP, was a feminist and medical doctor and an advocate of reform of Britain's health services.

Underwear, of course, wore out and during the war replacements were hard to come by, to the chagrin of many women. One of the official wartime histories explicitly acknowledged the problem: 'total corset production was inadequate. Production was never more than nine to ten million garments a year, whereas there were probably 18 million corset wearers; one war-time corset was hardly likely to last as long as two years. The corset industry had released a high proportion of its resources to the war effort.' Moreover, the garments available were generally of poor quality – and perhaps getting worse. Firms that had previously made corsets were by 1943 likely to be producing parachutes. (E.L Hargreaves and M.M. Gowing, *Civil Industry and Trade* [London: HMSO, 1952], p. 466.)

During a shopping trip to Kensington shortly after the end of war in Europe, on 15 June 1945, Kathleen and Joyce found little of value to buy until 'we ran to earth a "roll-on" [i.e., a girdle], which the assistant produced from some secret place, merely because she liked the look of our smiling faces I think. It is a lovely garment, absolutely pre-war in appearance and quality.' Three weeks later, on July 6, a hot day, she found visible reasons to remark that 'uncorseted flesh is most revolting in summer garb, and if the men responsible cast their eyes around (as if they need telling) they will see just where the women have had to suffer in this war. Surely decent corsets for women to keep their good health should be more important than putting fresh tyres on the market. After all it wouldn't hurt car owners to go without their cars for a bit longer, as they mostly use them now for pleasure.'

fell at Bexleyheath it seems, but we don't know anything much about that one. Went up to Paddington at lunchtime in the hope of seeing Win, but had no luck. I should imagine her train was late in at Liverpool Street, because she didn't appear and I waited till 12.45. …

Thursday, November 2. It is a year ago that Mother died, and somehow the time seems to have passed very quickly, although we haven't really got used to doing everything for ourselves. A couple of rockets this morning, one near the Marquis, another somewhere near Hampton Court I understand (this delayed one of our directors). Later, when I arrived at the canteen, heard more about the Shardeloes Road [SE14] rocket last night at 6.40, which fell on a row of houses, [and] also affected a passing tram [some 31 people were killed]. Vans from the canteen have been there all day, and when the last one came away the searching was still going on, and they were using Alsatian dogs. Thirty families were buried it seems, and this evening 15 families had been accounted for. Everyone at the canteen was talking rockets. One bright fellow (REME) [Royal Electrical and Mechanical Engineers] told me happily that the Germans might be able to send them over one every three minutes, which is a depressing thought. A lovely bright night when we walked home, but terribly cold. Mrs. B. was there tonight, and she told us that P., her son, is probably getting married soon. His fiancée has already let him down once, by becoming engaged to an Australian officer last year whilst still officially engaged to P. Then when the Aussie was killed she looked appealingly at P. again, and it seems that he has fallen. Odd affair. Not likely to be successful in my opinion (for what that is worth).

Friday, November 3. Such a terrific explosion this morning at 4.55 a.m. It scared the life out of me. It fell in Lee, practically the identical spot an earlier rocket landed the other day, and no one was killed again. Remarkable luck really. The British have strengthened their hold in Walcheren [the Netherlands], and Flushing is almost surrounded. In Hungary, the Russians are rushing on and are only 30 miles, or less, from Budapest. Met Mrs. R. She hasn't had any news from K. for over a fortnight, and is naturally worried about him.

[Intervening entry omitted]

Sunday, November 5. A simply dreadful day, only fit for firesides. I didn't venture out, but found the day passed quickly enough whilst I was working. Although I listened to several news bulletins, I couldn't tell anyone what they were about. I found myself not listening to them with concentration. Heard an amusing 'Spelling Bee' this evening in which Variety stars covered themselves with glory, whilst drama stars were not so hot. I feel myself that I couldn't spell <u>cat</u> in similar circumstances, and I am renowned for my poor spelling, so had sympathy with Mr. John Mills who didn't get one right. Dobson & Young were amusing again this evening (I forget which one does the talking so include them both).[17] A long warning tonight, about ¾ hour, and heard one doodlebug come down in the distance. This evening it looked terrible, black with pouring rain, and violent wind. Then add to that warning with doodles, or no warnings and rockets coming out of the blue, and one gives a fairly accurate picture of happy English homes at the present time.

Monday, November 6. I forgot it was Guy Fawkes Day yesterday, a day I always remember with horror from my youth. Actually, though we always had a lot of fun at home with our fireworks, etc., and although I was pretty scared of loud fizzes and bangs, the roast potatoes, chestnuts, and gorgeous bonfires made up for this fact. To children of today, used to fires of blitz size and the sounds of 1,000 pound bombs exploding and the sight of rockets exploding in the sky, the fireworks we used to have will seem insipid. Lord Moyne, Resident Minister in the Middle East, has been shot in Cairo, and is severely injured. His chauffeur was killed at the same time. Whatever the reasons for this crime, it is a dreadful thing. We were crowded with soldiers at the Club this evening, several wearing newly presented MCs [Military Crosses] and MMs [Military Medals]. Many of them are going home very soon, and when somewhat merry are very indiscreet about their sailing times. Joyce told me tonight about the War Damage Claim put in by J. for a recent 'Incident' in which his wife and parents lost most of their possessions (his mother was killed). In the space where one is asked 'cause of damage' he put <u>rocket (?)</u>, and a few days later this claim was returned marked 'incorrect – cause of damage <u>government experiment</u>'. As J. says, this so-called experiment proved rather costly for their family – and I am sure, and so is everyone else who knows about it, that this is nonsense.

Tuesday, November 7. Lord Moyne has died, but his assassins have been caught, and according to the Egyptian Government were foreigners [they were two members of the Zionist Stern Gang]. I am afraid they won't do whatever cause they were supporting much good by this act. Mr. Churchill paid a moving tribute to Lord Moyne in the Commons today. That of Mr. Amery, broadcast this evening, was not so good. Today is election day in America, and I think people here are as interested as any over there. The general feeling here I think is that it will be a bad thing for world peace if [Thomas] Dewey is elected, although I was much amused by *The Times* leading article, which is so written that whichever candidate is elected they will be able to say that they supported him. Very clever. Joyce brought home a file of letters from the 76 members of their office now in the forces, and we read them whilst she prepared some records. They were very interesting and came from every

17. Walter Dobson and Walter Young were the hosts of *Music with a Smile*, a four-part fortnightly series that began on September 24. This evening's broadcast was from a naval training centre in the North-West. According to the *Radio Times*, 24 September 1944, p. 6, 'Dobson (he talks while Young, one-time electrical technician, puts on the records) believes everyone can enjoy music. He has proved he is right during 3,000 lectures in four years.... It is their informal presentations of music, often streamlined by themselves before being played, that gets their audience and makes the troops glad they came.'

corner of the globe, and every service. I was amused at the general feeling that they all express, to get back to the boredom of everyday work. Almost without exception they expressed this view, and some of them I discovered had very unimportant and uninteresting jobs in Woolwich. One man, now a Major I think, put an interesting point forward, one which we at our office have often discussed – the question of men in subordinate positions who are now in positions of rank in the services, and their feelings when they come back. This fellow (a very intelligent one I know) shows that he is facing up to this problem, but I wonder if others in the same position are?

Wednesday, November 8. At 7 o'clock this morning Mr. Roosevelt was right ahead in the Presidential election, but by the 8 o'clock news Mr. Dewey had polled so many votes that he was still in the fight. However during the morning Dorothy's mother phoned us to say that Mr. R. had got in, Mr. Dewey having given up. I am almost relieved about this, and I think we all felt the same. I expect Mr. Churchill is one person really pleased about this result, as I imagine their friendship is very real. Picked up Philip's second uniform this afternoon, and was impressed once again by the difference in the service at men's shops. Here the pre-war attitude towards customers seems to be observed still, and it was a pleasure to be served – so different from that experienced in most of the shops I deal with for food and clothes.

Thursday, November 9. A couple of warnings this evening and heard one or two explode in the distance. We were at the canteen and the noise there deadens most external banging. They broadcast Mr. Churchill's speech at the Mansion House, after the 9 o'clock news. I thought it one of the worst I have ever heard – so hesitant and stumbling ['Review of 1944', *Speeches*, VII, pp. 7025–29]. However I was listening with only one ear, but Pop agreed when we got home. It is bitterly cold. An Eskimo would feel quite at home in London, and I hear that there has been snow in Kent and Stroud. What a grim prospect – snow in November. I suppose it has happened before, probably before my time though. The announcements by the Germans about the V2s which they have been launching against London have been given out by our announcers with a most naïve intonation, almost as if we (the public affected by these objects) and the Government are getting together in some quaint little parlour game. Anyway, the Germans apparently said they dropped one in Sidcup (they named the road which was accurate) so they are getting some good information it seems.

Friday, November 10. Mr. Morrison's pronouncement yesterday doesn't seem to make much difference really to street lighting. At least on paper most boroughs seem to be having a great deal of trouble with the lights, and can't hope for much brightness.[18]

---

18.   While higher standards of lighting were to be permitted in London, as was already the case in most parts of the country, some boroughs lacked the technical capacity to carry out the new policy.

Saturday, November 11. I have never really got used to Armistice Day without maroons[19] and two minutes silence, and I wonder if we will ever go back to this old habit. I suppose by the time this war is over we shall have more to be silent about. Mr. Churchill will no doubt be going to the great Armistice Day parade in Paris, a ceremony which will, no doubt, be very impressive. It must be very moving for the French people to be able to celebrate this day free once more. They have a great deal to remember, apart from their appalling losses in the last war. The *Star* this evening contains an account of the visit of Mr. Noel Coward and the Duchess of Kent to the New Theatre, and of their subsequent dinner with the Oliviers. This bit of news will certainly start up the talk about this pair again. Not so long ago everyone was saying that the Duchess and Mr. Coward were going to be married – a rumour which became front page news in America, so my Americans acquaintances told me. Personally I can't imagine him marrying anyone. Why should he?

Sunday, November 12. A grim cold day. I think I have strained my back and chest by carrying too much on Friday evening – a bread bin, obtained with difficulty after 18 months of endeavour, a quart of milk, my order of groceries, joint of meat, bag with book, etc., and a handbag – and I had to get in and out of trams with all this. I know I was stupid, but I wanted to get it all home. Anyway during the evening my back and arm ached, and now my chest feels as if a band were round it both when I eat and breathe. I am already imagining myself with congestion of the lungs, or equally unpleasant complaints, but will content myself with some rubbing. Joyce went over to the cemetery this afternoon, taking some lovely chrysanthemums with which the graves were almost entirely covered. It is practically the only flower plentiful at the present time, although I noticed that the gardens in our road have a very lovely show of roses. We have two as well. Mr. Churchill was given a wonderful reception by the people of Paris. The broadcast we had brought tears to one's eyes. I feel that a great bond of friendship can be made for the future if our statesmen are sincere. The French people are ready and eager for news of the British and what they have been doing since Dunkirk, and careful understanding of this desire will do much to bridge past misunderstandings.

Monday, November 13. As my back was still painful I rang the Club and told them I couldn't go tonight. Decided to take it easy at home. Joyce goes to see my Aunt on Mondays and usually gets in about 7.30, but as the evening went on we got worried, and when it got 9.15 I persuaded Pop to set off and to look for her. When he got to Well Hall, he found that Auntie Lila had broken her arm, and the plaster, which had been put on at the hospital, proving to be so tight that it turned the fingers black, Joyce had taken her up to the War Memorial [Hospital] again to have it loosened. This [involved] an old lady of 80, and in the blackout too, so no wonder she was late home. I think Auntie L. is marvellous. This is the second arm she has broken in about five years, yet she goes on.

19. Maroons are exploding fireworks. In 2005 Kathleen remembered these bangs as the firing of the big guns at Woolwich.

Tuesday, November 14. The *Tirpitz* has at last been sunk by the RAF. This is good news because she was such a powerful ship and could have still caused much damage to our shipping and that of Russia. Heard from Philip this morning, and he sounds much more cheerful, being much busier – and off last weekend for a visit to Miss Hendry. During last weekend's terrific storm he was out in the Irish Sea on a destroyer which was on her trials, and as well as finding it most interesting he seemed proud of the fact that he wasn't sick – a hopeful sign for the future I think. There have been a couple of rockets in our district this morning. One broke the windows of Joyce's office I hear. The one in Well Hall has caused much damage and on my way to see Auntie Lila this evening I passed it. I notice that Mrs. N's house is one of those right flat, and must try to find out what happened to them. Actually now we know people in all the incidents. I suppose that is inevitable when one has lived in a district all one's life. Auntie Lila looked fairly sprightly, although her hand is black and blue. She had a long morning at the hospital as several coachloads of injured from the bombing were brought straight in and naturally attended to first. Apart from the shock of the two rockets, this naturally made Auntie much more miserable, although she said it made her ashamed of her complaining about her own trouble. A warning on my way home.

[Intervening entry omitted]

Thursday, November 16. The British advance towards the Maas continues successfully. These bald words hide so much that is terrible though and seem so horribly inadequate, but so often that is the case and we should be used to the understatement of our communiqués by now. Margaret, Joyce's junior at her office, last night went to the New Theatre to see *Arms and the Man* with her youth club. There were representatives from all the London youth groups there. Afterwards some of them went round to the stage door, opened it, went in and sat down. Later Mr. Olivier came out and talked to them and asked their opinion of the play, etc., and was so pleasant that these children have come away thinking him quite the greatest man on the stage, and they will probably remain ardent fans of his for all time. Didn't go to the canteen tonight, and will probably visit the doctor tomorrow as my pains don't seem to be vanishing. I haven't had a week indoors in the evening for ages, but I don't seem to do much even so. Listened to the wireless this evening. Didn't think the *To Start You Talking* talk [on 'Our Future Homes'] was as good as usual. The opinions of the speakers weren't as clear cut and intelligent as I have heard them.

Friday, November 17. Several bangs disturbed me in the night, but they seemed a good distance away. Quite a few people I know are now sleeping in their shelters, but I wonder how they feel these cold nights going out into gardens. Personally I feel now that if I have to end my days as a result of a rocket, bomb or other horrible German invention, I would rather be comfortable up till that time. I expect though that many nervous people just can't get to sleep unless they are in some sort of shelter or downstairs. The advance on the Rhine is going well, and many hundreds of prisoners are coming in. I wonder what we are doing with them all? The papers today contain a dreadful story of German brutality in Holland, just typical of their revenge, when defeat is in sight. I often wonder whether any of the men responsible for these dreadful crimes will be punished – and regretfully think they will get away with it. Went to the doctor this evening. She thinks my pain is partly strain from carrying too much at one time, partly the cold, and partly acute indigestion, so she is treating the latter in the hope that it will put the other causes right.

[Intervening entries omitted]

Monday, November 20. Dorothy is still not at the office. Her cold is hanging on and she is still trying to get rid of it. The French troops fighting with the Americans are now at the gate of the Belfort Gap [near the Swiss-German border] and going forward. They are now all set to show the world their revival it seems, and certainly they will be much more entitled to respect if they earn it. The atmosphere amongst the men at the Club this evening, whether they be sailors, soldiers or airmen, was decidedly hopeful. In fact many said they thought the war would be over by Christmas, but this seems almost too good to be true. I feel that if the war is over by then the casualties may be very high. Have just finished reading *England, Their England* [1933], one of the most amusing satires I have yet come across. A.G. Macdonell had a great sense of humour. I wonder whether it was typically Scottish?

Tuesday, November 21. The French have now reached the Rhine. I wonder what the Germans think when they discover that they are being beaten by Frenchmen. I expect many of them quake, especially if they have been stationed in France, because I imagine that many people in occupied Europe will have long memories where the Germans are concerned. Major Lewis Hastings broadcast this evening on his return from the continent, and paid tribute most movingly to the ordinary British soldier who is doing such great deeds out there and as usual made one feel ashamed at the petty grumbles we are so often indulging in. Certainly we oughtn't to make such a fuss about rockets and doodles (I soon forget this resolution when I hear one).

Wednesday, November 22. A fellow in Joyce's office is just back from Holland, where he is an Air Transport officer, because his home has been destroyed by a rocket and he is needed to attend to affairs. He told them quite a bit of interesting information about life in that country and couldn't speak highly enough of the Dutch people, who are enduring so much with so little complaint. He said that it is pathetic to watch the queues of people lining up for food. After hours they usually get a piece of black bread, and occasionally a tomato, but they always say 'At least we haven't the Germans here now'. Also he said that when our troops have their meals they are surrounded by crowds of Dutch children waiting to pounce on the crumbs, and naturally our men are very generous, but are not allowed to give everything away. His principal impression of the Dutch is their eternal gratitude and their kindness to the

British, and he added that much could be done after this war to use this feeling of kindness and brotherhood towards the British if our politicians don't ruin it. General Eisenhower has called for a great united effort to defeat the Germans and has said that final victory may be delayed owing to a lack of shells – a fact which seems rather odd when one considers that America have gone over in such a big way to peace production. People here imagined that they had enough war materials to last 50 years. Several explosions in the night as well as a warning. I find I sleep through most noises fortunately.

Thursday, November 23. The Ministry of Supply have announced that there will be no shortage of shells for the British army, so presumably it is the American production which the Supreme Commander was hitting at. The French are near Strasbourg now. That city is well in the line of the battle at last. Today is American Thanksgiving Day and I noticed that most public buildings were flying American flags. There is to be a great celebration at the Albert Hall this evening, and [all] in all the Americans are doing the day in great style, as they do everything. A couple of last night's bangs were in our borough. No wonder they woke us. Quite busy at the canteen this evening. We had a convoy in. The men wanted to be put up for the night, but we had to direct them to Croydon, being the nearest canteen able to accommodate large numbers of men.

Friday, November 24. The French are fighting in the suburbs of Strasbourg at last and it is only a matter of time before the town falls as the Americans are inside too. The British advance is still going well although they are meeting fanatical resistance. The air war seems to have started up with more violence. We heard planes going out practically all day. A rocket fell in the river near Joyce's office. It shook all the windows from some of their offices on the riverside and people who saw it said the column of water which went up was terrific. What a bit of luck though that it went there – the best place for one to fall.

Saturday, November 25. Tokyo has been bombed by American Fortresses. No details yet, but I hope that no planes were shot down because one has a terrible fear of what will happen to any airmen who bail out after bombing a Japanese town, particularly Tokyo. I think these airmen are brave because they know the risks they take. A noisy morning, with three hefty bangs – one up in the City, in Warwick Street [W1], which is near Sergeant, so he must have had a shock, and later another around 12.30 which sounded [as if it were] in the next street but turned out to be in New Cross on a most crowded part of the main road, on [a] Woolworth's building. This is awful, because at any time of the day there is always a great mass of people and lots of traffic on the road, and at this time on a Saturday morning it must have been awful. One of the branches of Joyce's firm [Royal Arsenal Co-operative Society] is next door to Woolworth's, so they are all anxious to know what has really happened. Pop is in Colchester this weekend. Will probably get asked down for Christmas, a proceeding of which I approve because … it will mean that Joyce and I won't have to work the whole time, which is what we would do at home. Had a long letter from Philip. They still haven't been paid – this after ten weeks – which is a scandal.

Damage from the V2 strike on New Cross, 25 November 1944. Photograph courtesy of the Lewisham Local History and Archives Centre.

[Intervening entry omitted]

Monday, November 27. Tokyo has been raided again, this time with no losses. This makes good reading and makes one think with pleasure of what will happen to the Japanese when Air Marshal [Sir Arthur] Harris [Commander-in-Chief of Bomber Command] moves his bombers to the Far East. A thousand bombers over Tokyo or any other Japanese occupied city would bring joy to many an Allied heart, although many people here are firmly convinced that as soon as we start making any sort of headway against the Japs they will kill or ill treat our prisoners, and no doubt this is worrying the powers that be. Sergeant was indeed shaken by the rocket on Saturday morning as it fell only about 200 yards from him. Joyce tells me that the last time she was in communication with New Cross the death toll was 143, which is dreadful, but not so bad as the tale I was told at the Club, that 180 had been killed already, and this from a girl who hadn't the remotest idea where New Cross is.[20] As I was nearing home there was a terrific flash in the sky, presumably a rocket in the distance.

Tuesday, November 28. Rocket last night at Woolwich, and I didn't think it sounded very near. Doris N's father taken to hospital injured (he is a permanent night worker). Details of the 'gen box' revealed this morning, after they

20. In fact, around 170 people were killed by the rocket on November 25, the greatest loss inflicted by any V2 attack. Details of this catastrophe are presented in Norman Longmate, *Hitler's Rockets: The Story of the V-2s* (London: Hutchinson, 1985), chap 16, and *Rations and Rubble: Remembering Woolworths, Britain's worst V2 disaster, New Cross Road, 25th November 1944* (Deptford Forum Publishing for the Deptford History Group, 1994).

have been flashed over America by enterprising American journalists who are apparently giving American scientists credit for this wonderful discovery. In the statement by Britain it is said that this invention is merely a development of radio-location, which was originally discovered by a Briton and which has been improved upon by British and American scientists. Another case where the American press gets in first, and no number of quiet statements of fact can oust that first impression.[21] A dreadful explosion at Burton-on-Trent [Stafford-shire] occurred yesterday, where an arms dump blew up, causing an earthquake which was recorded on the special apparatus in London for recording eruptions, so violent was it. Tonight it was announced that over 100 men were still trapped in one section, and that casualties in the dump and surrounding districts were expected to be very high. I noticed a suggestion in the correspondence column of *The Times* that the British Treasury might create much good feeling in America if, after the war, they invited over here, at the country's expense, relatives of men so severely injured that they would be in this country for months or years before being fit to travel home. I think this is an excellent plan, and worth thinking about.

Wednesday, November 29. ...A White Paper has been published giving details about the war effort of Britain and is obviously a mass of figures and diagrams, and I can't imagine any of our allies being the slightest bit interested in it. The death toll at Burton-on-Trent is still expected to be high, although accounts vary amazingly and we don't yet know what really happened (if the authorities do). The son of one of the men at Joyce's place, aged 15, has been evacuated to Torquay since one week before the war started, and three weeks ago came home having left school. He started work at Erith Oil Works and after being there for ten days was involved in the rocket incident there last week and has had both legs amputated. This is a dreadful affair, and proves really that no amount of dodging bombs is really fool-proof. What a terrible thing to have happened to a young boy though. Ruined him for life. Whilst we were in the cinema this evening heard two rockets – one shook the place considerably. Saw a very funny programme, a British satire *Don't Take it to Heart*, with a great deal of humour in it, and a film with Donald O'Connor the title of which I forget, which was also terribly funny. In fact I forgot the war and the rockets etc., even when they went off, so heartily were we laughing.

Thursday, November 30. I didn't hear all the rockets in the night – five or six I believe – but some were sufficiently near to frighten many of my neighbours. Those last night were at New Eltham and Falconwood. During the night one at The Sun in the Sands blasted G. and several other people I know. Another at Blackfen. In fact it was one of the worst nights I remember (only I didn't hear them). Tokyo has been bombed again, this time at night, and a good deal of damage has been done I hear. Mr. Churchill is 70 today which is really a great age for a man with his responsibilities. Sir Archibald Sinclair's statement

21. The 'gen box' ('mickey' in the United States) was a device that permitted more accurate bomb-aiming.

regarding the explosion [at Burton-on-Trent] needs a bit of swallowing, or else we must think that the British press consists of madmen or liars and that newspaper editors are fools, because his figures certainly don't tally with either the press or the radio, and I am afraid I just don't believe what he says and I think everyone I have spoken to is of the same opinion.[22] Very busy at the canteen this evening. There is more trouble now because the vans have been serving bombed out [people], etc. at rocket incidents, and the various councils involved argue that we are 'doing them out of a job', which seems a petty sort of excuse for refusing active help to those unfortunate enough to be bombed, and I am afraid I haven't seen much evidence that the councils have facilities for sending round vans with tea and food for people bombed out.

[Intervening entry omitted]

Saturday, December 2. A bang this morning near Waterloo Bridge I hear. Caused some broken glass in the Strand and thereabouts. What a dreadful thing if it had fallen on the Bridge itself, especially as it landed so near. Princess Elizabeth has launched the biggest battleship ever built in Britain and the reporters seem to think that it will be got ready in record time. I wonder if it will be ready for my dear brother to go on it? What a disappointment that would be for him, as he wanted corvettes – something of a contrast. The River Saar has been reached on three points but the bridges are mostly down and crossing it will probably be a costly affair. How an army contemplates crossing a river under enemy fire seems an impossible task, but modern armies seem to take these barriers in their stride. A little bit of news from Crete in today's paper, where it seems over 10,000 Germans are bottled up in one corner by combined British, Greek and Cretian troops – truly a grand vengeance. Went to Croydon this afternoon to try to get a frock. Walked round for hours but didn't see a thing I would have been seen dead in. I have never been there shopping before, but although it is a long way from us, the bus goes direct from Lee Green, and we thought it seemed a better bet than Lewisham or Peckham, both sorely affected by bombs. There are crowds of shops in Croydon, but most of them seemed full of the most awfully tawdry objects. I suppose it is the same everywhere, but most people I know think highly of the shops there.

86. *Sunday, December 3.* Today the Home Guard are standing down and there are going to be processions everywhere, the main one being in London, where most people seem to think the King will take the salute. This evening we heard recordings of bits of the march, as well as parades in various parts of the country, and it made one look back a long way to the first days of the LDV [Local Defence Volunteers; i.e., the Home Guard], as did the King's speech,

22. Sir Archibald Sinclair was Secretary of State for Air. Some 68 people were killed as a result of this massive explosion in an underground ammunition dump near Burton-on-Trent on 27 November. The Minister did, in fact, acknowledge something of the scale of the accident (*Parliamentary Debates*, 5th Series, vol. 406, cols. 66–67).

and indeed we have come a long way since those days. I expect many Home Guards (I know a few) will be sorry things have finished for them, but personally I would never be surprised if they weren't recalled, especially if the Germans start sending jet-propelled bombers over here. The King seemed to have two or three bad patches in his speech, but goes on most valiantly where most others would give up altogether. I do think he is brave to speak to the Empire at all, as we are always looking for hesitation whereas we don't notice it in others. Mr. Churchill's last speech was much worse than this one of the King's, but apart from a few remarks such as 'He seemed rather merry' or 'He seemed tired', it caused no other comment.

Monday, December 4. Troops in France are to have seven-days leave after six months, and are to have all sorts of special facilities to get them home quickly. I agree with those who think this a bad sign, that the war is going on longer than we at one time thought, but it will be grand for the men involved, because many Americans have already had leave from France, and it causes a certain amount of bitterness this inequality. Dan has gone back to camp, and they are due to go back to Italy any time any time now. Eileen is very upset and hopes that something will happen to stop him leaving. They will miss him as he has been staying with them for some weeks now. We were very busy at the Club, and I had several most involved explanations of how the strategy of the war is evolved by Generals Montgomery and [Sir Miles] Dempsey, none of which penetrated my brains, or maybe the brains of those doing the explaining weren't so clear. Certainly some airmen think they know a great deal about soldiering.

Tuesday, December 5. … It seems dreadful … that the British Government still, after all these years of war, are going to support old and reactionary forms of government in freed countries, the people of which must have changed a great deal over these years, and they certainly don't want anything to do with statesmen and diplomats who got them in their luckless position in 1939. I suppose though that the people behind the Government here would rather support old regimes than allow new and young blood to rule – new blood I feel that would be very friendly towards Britain, if left alone. Berlin raided by the Yanks, who report terrific air battles over the capital, claiming to have shot down 86 German planes. This evening we had a warning, lots of flying the while, heard two doodles, and saw much flashing in the distance, in all very confusing. Our old Sergeant at the office is very ill. He came in this morning on his way to Barts [Hospital], where they told him he must rest for weeks, and probably mustn't work again. He is nearly 80 and is such an institution at the office. We shall miss him terribly. He is such a dear old boy.

Wednesday, December 6. British troops are assisting the Greek Government to put down the left (ELAS) troops, and it is now Civil War indeed. I feel dreadfully about this. It is awful that British troops should be used to fight Greeks with whom they were brothers in arms such a short time back, and it seems dreadful that British troops should be killed and injured fighting one of our allies.[23] Questions asked in the House about remarks of Mr. Stettinius [the new US Secretary of State] regarding the British Government's action taken over the possible appointment of Count Sforza as Italian Foreign Minister. I agree with the questioners that it would be better if the Italians were left to pick their own ministers.[24] Our country will find itself in bad odour, as unpleasant as it was in September 1938, if we are not careful, and I am afraid our Allies, America and Russia, will come out of both situations with a better record, as they are carefully keeping out of both matters.

Thursday, December 7. The rocket during the night is said to have fallen near Selfridges. I imagine this is true, as everyone has the tale. Judging by newspaper reports not much damage was done but this may not agree with actuality. British tanks and paratroops are now fighting the Greek ELAS troops, and I am afraid people here don't feel very happy about the whole affair. In fact I have yet to discover anyone who approves of the Churchillian attitude. We are not to have Portal [prefabricated] houses it seems until after the war – so said Mr. Sandys in the House today – but there are a variety of small and 'temporary' houses which are going to be erected with all speed. I hope Mr. Sandys is more accurate about this than about the flying bombs.[25] Anyway I think the homeless people of London would rather see a few of these houses than listen to all the speechmaking that has accompanied this re-housing campaign. As for continually calling them temporary houses, I find that general opinion is that they will last at least 20 years, just as the hutments of the last war did. Anyway, I hope the men who build these houses are a little more speedy than the men repairing the bombed houses at the present time.

Friday, December 8. Was up in Oxford Street today trying to buy a dress, and although I tried in every shop I couldn't find anything I liked under £13. Every shop had the same dresses in them, and by the time I had finished I was heartily sick of seeing the same things in each shop. All the Utility dresses (which constituted the entire stock of most shops) seem now to be made of such shoddy material, which was not the case when Utility clothes first came on the market. The damage to Selfridges is much more serious than I had imagined. It looks dreadful and great girders and windows have been flung out. The damage on the spot is much worse than many a doodle bug caused. Mr. Churchill got his vote of confidence in the House, the members behaving like sheep as usual, although many Labour members abstained I understand. I am

---

23. ELAS, the National People's Liberation Army, had emerged during the Greek resistance to German occupation and was Communist-dominated. Churchill, who supported the Greek monarch, George II (few others did), was determined to prevent the Communists from gaining power in Greece, a prospect for which Stalin in fact showed little enthusiasm.
24. Count Carlo Sforza (b.1873) was an anti-fascist politician and former Italian minister of foreign affairs (1920–21) who had lived in exile for two decades up to 1943, first in Belgium and from 1940 in the United States.
25. Portal houses took their name from Lord Portal, the Minister of Works between 1942 and 1944. Duncan Sandys became Minister of Works in November 1944. In early September he had predicted – prematurely – the imminent cessation of flying bombs.

afraid that Mr. McGovern expressed my opinion very forcibly,[26] but obviously the rest of the House gave their own opinions, not that of their constituents, if my friends and acquaintances are anything to go by. I see too that the Canadian Government also got a vote of confidence, on the policy of sending men overseas. I suppose this will cause much displeasure to the men who are involved – and the priests! A Naval officer, Captain [Ralph Douglas] Binney, has met an awful death in London today. He tried to stop some men who had just robbed a jewellery shop and hung onto the car in which they were escaping. No one could help it seems and he was dragged through the City and later died. This is a dreadful business, and he was a brave man to try to stop the thieves. But I am afraid it will need a great many brave men to stop the wave of wrongdoing that seems to be sweeping the country. There was an earthquake recorded last night and experts think it may have been in Japan, but wherever it was it seems to have been a terrific quake. I hope it was in Japan, but wonder if any of our prisoners were encamped nearby, a thought which is probably occurring to many people here.

Saturday, December 9. At the hairdresser's today. Mrs. M. (the proprietress) was very worried as she had just had a letter from her son after a gap of about ten weeks, to say that he had arrived in Greece, an event which didn't please him, or his mother. In fact she was naturally as bitter as anyone I know about the policy of the Government which is causing our men to fight against our former comrades. One of the coldest days of the year, but it was quite dry, so one didn't care much.

Sunday, December 10. A terrific frost this morning. I thought it was snow at first. Then it turned to rain, and by this evening the wind was howling and the rain was beating down. Heard a couple of thuds and we had a longish warning this evening, during which there were doodle bugs about, and it made me feel dreadful knowing that some people were being bombed out on a night like this. Frank Owen [at this time a military correspondent] gave the *Postscript* this evening, talking about the 14th Army, and although I admire him very much and thought his talk excellent, I think his voice is awful. The accent irritates me. RAF bombers have been used against the ELAS troops in Greece, but they are not by any means defeated yet.

[Intervening entries omitted]

Wednesday, December 13. Were told about our Christmas bonus today. I have £15, from which of course income tax has to be deducted. I know this is a lovely present, but if only these large amounts had been paid out in peacetime we could have done so much with them. I know there is sound economic argument as to why we can't get high bonuses and wages in peacetime, but like

---

26. John McGovern, Independent Labour Party, was MP for the Shettleston division of Glasgow. He spoke in opposition to British military intervention in Greece (*Parliamentary Debates*, 5th Series, vol. 406, cols. 966–72).

most women I don't want to know why – I just wish. Money has certainly changed in value. When before the war I got £1 or £2 as a Christmas box, I could go out and buy a pair of shoes, stockings, gloves, etc., all for one or two pounds, now my bonus would buy only a decent dress, judging by what I have seen recently. A rocket this morning in Well Hall, at the top of our old road, so once again we are glad we didn't return there. This evening Joyce came up and we saw *It Depends What You Mean*, which we enjoyed very much, particularly as we listen pretty often to the *Brains Trust*, which certainly added to the amusement.[27] I thought the acting grand. I always like Angela Baddeley, and although she is no glamour girl, she has a lovely expression and voice. I found the dialogue most amusing, and only regretted that that the terribly high price Mr. [Robert] Donat sees fit to charge for most of his seats will prevent many men and women on leave from seeing a good clean show, which they would almost certainly find most entertaining. We got back to Charing Cross at 9.10 and midst a great mass of people waited for trains to loom in out of the thickest fog we have had for ages. Finally we caught an 8 something train which went out around 10, and got to Lewisham around 10.30 only to find that trams and buses stopped around 6. Just as we were preparing for a long, dark, unpleasant walk, a car drew up and gave us and some others a lift. The driver had been into the pictures for three hours as he couldn't move, and was now making a desperate effort to get home. We had a nightmare drive, often on the pavement and usually on the wrong side of the road, but since he was the only moving vehicle in South London I should think, we survived. We felt that we had been very lucky. Pop had to walk in front of the car all the way from Bexleyheath, and got home around 9, and he went wrong once or twice. He said that all along the road there were American lorries and cars, absolutely stumped by fog, which is something new to many of them. When we got in there was a letter from Philip, the first for over a week, telling us that he is in hospital, suffering from tonsillitis and abscess in the throat, for which they are giving him 500 units of penicillin every five minutes. We are naturally worried, but had imagined that he was out on trials or something. I hope he will keep us posted, but as he has been in hospital for nearly ten days he must have felt pretty grim not to have written.

Thursday, December 14. I rang Miss Hendry [in Scotland] today and she also had had no news of Philip, but she is probably going to see him tomorrow, or she will ring the hospital and write and tell us straight away how he is. It is quite a relief to have someone so near him, and she is very good. I wrote him today and sent off a book of Fougasse [i.e., Cyril Kenneth Bird] cartoons which I was keeping for Christmas for him, but I feel he needs cheering up a bit now. We were paid today and I felt most rich going home. A good thing I wasn't robbed on the way. Very busy at the canteen, and we have been warned that we are going to be much busier very soon. In fact they threw out all sorts of dark hints as to what sacrifices the volunteers would be called on to make – rather odd at this stage of the war. So great now are the calls on the YMCA that

---

27. The playwright was James Bridie, the pseudonym of Osborne Henry Mavor. The play uses a 'Brains Trust' format and conventions to dissect the institution of marriage.

the Ministry of Labour is releasing women from war work to take up voluntary work – very necessary because we are terribly short staffed at Lee Green, and we must be typical. Another interesting bit of work has started at Lee now. The YMCA is involved in this new scheme to buy flowers for men overseas who want them sent to their relatives here. We are dealing with a great area of South London, and many pounds worth of flowers have to be bought and delivered by our ladies and vans – a very good work. Some of the messages sent by the men which we attach to the flowers when bought bring tears to the eyes. I read all about this in the papers, but the credit was all given to the Women's Voluntary Services when it appears now that the YM is doing at least as much, or perhaps more, with, as usual, no praise forthcoming.

[*There is no diary entry for December 15.*]

Saturday, December 16. The rocket yesterday evening fell in Great Dover Street [SE1], near the factory at which Philip toiled for some weeks last year. It must have been a nasty business. The searchlights were still on the job when I came up this morning, and it seems that a wall collapsed on rescue workers at one point. This morning our doors were opened rather quickly. We thought the rocket was much nearer than it turned out to be, but near enough to jolt me out of my sleep. The Government's attitude to Poland is interesting, and it is obvious that they had to give in to Stalin's wishes in this matter, and I imagine the Russians will behave in the same way with regard to most of the Balkan countries. Although I have little time for the Poles in London, they seem to be quite unrelated to Polish life in Poland. I do feel sorry for the Poles when I look at the map of their country, as proposed by the Russians, but I suppose no one will be able to do anything about it, and if all one hears about the massacres of Polish people has been true, I shouldn't think that they will even fill what the Russians are allowing them to keep of their country.

Sunday, December 17. In Italy the advance is going well towards Faenza [south-east of Bologna], and its capture seems imminent. I notice that General de Gaulle has banned night clubs and dancing in France till the war is won. Judging by tales and letters coming from soldiers and airmen in France, the night clubs, etc. were certainly up to pre-war standards as regards dirt, and I hear that shortages of supplies of clothes has rather helped some of the strip-tease shows. I wonder how one enforces a law like this new French one, though one has only to think of the effect it would have over here to realise the difficulties the police would have in suppressing dancing, although sometimes I think it would be a good thing when I see youngsters coming out of the dance halls, kids of about 12 to 14 dancing till all hours. Like the black market, I would back dancing to win though. The authorities can't suppress the former because the feeling of the population isn't really against it.

Monday, December 18. Posted off some oranges to Philip, and some I have taken to the office to send up to Sergeant. We got so few that it didn't seem worth keeping any at home. Faenza has been captured by New Zealand troops, so they are still in Italy. I wondered if they had moved to Greece when I heard that several fellows in regiments attached to the New Zealand army had moved on to that country. Dan has now left England and is on his way back to Italy. Eileen and he have a secret arrangement whereby she goes out to New Zealand to him when he gets back from the Jap War. A remote prospect, and I am afraid she takes a dim view of ever getting there. I tried to cheer her up, but myself think that now it may be two years at least before that war is even partly over. [Field Marshal von] Rundstedt is throwing great masses of troops and tanks against the Americans and there seems something of a break in their lines, but this is not revealed because they have imposed a security blackout on news from the Western Front. This is terribly disappointing for everyone because even when this attack is driven back (as it will be eventually), it will be at considerable cost in life, and will make the war last just a little bit longer. We were not too busy at the Club this evening, and think it is due to the fact that another New Zealand Club, the Fernleaf, has been opened in Lowndes Square [SW1], which resembles the Ritz and has wonderful facilities to ensure comfort. I expect later on they will both do well again, but tonight we indeed noticed the difference. No news from Philip yet, but Christmas cards have begun to arrive.

Tuesday, December 19. The Germans have penetrated for several miles into the American lines, and their air force is coming up in larger numbers than have appeared since D-Day. Obviously they have been saved up for some occasions of this nature. In Athens fighting is still pretty violent, and today the Government here had to agree to a further debate on Greece tomorrow. This is another example of the fact that feeling is still very high in the country on this thorny subject. This evening I made sweets for Christmas with our extra sugar ration. Tried some fondants, and acting on instructions began to knead the ingredients with my hands, and soon found the mixture up to my elbows. It all had to be scraped off, and in so doing set quite nicely. Home made sweets seem lovely to us, until I compare them with those sent from Philadelphia that we are eating at the office.

[Intervening entry omitted]

Thursday, December 21. The fog has cleared a little today [it had been 'very foggy' the previous evening], although it is getting very cold. The Americans are making several stands, but the German advance is now well into Belgium [this became known as the 'Battle of the Bulge']. Some people are going to have a tragic Christmas so soon after liberation. Philip telegraphed that he is arriving at Euston tomorrow morning, presumably by the train arriving at 6.30. We decided (Joyce and I) to go up to meet him. Because he isn't feeling good he may like some company. Terribly busy at the canteen. We took a record amount of money, and we felt really beat when we finished.

Friday, December 22. Joyce and I got up at 5 a.m. and managed to get to Euston in the drizzling rain soon after 6.30. The trains were running hours late, and crowds of people were waiting for them. A train ran in at 9.05, which was due at 5.33 a.m., and I searched it but no Philip, although I was practically brushed aside by a haughty German prisoner who looked both healthy and well trained, who was attended by two undersized British soldiers. Someone called out to him, 'A fine Father Christmas you are', but didn't get anything but a scowl from the German. I left the station at 9, but Joyce stayed till 9.30, but later went on waiting, considering she might as well meet him and be really late. His train came in after 10.30, and the passengers were absolutely tired out, including brother Philip. He looks far from well, and has obviously been quite ill. When I called at the butcher's to get my meat he told me I had won a turkey in his ballot, so there are legal turkeys to be had. It was a large bird, and will be heavy to carry tomorrow. Joyce and I took our Christmas parcel to Auntie Lila this evening. This year it was a Christmas pudding, lemons, sweets, biscuits, tea and cigarettes, and they were well pleased. They were very generous to us when we were small, so we like to give them things now that they are old and less well off.

Saturday, December 23. The news from France is still serious, as it often is at Christmas time. But this year I feel that it is serious because it is so unexpected – at least it seemed unexpected by both high command and civilian. I imagine that many homes in America will not be very happy at this time, for it must be so much worse to be so far away. At least we are near enough to the continent to be bombed, and for that reason seem a little nearer to the fighting. Had such a rush to get off today, as I had to go out to buy some flowers for Pop to take over to the cemetery, and transport seemed so slow. We packed all the food for our holiday and it seemed to weigh a great deal. Philip finally went off to meet Joyce at Liverpool Street around 2.30, and Pop and I left home just after 3 and caught the same train by the skin of our teeth, although we had to stand. I got half a seat at Chelmsford, wedged between an able-seaman and a lieutenant-commander. My Grandmother seemed very glad to see us when we finally got up there, and Aunt Sue was thrilled to have us there, and they both seem determined to give us a good restful time. Talked for some time and then went off to bed. Joyce and I went off up the road to Sue's house, and Philip and Pop stayed at Grandma's.

Kathleen and her family stayed for four nights in Colchester, and mostly enjoyed their holiday – chatting, sitting by the fire, and eating well. Kathleen again remarked on the exaggerated (from her perspective) sense of danger exhibited by non-Londoners – compared to the real dangers in London. The bombings in Essex seemed to her to be of minor importance: 'these people who have so little to endure make us very tired, when we think of the way old people and young are putting up with so much in the capital' (December 24). She was aware, though, that non-Londoners had to contend with more traditional sorts of privations, such as unmodernised housing. Her Aunt's 'small house', she wrote on Christmas Day, 'is quite rustic and has no conveniences in the way that these picturesque places seem to lack them. She has two rooms downstairs with a sort of out-place built on, in which is her sink and one tap (cold) which froze this morning and had to be thawed with hot water from next door. The

141

whole place is falling down and there are huge holes through walls and roof. The lavatory is outside and is permanently frozen in the cold weather. I feel very sorry for country, and town, folk who have to live under these pretty primitive conditions, particularly when we have a cold spell like the present. I know we have no comfort to speak of at home, but any day I would sacrifice comfort for a few modern conveniences. In fact I would rather have hot water and a bathroom than all the soft chairs and carpets in the country.'

Her holiday ended the day after Boxing Day.

Wednesday, December 27. Was up at 6.30 this morning and walked the two miles to the station in pitch dark. The roads were like glass too so I had to pick my way carefully. The station was crowded with sailors and soldiers, and trains in a muddle, and everyone was freezing. Our train ran into Liverpool Street about 9.40, about one hour late. Joyce came up next, and had to stand all the way and her train was not in till about 12, nearly two hours late, so she was well nigh exhausted. Philip caught a 'Forces Only' train, so travelled up in comparative comfort, but Pop had to stand in a packed train a little later. It has been foggy in London all over Christmas, and we were very lucky at Colchester to have it so clear. It looks as if it is going to be really thick later on today. Someone at work told us with obvious pleasure, and a complete disregard (or ignorance) of conditions in this country, that they had for Christmas three turkeys, three chickens, two pheasants, four rabbits, etc., and didn't start to tell us of the ordinary meat. Odd how different conditions are in this country – so many have nothing, and so many have too much. We found the pipes frozen when we got in despite layers of lagging, and not until 9 o'clock did we get the lavatory and other pipes to move. Fortunately we have two 'handy men' at home today. I can't imagine how I would get on if I had to face this type of crisis alone.

Thursday, December 28. It is still bitterly cold. I never remember frost so white and so continuous, and our coal will now only last us about a week. The coalman has neglected us for weeks.[28] The conference in Athens has ended with some of the delegates walking out, so a deadlock seems to have resulted. It must be terribly difficult trying to agree after so much bitterness, especially with the sounds of gunfire, etc. as a background. At the canteen as usual this evening. We were very busy. In fact they said that at Christmas they were full each day, and this is not what happens as a rule. We walked home with a nice full moon shining on the whiteness below. It looked like a fairyland wherever we passed trees and shrubs. Was not early in bed as a result, despite my good intentions. We have been visited by mice and I have declared war on them, the only member of the family who really loathes them.

[Intervening entry omitted]

28. Coal production had declined during the war, and demand sometimes exceeded supply, notably in cold weather. Households in south-east England were liable to be under-supplied.

Saturday, December 30. Just after breakfast this morning a little rain fell, which froze as it fell, and as a result the roads and paths were like a skating rink. I went out shopping and was practically the only person to be seen, and those out were, like myself, slipping all over the place. It was most dangerous and I saw several elderly women fall down. We are certainly experiencing every sort and kind of weather this year. Let us hope we get a good summer as compensation (for those still alive). There were several rockets this morning. We are almost getting to expect a bad patch at the weekends now. This evening we came up to see *Private Lives* [1930], a play which has dated quite a bit, and we found patches which Mr. [Noel] Coward obviously wrote with all serious-ness absolutely uproarious. I don't know who enjoyed the play more, the audience or the cast, which at times couldn't continue for laughter. Odd how tastes change so violently. If this play weren't witty it would be pathetic. And much of the sentiment is just not to the present taste.

Sunday, December 31. The cold is still intense, and we now have only enough coal for about three more days. The communiqué reports slight improvement in the situation in Europe, but that probably is out of date, and according to this morning's maps the Germans have made amazing advances and will certainly need some driving back. C. came to tea today and we were also visited by B., who has a habit of calling at inconvenient times. C. is Bohemian (she thinks) and is out to gain as much experience in the world as she can before she is too old, and to some extent is successfully carrying out her intentions. She is very unlucky in her men friends, however. They all seem such utter rogues. It is a good thing that at heart she is a moral girl, or she mightn't be such a pleasant girl now. Philip thinks she is very nice, and more so because she is so intellec-tual and amusing. These things rarely go together, he informs me. This evening whilst listening to the Old Year programme a rocket fell, and we felt very miserable. What a time to be bombed out. I expect the people were happily listening to the wireless and then that.

1945

Monday, January 1. Didn't go to the Club again this evening as Philip accepted an invitation to go round to Dol's this evening. We arrived about 7.45 and the three children were in bed but waiting to see us, so Joyce and I went up to them and spent the next hour very pleasantly. They are so jolly, and looked sweet all in bed together. Their mother keeps them together now so that if needs be she can pick them out of bed quickly and doesn't have to go into several rooms. We all soon collected up there and it was with difficulty that we got away and downstairs to talk. They were awake for a long time, but gradu-ally drifted off to sleep. We talked until very late, and finally got away about 1.30, several hours after my natural bedtime, so I don't look forward to getting up tomorrow.

During the next three weeks Kathleen wrote often about the military matters – advances by the Germans and later the Allies in Western Europe, the civil war and political intrigue in Greece, American progress in the Far East, the

143

capture of Warsaw by Russians. She also commented on or wondered about political matters at home (speeches, rumours, press reports). Rocket attacks persisted. 'On our way home [from the theatre] a rocket fell not far away, to remind us that we were once again in wartime England' (January 2). 'Several rockets today,' she reported on January 14. 'One opened our back door, but no doubt was miles away.' (The next day she noted that it had fallen in Camberwell, 'at least six miles away'.) There were also minor nuisances. 'I am still trying to catch the mice at home, but they are very cunning and seem to avoid all the bait and traps put down for them. I think this cold weather is sending them in, because other people are complaining of them too, so mine isn't a lone cry in the wilderness.' (January 3) There were also festive moments. 'This evening [Thursday, January 11] we had our annual party at the YM, and once again it was absolutely packed – over 200 I think in a very small hall, and as a result most games and dancing were an ordeal. The food was absolutely marvellous again – lovely cakes, jellies, trifles, and gorgeous Christmas cakes. In fact it looked a pre-war affair, and everyone thoroughly enjoyed it. I noticed however that people cannot eat much of this rich stuff now, and think that after the war, even were the food available, we will never be able to eat as much as we did, and a good amount of "real" eggs, milk, etc. will make us ill. How men like "kissing" games, and they seem to bore the girls! Had a good gossip with people I hadn't seen for ages, and walked home through the snow quite late.' Shopping, as usual, was mentioned as a problem. 'Joyce and I went to Peckham this afternoon [Saturday, January 20] to buy a skirt for her. Everywhere shops declared they would be well stocked in a fortnight, when the new coupons are valid, so we can look forward to a dreadful rush at that time.'

Kathleen's diary for the next few weeks is reproduced with few omissions.

Monday, January 22. One of yesterday's rockets fell in Herbert Road [Plumstead, SE18], about 50 yards from the one that fell on my poor Grandmama, and now the natives are calling their district, which is rapidly being demolished by bombs, flying bombs and now rockets, 'Hell-fire corner' – quite a good name I suppose. Lots of drunken girls and men in the Club this evening, and although we were busy they made me feel very sick. Some of the ATS girls too were quite a nice type (or would have been sober). On my way to Charing Cross I was stopped by a young Canadian airman who had just arrived in London on 17 days leave from the Middle East. He had arranged to meet some friends at the Beaver Club at 10 p.m. and had apparently been wandering round Trafalgar Square for half an hour. I was in good time so was able to take him round and deposit him on the doorstep [Spring Gardens, SW1], and he seemed quite surprised that I should have done this out of the goodness of my heart!! I hope I didn't offend him by refusing his offer to take a meal at the Beaver! Anyway he was a nice lad, and reminded me of R., which is probably why I was helpful. Joyce when I told her said I was lucky not to find myself murdered in the gutter, which I suppose would be the reaction of most 'nice girls' nowadays, and I really think they are the wise ones.

Tuesday, January 23. A loud rocket this morning. Found out later that it was at Hither Green [SE13], and no wonder Rene said the flash was terrific – it wasn't far away. Managed to get two tickets for the New Theatre this evening for *Peer Gynt* [by Henrik Ibsen]. Met Joyce, and we just managed to get into the theatre as the curtain went up. I did enjoy this play, although there was much in it that I didn't wholly understand. Ralph Richardson was simply wonderful, and was wholly convincing as both the bouncing young man and the doddery old man – a grand performance. Bits of the play I thought a bit crude, but I suppose one can put these down as 'art'. The Troll King I thought revolting, and maybe Nicholas Hannen enjoyed making him so. The American soldier and the young striptease dancer have been sentenced to death at the Old Bailey. I don't agree with capital punishment, but if the system is still in force I shouldn't think two people have ever so deserved to be hanged. They are a dreadful pair.[29] It was bitterly cold in the theatre this evening, and continues to get colder.

Wednesday, January 24. The papers today contain further accounts of other criminal activities of the pair sentenced to death. It seems they tried to murder or rob several other people, but luckily they didn't quite complete the job. Thick fog this evening at home. It has been getting thicker all day in London, and what with the snow, etc., we are having a packet of bad weather. A rocket fell at Greenwich this afternoon during shopping time. Let us hope the casualties are not too numerous. The British have entered Heinsberg [just inside Germany, west of Cologne], and with the Americans and Russians both advancing, the position looks much more hopeful than it did three weeks ago.

Thursday, January 25. The Russians are in the suburbs of Breslau, and are now only 150 miles from Berlin as the crow flies. The coldest day of the year I should think. This evening at the canteen we had two fires, and I had trousers on as well as costume yet I was still shivering, and as we went home it was bitter. Several fellows told us that they are not allowed to have fires in their billets, which seems rather hard, so they come for miles to sit by the canteen fires. Mr. Joll has died aged 59, a terrible loss to surgery, and so young too. I wonder what was wrong with him. He seemed always so virile and young. He seemed almost to be one of the family. We talked about him so much, and he did so much for my Mother, and she trusted him so much.[30] This evening Major Lewis Hastings talked [on the radio] about the Russian advance, and I was amused to see the men at the canteen listened for a change!

Friday, January 26. The little man who repairs our telephone at the office is a great admirer of the Russians. Who isn't? He amused us today with his experiences in the last war, and his trip to Cologne with the Royal Flying Corps,

---

29. Elizabeth Jones, 18, from Hammersmith, and Karl Gustav Hulten, 22, a US paratrooper, were tried for and found guilty of the murder of George Heath, a tax-driver. He had a cleft chin, hence the references at the time to the 'Cleft Chin Trial'. Press coverage of this murder was extensive.
30. An obituary of Mr. Cecil Augustus Joll, 'An Eminent Surgeon', was published in *The Times*, 26 January 1945, p. 7.

when they occupied the German aerodromes. The Americans are drawing nearer to Manila, and when they capture this base it will be quite the juiciest prize they have, because although Paris was a great victory, it was mostly a French one, and Manila restored will mean restored pride.

Saturday, January 27. Very cold again, and the electricity is pretty weak. It took me three hours to boil some potatoes today. Fuel was cut again in England south of the Wash, but ours didn't go off completely. This all seems so stupid, because people don't use fuel at home just for fun. In the London area most people have windows, doors or roofs missing, and nothing fits properly, and naturally they need a little heat to keep warm and well, and certainly at the present price no one, at least of my acquaintance, can afford to be extravagant. We have very little coal – about two buckets – and only a few buckets of coke. Up till now Pop has helped himself to the coal in Mr. L's shed, but feels that he can't do that any more, as the careful list he has kept of borrowed coal is becoming rather long. Our coalman has just not arrived, and at the office they say they have none at all. We huddled round a few embers this evening – annoying because we wanted to listen to the excellent production of *The Corn is Green* [by Emlyn Williams] in comfort. Rockets yesterday and during the night at Woolwich, Charlton and Sidcup, and I didn't hear the loud ones in the night. Two MPs, Capt. [Robert H.] Bernays and Mr. [John D.] Campbell, are missing in a plane over Italy, and from the way this news is given I should imagine they are definitely lost [their plane crashed on 23 January].

Sunday, January 28. Berlin raided again last night, which is good news to shivering Britain. Stayed indoors all day and tried to keep warm, and heard several rockets in the distance. [American journalist] Joseph Harsch's *American Commentary* this evening was most interesting. He talked principally about the rejection by the American Senate of Mr. [Henry] Wallace as Secretary of Commerce, and I felt after listening that I understood some of the reasons for his rejection, and also why President Roosevelt wanted him there [*Listener*, 1 February 1945, p. 125]. Mr. Wallace seems a good man, and I hope the President fights to keep him.

Monday, January 29. Several rockets this weekend, it seems, in East Ham and West Ham. They are suffering most terribly from this weapon. Berlin raided again during the night, the fifth time in three days. The Russians are now only 90 miles from Berlin, and the map of Germany with arrows drawing near the capital is now a regular feature of the daily press. Today is the 12th anniversary of Hitler's ascension to power [actually, it was January 30th], and what an amazing period it has been, and how his position has changed since that day. Quite busy at the Club. Talked to a terribly burned boy. His face was quite grotesque, but he was cheerful. His hands worried me more. They were so terribly disfigured, and looked much worse. One never knows quite how to treat these boys, whether to look them right in the eye as if they look like [the actor] Robert Taylor, or to avoid them. Anyway they must get tired of sympathetic looks. Major Lloyd George drivelled in the House today, saying little fresh except to appeal to the non-bombed areas to economise with fuel. He should save his breath for the good he does.[31] The British 14th Army are only 12 miles from Mandalay [Burma] – a piece of news which is wonderful, but which gets an odd corner of the news.

Tuesday, January 30. We measured seven inches of snow in our back garden this morning, which may be exceptional because it is somewhat sheltered. It was however a good six inches thick on the roads and my shoes just vanished, although I tried walking in other footsteps and finally in a car track, but seemed rather top heavy. I waited for a bus or tram for more than half an hour, and just as I was trying to decide whether to tackle a two hour walk to the station or go back to my warm bed, a car drew up and offered me a lift, together with a couple of [other] people waiting. I was thankful, for although my walk actually would have been about three miles, it would have been difficult going. So I was at work first. My boss, arriving at 10 o'clock, had skidded in a bus somewhere near Hyde Park Corner, and had to wait '25 minutes on the sidewalk', which just shows how the aristocracy suffer during this war!! Dorothy is ill with aspirin poisoning, whereby she swells up and is covered with blisters – very unpleasant – and in all six of the staff mustered. Rene was very late, having walked home from the FAP. Then she had the journey up to town. The Strand was unbelievably dreadful at lunchtime, because the thaw has set in and one was up to one's ankles in filth, and it was really comical to see people walking with a sort of goose-step, [and] not so funny to see cars just skidding into pavements. Cuts in the coal supplies for February are announced, and it seems that London and the South are going to come off worst, because not only do the cuts in electricity affect the people here, but they also have less coal than the rest of England. Russian news is still wonderful, but the weather, and all our own sufferings and experiences whilst enduring same, are rather uppermost in our minds!!

Wednesday, January 31. The Russians are 60 miles from Berlin, and judging by the calm way we seem to expect this sort of news, I have a feeling that the day the papers say 'Berlin captured' we shall just treat it as a matter of course, although Rene is expecting Russian National Anthems to be broadcast continuously from the BBC. The snow has almost disappeared and it is much milder, although a chilly wind is treacherous. Rene was telling me today about an article in one of the Sunday papers in which it discussed the numbers of spinsters and widows there would be in England after the war. Apparently it said that four out of five girls would be in one or other of those classes, and it is a grim thought. My view, and the view of several of my friends to whom I have spoken, is that it is grand to be unmarried if one has a small income so that you can be independent, and so that your company is sought. The side that isn't so pleasant is much more common, where girls have to go on working till they are

31. Major Gwilym Lloyd George was the Minister of Fuel and Power. This debate in the Commons actually occurred on Tuesday, 30 January, not the 29th. The Minister was under attack for the flawed distribution of coal in London during this cold season. (*Commons Debates*, 5th series, vol. 407, pp. 1275–80.)

pretty old, and have to work so hard to keep interests and friends, and in their case all the seeking has to be on their side. I see this happening to several of my acquaintances. They are always rushing around so that they shan't be considered old or unsuccessful or friendless. I suppose this is a pessimistic view, and probably I have exaggerated, but it really is a depressing thought for the future. The solution would be 'pensions at 40 or 45' I think, or earlier, so that one could enjoy at least a third of one's life without working.

Thursday, February 1. My wet feet have started a very sore throat which seems to be getting worse. This evening at the canteen I could have passed out, but we were so busy I had to stagger along. All the evening our kitchen was the scene of a procession of women from houses nearby, all of whom had broken pipes and had to rely on the canteen for their water two or three times a day. Heard about P's wedding, which was a grand affair it seems, with a large picture in the *Sunday Pictorial* to crown it all. Mrs. B., talking to Joyce, said, 'I may be behind the times, but who are these people to go round having weddings as grand as this, and what are their prospects after the war?' P. was an errand boy before the war. He is now a Sergeant Air-gunner. His bride worked in a shop, and is … possessed of a little money I think (her people keep a shop). Yet this couple, with little or no money, have an elaborate wedding, with white bride, several bridesmaids, grand reception, beautiful photographs taken at all angles, etc., and we who know all the circumstances are expected to look on and marvel. Are we merely sour grapish I wonder? Heard from Win today. She has been ill with some trouble in her nose. Everyone now has something peculiar wrong with them. Our Coal has arrived, so now we can have something like a fire – and it seems much milder. An amazing tale from Luzon [in the Philippines] today concerning an American Commando raid which freed a couple of hundred prisoners, including about 20 British, whose names are given in the evening papers. Wonderful news for their relatives, although the reports say they are weak and ill.

Friday, February 2. Overslept this morning. It was about 7.30 when I woke, and we had such a rush around. My throat still feels bad, and I have tried everything. Tried to buy birthday cards today, and found it almost impossible. Rene is away with a chill, caught on Tuesday morning in the snow I think. Heard from Philip, written with a terrible hangover, caused by too much gin at a submarine party, followed by more whisky at a Wren party. He said he felt quite prepared at the time of writing to sign the pledge. I know he is only young once, but I don't really approve!! Dorothy told me today about a friend with three young children. The baby has bronchial pneumonia, and the doctor last week gave the mother a certificate for coal, she being without any. She went to the town hall, filled in forms in triplicate, attached the certificate, went away and awaited coal. Neighbours helped her with buckets of coal, but after a week and no coal she returned to the office, and after telling a youth what she thought about him and the liability of the Council, etc. if her baby died, she insisted that they find the form. A search involving two people took over two hours, and they discovered her form, with medical certificate, thrown into a box, just as she had left it. Isn't this disgraceful? She is hoping the scene she made will do some good, but I feel that this is typical of the public service a civilian gets these days.

Saturday, February 3. In yesterday's evening papers there appeared three more names of prisoners released by the American Commando raid, and one of them was Corporal Dennis Keating, aged 26. About ten years ago, when we used to go to the Oval in the summer and before we were members, we used to sit with a boy called Dennis Keating (Bugs), and he is, I am certain, this released corporal, as he tallies with everything in the paper. The air today has been filled with planes, and both the RAF and the Yanks have been out. One of the best days for months, fine and sunny, and fairly warm. I went to [the] hairdresser's, shopped, paid rent, had lunch, then met Joyce in order to see *Western Approaches*, but when we saw the length of the queue, my cold was excuse enough to walk away, so we saw *Laura*, which I had been more keen to see anyway, but my feeling that one should see *Western Approaches* has made me agree to go there first. Enjoyed *Laura* immensely. It was nice to see a film in which the characters didn't appear in the final scenes in uniform. Nor did they fly, sail or fight. In fact it was a tonic, as well as entertainment. A most unusual and intelligent film. Actually I find these thrillers, in which one is expected to exercise just a little mental power, more satisfying than ordinary 'Who done it?' films. Maybe the cinema is growing up. I thought the acting of Dana Andrews and Clifton Webb of a very high standard, and Miss [Gene] Tierney is all that a man could ask for.[32]

[Intervening entry omitted]

Monday, February 5. Rene is still away. Her chill is stubborn. The Americans on Luzon are doing well. They have entered Manila, and released many hundreds of internees, including a good many British. A damp nasty day, more treacherous than cold. We were very busy at the Club this evening, and I had a good gossip with Eileen and several other people. A handsome young Fleet Air Arm pilot, who was my ideal of a beau a year or so back, became affectionate this evening (he was fairly drunk) and endeavoured to escort me home. Eileen and Mac were tickled at my gentle refusal, as, knowing my weakness of earlier days, they said, 'Two years ago you wouldn't have said no'. I think my taste must be improving. Anyway I loathe drunks, or semi-drunks, seeing me home. Even if they behave they are apt to draw attention to themselves and their escort. I suppose one should endeavour to remain discriminating, but it really doesn't help matters. The rakish young men don't immediately improve, they just look around to find some girl who doesn't mind them drunk. A boy in this evening, pretty badly disfigured, and he is the first I have seen whom I knew before their accident. You just wouldn't know him for the same boy.

32. *Laura*, directed by Otto Preminger (1944), was a murder/romance story, in the film-noir tradition. *Western Approaches* (1944) was a wartime documentary made under the auspices of the Crown Film Unit; it was in part a tribute to the Merchant Navy, and was highly regarded at the time.

Tuesday, February 6. Philip's 20th birthday. I expect he will celebrate it in good style with kilted lassies. Odd to think he was such a little boy when the war started, in short trousers, and now he is 20, at which age many a boy is married with a family. The Big Three are meeting officially, although their meeting place is not mentioned. Heard from Aunt Sue in reply to my letter sending her some starch. She says that Grandma is up in the town buying a new coat. She has more clothes than I have and takes much more interest in decking herself up. Dorothy says that my Grandmother should be thinking of higher things at her time of life. Listened this evening to some recordings made at the first night of *Meet the Navy*, the Canadian show at the Hippodrome, and what we heard made us keen to see it, so we may try to get some cheap seats for a performance. Quite warm today, and I have now removed some blankets from my bed. I expect fuel consumption has dropped quite a bit. Our own house is typical. We haven't needed a fire in any bedroom for a week, and as the evenings draw out, need for lights is slightly lessened.

[Intervening entry omitted]

Thursday, February 8. Went up to the Hippodrome at the lunch hour to try for two cheap seats. After pushing around the box office, I joined a queue and just as I had been warned I listened to females in the box offices being downright rude and insolent to any poor civilians in the queue and as sweet as honey to all those in uniform. I stood beside a man in civilian clothes who turned out to be a sailor on leave, but he got short shift from the lady and was quickly on his way after a blunt refusal. Sticking to my guns I managed to get two revolting seats for a date in March. I was rather shocked to see the way a man who seemed to be regulating and directing queues treated the many Canadians who walked up to him during my ten minutes there. One wouldn't have thought it was their show. There has been a plane crash involving a party of men and one girl on their way to the Big Three conference and 15 of the occupants are either dead or missing. This must cause a great deal of trouble to the British delegation, apart from the very great personal loss the deaths of these men will be to Mr. Churchill and the other chiefs-of-staff, and is just another instance of the grave risks taken in the course of duty, and another proof that flying is still a very risky game – and always will be in my opinion.

Friday, February 9. … Heard from Philip today. He celebrated his birthday quite pleasantly I gather. Scotland is beginning to lose its attraction for him I feel, but maybe when the weather improves he will like it more. One of the rockets last evening fell in Charlton and has done quite a bit of damage I hear. One of the young girls at Joyce's place was involved she heard, and her young brother, aged six, had both his legs blown off. What a dreadful thing, because no wonderful artificial limbs can compensate such a young child for what he has lost. I imagine any folk who know these circumstances will be getting much satisfaction from the sufferings of the Germans at the present time. One rocket this afternoon around 4.15 seemed very loud. I thought it must be in the next street.

Saturday, February 10. More rockets this morning. They seem to get more numerous at the weekends. During the night they were at Sidcup and one at Welling opened our doors. A filthy day. We had snow, then a lightning and thunder storm which soaked Joyce, who was up in town at a show with some friends. Was much amused this afternoon when I was shopping at a queue in Marks & Spencer for ice cream. It was four or five deep and ran twice round the shop. There must have been three or four hundred people in it. What shocked me however was the sight of small children, some only about six or seven, asking for 'two 1s 8d ones' and producing 10 shilling notes from their purses or bags. I told them at home about it. When we were 12 and 13 we still received only a half-penny or at most a penny a week for sweets, and thought ourselves very lucky to get that. I don't really think it is right that children should not get some fun, but really nowadays I feel they get too much money at least. The advance still goes well, although mud seems to be making the going terribly difficult. In many cases the men have had to dump their transport and go on foot. Listened this evening to *Strife* by John Galsworthy, which, although written 20 years ago, is still fairly topical. Listening to this play it was clear, even to me, how a great master constructs his play, putting arguments to every side, so that the interest is kept right through the play – and many of the problems of this particular play are still unsolved to this day.[33] Once again I thought how well the BBC put over these plays. The [radio] licence is worth the drama we are given alone.

Sunday, February 11. The British and Canadians are fighting in the streets of Cleves [i.e., Kleve, Germany, five miles south of the Dutch border], a most romantic sounding name, and are meeting fairly stiff resistance. It looks as if this advance, coming as it does during the meeting of the Big Three, means business, and one feels now that really it is the last stage of the war. A beastly day. It rained on and off all the time and there were quite a few rockets, which inclined one to morbid thoughts. B. called to see us this afternoon, armed with photographs and gifts sent by her brother K. from Holland. She has recently started work, and as she is rather the old-fashioned type of girl, carefully brought up, I was amused at her reactions to office life. Originally she wanted to become a nurse, but her parents disapproved, so she is now in an office. Recently her parents booked some seats for the theatre, for a matinee during the week, and B. seemed to think it quite in order to go to her boss and ask for the time off, which he granted after a slight scene. She asks for time off quite frequently, and seems to take it as a matter of course. This is merely an example of the way conditions have changed, because when we all went to work to begin with [in the 1930s], we wouldn't have dared to ask for time off merely for theatres, and certainly wouldn't have got it. She hopes to take two weeks holiday this summer, and has made all her plans to go away in August – this despite the fact that there are others in her office, and surely they will have first choice. I feel very old and old-fashioned when I listen to this talk. Things

---

33. Galsworthy's *Strife*, which was first produced in 1909, focuses on labour relations in a tinplate company. The play highlights the class and personal tensions underlying a strike and avoids simplistic judgments.

certainly have changed, and sometimes I don't think for the better. Joyce told me today about M.F., wife of a boy who worked in their office before the war. He is now a prisoner in Japan. This girl (possessed of a lovely nature, very popular, and an affectionate wife) was obliged to work once again, and came to the office to take her husband's place, from where she was called up and sent by the Labour Exchange to work in an all-masculine atmosphere in the Barracks. Her lovely nature it seems could survive the old office, but these lonely soldiers, who worked with her in droves, combined with the fact that she was lonely herself and had no female company all day, must have affected her, because she formed an alliance with one of her companions, and is now in Scotland in process of having a baby. I suppose this really can be put down as a war disaster, because such a nice girl would never have done anything like this unless circumstances were against her, as they have been. But it made me feel very miserable nonetheless.

Monday, February 12. A new Belgian cabinet has been formed to try to deal with the mighty tasks of reshaping their shattered country. I know it is easy for us to criticise, but what mammoth tasks do await governments who follow liberation, and they have so little to assist them in these tasks too. Goodwill isn't really much good. Came up in the train with a friend who showed me a hanky brought from Brussels by her son, who paid £1 for it. When challenged by his mother for his extravagance, he said, 'Well you wanted something from Belgium didn't you, and it was the only thing I could afford'. I hate to think of them wasting their money, but I know how they love to bring home these presents. At the Club this evening a sailor gave M. a pound [of] lovely butter from New Zealand – a lovely present. She is a nice girl, and so anxious to get married. Eileen and I are doing our best to get her a husband, but matchmaking is a difficult task. Eileen is full of Dan's news that when he gets home, which may not be for many months now, Eileen will be able to travel to New Zealand at the Government's expense (naturally they will have to be satisfied that her journey is genuine and that she is going to marry Dan), and also she will be put on the priority list for a passage, which is the best bit of news really. When I got home Joyce told me about the special announcement issued from Yalta, which indeed looks as if Mr. Stalin had a good deal of his own way in the deliberations. The Lublin Poles [creatures of Moscow] are recognised, as is the Tito-Subisich [Subasić] agreement,[34] and it seems obvious that Russia is going to have most to say about Eastern Europe, justifiably so I feel.

[Intervening entries omitted]

Thursday, February 15. Mr. Churchill is in Athens, and has addressed popular crowds of people, been given the freedom of the city, etc. etc. He obviously means to make himself popular there. The Germans are making something of a stand in the Reichswald Forest area, but with very little effect. The Russians

---

34. An internationally recognised coalition government was now in place in Yugoslavia, with Josip Broz Tito as premier and Ivan Subasić as foreign minister.

continue advancing all around Berlin, obviously getting into a favourable position for advancing on the city. Berlin got another raid from the RAF last night, just to let them know we still have an air force. The Yugoslav cabinet has gone back to Yugoslavia and are going to join forces with Tito in Belgrade, having left the King here still not satisfied with the agreement, but I suppose he will finally be wangled back as King George of Greece will probably be too. Quite busy at the canteen this evening. The fog had cleared up when we went home, although it got very thick in London this afternoon. Travelling continues to be bad. I get so tired of standing packed in trains and would love to go up by car, which as worked out by my father would cost just about what I have to pay now in train, bus and tram fares. The only drawback, as I see it, is garage expenses. I don't think parking in the streets will be allowed after the war, but feel that if I could buy just a little car I wouldn't be out of pocket and I would find travelling much more attractive. This is something to think about after the war.

[Intervening entry omitted]

Saturday, February 17. Rocket last night in Avery Hill, one of the lovely parks in Eltham, has blasted the College, now an NFS centre, and many houses and shops nearby, but I don't think any fatal casualties occurred, which is something for us all to be thankful for. Tokyo and Japan are still being bombed by great numbers of carrier aircraft, with little loss according to American reports. This is a fine sign for the future, and I felt when talking to Mrs. S. this morning that she felt much more hopeful about the Far Eastern War. She has her eldest son a prisoner-of-war in Siam, together with her brother, who is now in another camp. They were together originally. I think she is very brave, but some women are like that. …

Sunday, February 18. A spring-like day. I felt quite comfortable in summer clothes, but I realize the dangers that this weather can bring. Quite a few rockets today. One was pretty near. It caused Joyce, who was drinking a cup of tea leaning on the back door, to spill it all over the floor. Pop went over to borrow the stirrup pump from Mrs. M. this afternoon, and was shocked to hear that her husband has been killed in Holland. She was so good to us when we first moved into this house [in 1943] after we were bombed – a real good Samaritan, because she didn't know us at all. And it does seem unfair that such a woman should lose her husband when these little bits of girls who just marry any young man for the sake of it, and who perhaps don't care twopence for him afterwards, should get them home safe and sound. I know this is very poor reasoning, but these thoughts crowded into my head when I heard about it. Actually he wasn't a young man, nearly 40, and was home from Holland for a few weeks before Christmas when their business was rocket-bombed and he had to help look after things. Grandma came over this afternoon just as we were in the middle of cleaning the bathroom. She told us that Dol and the three children had gone away to Deal [in Kent] this time for a holiday. She is now looking after Charlie, a happening of which she takes a poor view.

Monday, February 19. ... Another lovely summer day. It really is warm enough for summer clothing. Our ration books have turned up, having been lost at the branch on Friday. We had to go to all the trouble of applying at the food office for new books, get our forms signed at the police station, and then the wretched branch manager rang Joyce today to say that they had turned up. I am glad but what a lot of trouble their carelessness has given us. Several bangs during the day. The loud one last night was in New Eltham, and one today exploded over Woolwich, doing damage to various factories around. Apparently it exploded rather low and lots of people were injured by falling stuff. Many of the windows at Joyce's office were smashed as they were directly underneath, and she said it was mighty frightening. Another fell at Blackheath and another at Bellingham. Altogether a nasty day. Quite busy at the Club this evening. Dozens of sailors in. They outnumbered all the other services. One young sailor amused us. He was trying to get married this evening and couldn't find a wife. I was tickled when I heard him tell Eileen that she would do as she would just fit inside his sea-bag! I often wonder whether sailors were ever innocent young men. They are certainly not innocent for long once they get into the navy, yet they succeed in looking the cleanest type of young man. Not that I am deceived by this look now.

Tuesday, February 20. Terrific rocket in the early hours of this morning. Later I heard that it fell on the Brook Hospital [in Woolwich]. The main damage seems to have been in some empty wards, so we must hope that the casualties were light. It is awful for this district. There have now been three rockets within about 100 yards of this hospital, and apart from the patients there, the Herbert is nearby and that is occupied by wounded men from the battlefronts – hardly a nice place for them to recover. The Germans are making a great effort to stem Russians advances, and at places are advancing a little, although the Russians don't seem to be retreating. Mr. Churchill was in the House today, answering questions, etc., and appears now to have a crisis with France to settle. General de Gaulle has caused some rather nasty comments to be hurled at him from all directions as a result of his action in snubbing President Roosevelt. It is obvious that he is a most high-handed and violent man, even if he is the saviour of his country. The two involved in the Cleft Chin case have had their appeals dismissed, a fact which seems to be applauded by everyone I have yet spoken to. I hadn't realised the amount of feeling in the matter.[35] Our Chairman [George Macaulay Booth] broadcast this evening on air transport and sounded absolutely used to the microphone, so easy was his manner.

[Intervening entry omitted]

Thursday, February 22. The Russians admit that they have lost a little ground in East Prussia, but I should imagine they will have some good news in time for Red Army Day tomorrow. Perhaps they intended to have Berlin by then?

---

35. See 23 January above. The sentence of death on Elizabeth Jones was later commuted to life imprisonment (below, 5 March). No woman had been executed in Britain since 1936.

One of Joyce's men went to the reception at the Admiralty yesterday in connection with King George's fund for sailors, and said it was an impressive do. The Duchess of Kent was there, and he said that it was quite a treat to see a royal personage tuck into her tea so heartily. Joyce also got some lovely apples today – Newtowns I think they are. But the important thing is that they are beautifully sweet and will be a treat. We sampled one whilst we were at the canteen and it was delicious. Our poor manager is still worried about the vans, etc. They are in such a bad state of repair, and the garage does absolutely nothing in the way of service. Their staff is almost entirely made up of boys aged about 16 who are earning high wages and have no technical knowledge. They just know about as little as is possible in such work. What will happen to all boys like this when skilled men come back from the forces? They will be left with no work and will have to get used to very much lower wages. I know for a fact that Mr. C., who owns the garage, is paying these lads considerably more than he paid some of his grown men before the war – a disgusting fact, but one which should be thought about a little more. Pop went to a *Brains Trust* at Woolwich Town Hall this evening. It was apparently a success, with local teachers giving good accounts of themselves. Amazing how popular this form of entertainment is nowadays?[36]

Friday, February 23. Red Army Day today and in London there were crowds of collectors – mostly bus drivers, conductors and conductresses collecting with much keenness. Much more enthusiasm was being put into this collection than is put into their work for the public as a rule. I thought I would love to tell them what I thought of them. These transport people haven't hesitated to hinder the war effort on occasions, and thereby hinder the Russian war effort, with their strikes for this and that. Rang Miss Hendry today, now that she is down in London for a few months. She hasn't yet told us why she came down so suddenly on Wednesday, but I expect we shall hear in time. Philip is much more contented up in Scotland she said, which is good to hear. I had a lovely ice for my lunch today – really creamy like a pre-war effort. My ration books were at the shop with the order today and he was very apologetic, but now I have deposited all the pages with him. This will save me trouble.

[Intervening entries omitted]

Monday, February 26. Berlin has now been raided six nights running and today great forces of Yanks were over the capital. I read somewhere an account by a man in Sweden of life in Berlin nowadays, and an odd sentence amused me. He said German women now wear by day and night ski-suits and turbans, and he seemed to think that was a sign of real suffering. I shouldn't imagine

36. This 'General Brains Trust' was organised by the Woolwich Borough Council and drew an audience of some 200 people. The members of the 'Trust' were six prominent local citizens, including three teachers, a doctor, a social worker, and Councillor Henry Berry (mentioned above, 8 September 1944). Councillor Newman acted as 'Question Master'. Questions posed by mail by members of the public were answered by the 'Trust' in the manner of the BBC's *Brains Trust*. (*Kentish Mercury* and *Kentish Independent* for 2 March 1945.)

those left in Berlin have time left to think about mere body covering. Quite a bad morning at home for rockets I understand. One at Plumstead at 9.10 which has done quite a bit of damage, and one at Belvedere a little later, and Pop said he heard seven within the next hour, some far away however. Very busy this evening at the Club. They now have a professional pianist who comes in several nights a week to play, and he certainly kept a crowd in. I was amazed to watch him though. He was a little dirty man, but he could really play well (dance music), and I can't really understand how such a dirty low man can have such a wonderful gift. A tough Canadian Sergeant home on leave from Holland told me several of his experiences during the course of the evening. He produced money, some of it Hungarian, Rumanian, Austrian, etc., all of which he obtained from a German soldier – also a lovely German watch with a silver chain. I asked him how he came by these things, and he said 'Oh I got them from a German'. I asked him 'Was he dead or alive?' and he avoided the question but said 'Well it was five miles back to the prison camp – what would you have done?' Oddly enough I didn't feel shocked at all. He told me that he was going back to Europe tomorrow afternoon and wasn't at all keen on going, as it was hell where he was.

Tuesday, February 27. An important day in the Commons as Mr. Churchill made his much awaited statement on the Yalta conference [*Speeches*, VII, pp. 7107–24]. I thought it one of the best speeches he has ever made. There seemed little of the trouble-making contents of earlier ones, and I feel that most people will feel satisfied with what he said. It is a great pity that we can't all believe all that Mr. C. and other public men say. I mean, on the face of it this speech implies a great love of his fellow men and a genuine effort at world cooperation, but somehow we are so used to statesmen saying one thing and doing exactly the opposite that we are rather wary. I feel that Mr. C. got over the Polish problem rather well, and with a certain amount of dignity. Pop rang Joyce to say he would be working all night, so after we had listened to the *Brains Trust*, which was rather better than usual, we went off to bed early. We have been discussing our financial position. At least I have, and have come to the conclusion that that I must earn some more. My job is congenial and has many advantages, but it is not terribly remunerative, and my chances of promotion are nil as the only two above me are young and unlikely to leave. I could of course change my job, but that is difficult, and at this stage of the war would probably pay as little as my present one. One thing I have considered is Saturday afternoon work at a local greyhound racing track. Several girls at Joyce's place go there and are able to earn several shillings for a few hours work, and she brought home the prospectus for Charlton track and we studied it this evening. We think we will try it for a few weeks anyway starting in a fortnight, and give it up if it is too much or too unpleasant. I told Eileen about it on Monday and she agreed that it was a good idea. She thinks it absurd that she should earn more [in the civil service] than I do, but agreed that my conditions of work should be taken well into account.

[Intervening entry omitted]

Thursday, March 1. Several rockets this morning and during the night fell in the Dockyard, Arsenal and one in Well Hall which absolutely rocked our house, although we didn't hear a sound of the explosion. I looked out of the window and could see great pillars of smoke coming up from Well Hall – could almost see the road where it fell. This evening whilst we were at the canteen it was announced that the Americans have captured Munchen-Glad-bach [west of Düsseldorf], a most satisfactory piece of news for me. (Our old geography mistress lived there after marrying her German doctor ....[37] She must be feeling pretty sour if she is still there, although she possessed much allure, and may find it useful in dealing with our American allies.) A new service has been started whereby men serving overseas can now send money home to friends or relations. The man pays the money on the battlefield (or foreign station) and we at our YMCA have to send money or stamps or however the gift is to be made. This is a most difficult service to run, because sometimes three or four visits have to be made before the recipient can be found indoors, and since the gifts are valuable they must only be handed to the person named on the form. With the floral service flowers can be left with neighbours. This is merely another of the forms of service performed by the YMCA, and for which they get very little recognition.

Friday, March 2. A bad night. I don't think I slept much at all. We kept being wakened by explosions. Everyone on the train said exactly the same. Some of them sounded rather near too. My bedroom windows had been jerked wide open, and my goodness, was a wind blowing in. Joyce rang me during the morning to say that one fell in Kidbrooke Park Road, not a quarter mile from us, and later on in the day she rang again to say that they had another which fell about the same distance from us, near my Grandmother's house [in Plum-stead]. I called there on my way home. The damage seemed quite bad. Some workmen were killed. Her flat lost windows, the upper one lost roof, and soldiers were hard at work all around doing what they could to help. She is unlucky (or lucky to escape I suppose) but everyone I spoke to seemed fed up with all these horrors. I feel that we had hoped that they were almost on their last legs.

Saturday, March 3. Woke up in the middle of the night thinking I was having a nightmare. The final strains of the warning were sounding. I turned over to sleep again, then heard a flying bomb coming towards us, and when it turned off I popped under the bed-clothes like lightning. I woke Joyce, who wasn't very pleased, and we both went off to sleep again before the all-clear. It seems that rockets, flying bombs and piloted aircraft were over during the night – a dismal thought for all those who imagined the war almost over. Out shopping this afternoon. There were two warnings and each time we heard and saw doodles. The second time we were talking to M., who had just arrived back in London after a year in the country with her baby. The baby had never heard a

---

37. This deleted passage contains an assertion about her former teacher that, as Kathleen later learned, was untrue.

siren and yelled to high heaven – not that I blame it at all. I understand that North as well as Southern England was bombed. What a shock for those folk who thought themselves well out of range of the Germans. One rocket landed intact at Abbey Wood yesterday. I should think that will be useful to the authorities.

Sunday, March 4. More flying bombs and rockets, but still more violent raids on Germany. I shudder to think of what we would be like here if we were at the receiving end of the RAF. We make enough fuss now. At lunchtime were almost deafened by 12 four-engined bombers which came over [at] roof-top level, diving here and there. I don't feel safe even when I can see friendly markings on planes overhead. Six planes shot down last night. My Father went to order a new suit yesterday and when he went to hand over his coupons he found that his new book, absolutely intact with 48 coupons and 10 industrial coupons in it, had been stolen. His old book, with two or three in it, was still in his wallet. He felt pretty silly, and will now have the bother of getting it back, and will then have to go along to the tailor's. We are unlucky just now with ration books, etc., or perhaps careless. This evening we were told about the new food rationing in Germany, with emphasis on the shortages there. I am afraid we take that sort of thing with a pinch of salt these days. The photographs we see in the papers, the accounts by reporters who look inside German larders, and the condition of prisoners make one think that conditions there aren't much worse with regard to food and clothes than they are here. In this country most folk are ashamed to be seen in their underclothes or night attire. Even men now are short of these things. All my friends now pray that they will never be involved in a street accident necessitating their conveyance to hospital.

Monday, March 5. More raids on North and South England. We are touched down here by the stories of bombs on Northern towns which actually penetrated roofs. To people who are seeing such devastation caused by rockets, coming in the same districts time and time again, this sort of report brings forth bitter remarks, and the publicity given to these hit-and-run raids is out of proportion to the damage they seem to have done. To people bombed by rockets, machine-gun raids don't seem very terrifying, although I expect they would scare me to death once again. I know I was frightened whenever a plane came low enough to machine-gun during the first week of the Blitz. The announcement that Princess Elizabeth is to join the ATS has caused quite a bit of discussion at the office, where they think it is a farce, and this evening at the Club the opinion was more or less the same, if less thoughtfully expressed. We feel that whatever they say she can't be treated as an ordinary recruit, and imagine that her circle of friends and ladies in waiting have probably joined too so that she will be surrounded by friends of her own class. Perhaps too this is only a means of getting her more or less legally into uniform. I feel, though, that Princess Elizabeth, with all the care and attention given to her education, must be a very clever and talented girl and will be wasted as a driver, which is why I think the job is a sinecure. … When I got home this evening the Mulberry programme ['The Harbour called "Mulberry" '] was half over, but what I heard was most impressive [see below, 21 March]. This evening at the Club a sailor showed me some photographs he had taken when the censor's back was turned of the various actions he had been in. There were some wonderful ones of Italian ships sinking, survivors being picked up, and some beautiful pictures of many of our great battleships, etc. He is probably breaking the law, but I wouldn't give him away. He also had a couple of good snaps of Rommel, taken by a South African friend of his.

[Intervening entry omitted]

Wednesday, March 7. Cologne has been captured by the Americans and is in a terrible state, although about 100,000 people are said to be still living in the city. This morning's papers carry stories of the Prime Minister's visit to Germany and show pictures of him there. The one that is causing most comment is the one of Mr. C. drinking a toast with various notables beneath an ancient bridge and General Montgomery is sitting very obviously outside, looking fed up, or disinterested as one paper puts it. I imagine he must be rather tired of these visits, which are somewhat unnecessary. I should think he would rather get on with the war. Several rockets around – one last night in New Eltham on a factory (that caused the fire we could see); one at New Cross has fallen on some tenements, and the scene looked pitiful as we passed in the train this morning – the casualties are said to be rather high. Another fell at West-combe Park [SE3], and passengers in a train were injured. [The] mother of a friend of ours, a nurse on her way to work in the train, was obliged to do her best with the aid of a medical student passenger to render help to the dozens of people injured by glass. Pop said one fell outside Wandsworth prison. Mrs. Elizabeth Jones [the 'Cleft Chin' murderer] has been reprieved, but not the American soldier. The comment of our charwoman at work when Rene spoke to her about it was, 'It is a scandal to let her off. If she were my daughter I would think she was in the right place if they hanged her.' Rather hard, but many of these ordinary people feel rather like this. Much flying this evening.

Thursday, March 8. Today is still mostly rocket talk. This morning one landed around Smithfield Market in Farringdon Road. It shook this office and we could see the smoke billowing up from the roof [around 110 people were killed]. Another at lunchtime in Blackheath village has caused much destruc-tion, even blasting the canteen. People all seem very fed up this evening, and even the troops seemed to share the feeling. I talked to one soldier who had only been down in London for a few days and he admitted he hadn't slept prop-erly all that time as a result of the rockets, which he said frightened him. We now have a new manager at the YM. This time Mr. Watson, official artist to the YMCA, is to do the job more or less permanently. We were very busy this evening. Crowds of soldiers in. Many of them have only been down here a few days. I wonder if they are getting a little more barrage in case of more raids. Had a long letter from D. today. A wedding day now seems possible for her I am glad to say, as she is one girl who will never be happy unless she is married. The man in question is a soldier she met about a year ago. He was married but his wife had deserted him – a tall story which Joyce and I thought the same old line. But after he and D. decided they were meant for each other he started proceedings for divorce, only for the Army to discover that he was never 'legally' married as his wife had committed bigamy, having already married another man. It seems however that although he wasn't really married he isn't free to marry again until some legal procedure is gone through, and his wife is now being sought by the police. What a muddle. But perhaps sense will come from it after all, and if D. is happy that is all we care about.

[Intervening entry omitted]

Saturday, March 10. … A good letter in *The Times* today about smoking in trains, which puts forth quite calmly the arguments most non-smokers feel but perhaps can't express. I have listened to some awful arguments in trains, caused by some innocent individual asking a smoker to put out his cigarette in a non-smoker [carriage]. I am still waiting for someone to pull the communication cord to get his point. It does seem to me that smoking is overdone in trains, etc. these days. After all it doesn't need much imagination to see what a foul atmosphere is caused by several people smoking pipes in a tiny space, and sometimes I know my friends or myself often feel we could pass out. Had my hair permed today. It took four hours and cost £2 2s 0d, whereas before the war I used to get a lovely perm for 10 shillings. *Bird in Hand* [by John Drinkwater] was terribly well done this evening [on the radio]. I did enjoy it.

Sunday, March 11. The story on the news last night told by a Canadian reporter has filled me with grim thoughts for the future He told how a small German boy approached a Canadian soldier and asked him for chocolate. The soldier, although knowing he was going against orders, put his hands in his pocket to look for some sweets, and whilst doing so the small boy drew a pistol and shot him. This story it seems is vouched for by a medical surgeon, and one wonders how on earth we can tackle this huge problem of re-educating German youth. The day passed very quickly, and however we arrange the work we can never get through until teatime. Perhaps we should get up earlier on Sundays, but since we gave up the canteen [on Sundays] we have been having a little 'lie-in'. The allotments at the back of our house have been alive with energy today, both male and female. It annoys me sometimes to look out and see it, and I realise how happy all the ladies of the various houses must be when gardening time comes around, as these men must be bored in the winter, [when] they probably find as little to do as my father does.[38] The story of the capture of the Remagen bridge [south of Bonn] is exciting, and it seems incredible even now that the Germans failed to blow it up – shades of the Dutch bridges, which failed to stop the Germans in 1940.

---

38. Kathleen's father, Charles, was, in fact, a dedicated and successful gardener – the Tipper family rarely had to buy fresh produce – and 'wonderful' around the house (Kathleen recalled in 2005).

Monday, March 12. The loud rocket last night was in Lewisham, near the technical school, and a friend said that crowds of people in trams and buses were injured. This morning there was a loud explosion around 7 (the first I had heard, although there were several in the night I hear). [It] was in Eltham. It fell on the links, but has done considerable damage nonetheless. The Russians have captured Kustrin [40 miles east of Berlin] it is announced tonight, and we are now perhaps getting ready for an out-and-out attack on Berlin. People seem very disturbed about the escape of 70 German prisoners from a camp in Bridgend – very unpleasant for people in the lonely country to have tough Germans roaming around. I expect we will be very kind to them all once they are rounded up. It wouldn't be our way to punish them. I have heard several people say we ought to treat them in the same way that they treated the RAF and Allied air-force officers last year. Sentence of death was today passed on the driver of the car which killed Captain Binney in the City a few months back [8 December 1944]. His assistant got seven or eight years imprisonment I think. What a lot of dreadful people there are about. This case, for instance, aroused a lot of interest generally. Maurice Chevalier has apparently been invited to England to perform on the stage, but there seems to be some objection on the part of the Home Office to his coming here. I wonder he has the impudence to come to England at all. His patriotism is still rather a vague quality to many here [see above, 27 August 1944].

Tuesday, March 13. A really beautiful day, bright and sunny, and the airmen seemed to be out in great style. We heard them in London on and off all day. A talk this evening after the 9 o'clock news gives rather a new impression of our bombing raids on Germany. A reporter had sent in a story of what he had seen in Germany so far, and told of the bomb-proof shelters in which most of the inhabitants of these towns have spent the past two years. He said that they were almost bomb-proof, and said that places of work were equipped with similar shelters. It is obvious from this report that life in Germany is going on mostly underground but I think now that air-raid casualties are probably lower in Germany than they were here. In fact I think we shall find most civilian Germans alive when we get there, in their fine shelters. One wonders now how the war can be brought home to these people. The reporter said that our shell-fire was going over them just as our bombs had done. Pop is now occupied in filling in his form for return of lost coupons, for, as he didn't report their loss to a police station, he can't say they were stolen. News from the Western front is still of more troops over the Remagen bridge, but of a lull on the British and Canadian front, a lull which will end very suddenly no doubt. Joyce's boss's little son aged 13 has now died in Wales, and she has been asked to go to the funeral tomorrow, and feels that it might hurt their feelings to refuse. I feel very sorry about this. He was such a little boy, and it seems suffered terribly whilst he has been lying ill. Odd how old people go on and on, yet young lives are taken in this way.

Wednesday, March 14. Most people are discussing the talk last evening about the shelter accommodation in Germany. It seems to have been heard quite generally. Late this evening it was announced by the Air Ministry that ten-ton bombs had been dropped by the RAF on Germany. They are carried by Lancasters, specially planned to carry this dreadful weapon. Our horror at this new destructive instrument is tempered by the thought that most Germans would be well out of harm's way under the ground. I wonder whether this latest announcement was published today to stop the surprising amount of talk about last night's talk? We felt miserable tonight so went off to the pictures. We saw *The Man in Half Moon Street*, which chilled my blood, but interested us partly because Nils Asther was in it, and also because, despite what the critics said, the London atmosphere was fairly well captured. We saw also *San Diego I Love You*, an amusing film which deserved a better title. The newsreel was interesting, showing the Prime Minister in Germany, also some shots taken in Cologne, which I suppose would interest those who knew the city, but to me one German town looks very much like another – on the newsreel.

Thursday, March 15. This morning's papers contain sketches of the new bomb, and stories about the damage they do, and the inventor thereof. Mr. Churchill at the Conservative Party Conference made a long and very 'party' speech, in which he talked bitterly of the insults he has had to endure from opponents, presumably referring to Mr. Stokes this week. I wonder if Mr. Churchill has forgotten the time he made equally insulting remarks to his opponents, when he was in disfavour and on the opposition side of the House? It amuses me to see [how] these men, who in their time threw many of the most insulting phrases at Ministers of the Crown, seem to dislike criticism when they themselves hold those positions of authority.[39] Very busy at the canteen this evening. We were 'standing room only' most of the time. Several rockets this evening around midnight, when I finally got to bed. I read somewhere that people of Southern England are obsessed with rockets and bangs, and reading my diary sometimes I am sure this is true.

Friday, March 16. Two rockets at Cricklewood, not far from Dorothy, one last night and another some hours later. Miss Hendry with whom I had lunch had had a disturbed night, because she is staying in Golders Green and she doesn't care for these noises. We talked a good deal, and will meet again soon. The Duke of Windsor has resigned his post as Governor of Bermuda [actually, the Bahamas]. Someone remarked in my hearing today 'He never sticks to anything'. I wonder if this is becoming a general view? It is my own, but at one time no one else would agree with me. Collected my shopping tonight and had a job to get through an enormous queue, which was formed for grapefruit. I

39. Richard Stokes, Labour MP for Ipswich, was a frequent critic of the Government. In this speech, Churchill declared that 'we have endured patiently and almost silently many provocations from that happily limited class of Left Wing politicians to whom party strife is the breath of their nostrils, and their only means of obtaining influence or notoriety. Many are the insults and slanders which we have allowed to pass, I will not say unnoticed, but unanswered, for the sake of concentration upon the war effort. Even the almost ceaseless series of attacks which have been made upon us in the official Socialist and Liberal newspapers with their bitter writers, have extorted from us neither protest nor reply.' (*Speeches*, VII, p.7129.) He also spoke against the nationalising policies of 'the Socialists', while accepting the need for some controls. (p. 7131)

didn't join it, but later Joyce told me that she would be able to get some tomorrow anyway. Did some work tonight. Then listened to Eric Barker [a comedian], who was better than he has been recently.

Saturday, March 17. Two or three very loud rockets during this morning, and when I am at home alone I don't care for them. One fell near the Prince Imperial Monument on the way to Woolwich. Joyce was in the tram on her way, but fortunately wasn't too near the incident. Another fell at Millwall, and yet another in Commercial Road. We couldn't help being aware that it was St. Patrick's Day today. The BBC did the Irish proud, and we had jigs and Irish brogues all day. Joyce had some shamrock sent her from Ireland, and there seemed to be a good deal about. The play this evening, *General John Reagan* [by George A. Birmingham, and set in Ireland], went off for the first quarter hour, but when we finally could hear it we enjoyed it very much.

Sunday, March 18. … [A]t this time our papers are full of talk about cuts in our rations, because America won't have cuts in hers. We all know that, compared with us, America is still living in luxury – merely taking, for example, the goods and food that kind Americans send to people over here – and it certainly leaves a bad taste in our mouths to know that we shall probably have to eat less, because Americans at home just won't realise there is a war on, and don't realise how very lucky they are. I know that we are well fed compared with the people in occupied Europe, but the health of the people here is not so good now, and one feels that there is a limit beyond which we couldn't go. The troops here are very well fed, and no one begrudges them, but sometimes I wish someone would put in a word for the poor old civilian.

Monday, March 19. People say that the rocket yesterday morning fell in Hyde Park, and I hope that is so, although if it had fallen there later in the day it might have been something of a massacre. … The Club this evening was full of Australians and sailors. Many old faces turned up again. Eileen has more hope now of getting to New Zealand within a year of Dan's arrival there, and now she is impatiently awaiting to hear that he is on his way. His departure is now delayed whilst reinforcements are allocated to all divisions. Heard from Philip. There is a possibility of some leave at Easter – nothing definite, but he is hoping for a break. When I got home there had been a bad rocket incident today, in the Arsenal this afternoon, and this is an unfortunate time for it to fall. Joyce said they heard glass crashing all around, but nothing came in their own office fortunately, because there are masses of windows in it.

[Intervening entry omitted]

Wednesday, March 21. Went to see the Mulberry exhibition with Eileen at lunchtime, and we both came out overwhelmed by the imagination behind this great enterprise. How engineers could have planned all this is beyond my simple comprehension. To think that it was made piecemeal, and some great brains could actually plan how it was to be put together and then taken over to France – well I just haven't the knowledge to grasp it. We saw the Ministry of Information film, *A Harbour Went to France*, which I had already seen, and after looking round the exhibition it did mean a little more to me. We in England should be indeed proud of the men who built this, and no task should be too difficult for men to tackle if they can do this. Somehow the problem of building houses in Britain and rebuilding Europe must seem like idle nothings to the men who invented and planned the Mulberry.[40] An American task force has engaged the Japanese fleet in its own waters, and has damaged or sunk many warships. News is scanty at the moment, but it seems to have been an audacious action.

[Intervening entry omitted]

Friday, March 23. Met E.H. this morning on the train. She has been married about three years, and formerly worked as a telephone operator with the GPO. She has a little boy about two and has now started back at work again, because she is so tired of living at home. She takes the child to a nursery at about 8.30 and picks him up again about 5, and when she has to work on Saturday morning she takes him to work with her. I was amused to hear about all this, but I felt rather cross because I know many girls who would be amply satisfied to have a husband, baby and undamaged home, and would not rush out to work to brush away boredom. … She has been told by her employers that she can stay on after the war. Is this the sort of thing that is going to face young men and women returned from the war when they are searching for jobs?

[Intervening entry omitted]

Sunday, March 25. The Rhine crossings are going well, with Mr. Churchill there to see what is happening. Discussion today about Mr. C's presence at Monty's headquarters seems rather critical, and the general opinion might surprise him, namely, that he is out to snaffle Montgomery's glory. Personally I think he is a silly old fool, who should remain at home and look after the politics of the war, leaving the battles to 'them that knows how'.[41] We were interested to see that Sarah Churchill's divorce is coming up this week,

40. Mulberries were artificial harbours built to facilitate the Allied landings in Normandy. The Mulberry was designed to provide both shelter from rough waters for ships and floating platforms on which to discharge vehicles and supplies. Details on these innovative devices may be found in Guy Hartcup, *Code Name Mulberry: The Planning, Building and Operation of the Normandy Harbours* (Newton Abbot, Devon: David & Charles, 1977). Mulberries allowed for major landings away from the heavily fortified ports on the French coast, thereby bypassing the main German defences.
41. Sixty years later, after re-reading her diary, Kathleen was critical of some of her wartime political judgments. 'Like many better qualified than myself, I seem to have been over-impressed by the Russian efforts and sometimes not very appreciative of poor Mr. Churchill, who was the recipient of some of my worst barbs.' (Letter of 17 July 2005.) See also Epilogue, note 1.

but what really surprises us is that Vic Oliver [her considerably older American husband, an entertainer] is suing for the divorce. Makes one think more than ever. Ninety planes were lost altogether yesterday, and although that seems a very great price to pay, I suppose really it isn't overpowering, although that 90 will bring sadness to many hundreds of people involved. Joseph Harsch's *[American] Commentary* tonight interested me, particularly his first remarks about his stay in Berlin as an American war reporter until Pearl Harbour. He said that all the Germans he knew – kindly, attractive, Nazis, in fact all of them – enjoyed the German victories, and what is worse enjoyed all the spoils of victory, and he said they do deserve this dreadful vengeance which is overtaking them. The rest of his talk, devoted to the meat question, convinced me I think ['American and the British Food Position', *Listener*, 29 March 1945, p. 349], but I wonder if all the people who are abusing the American action listened to this talk? I do doubt one of his statements (knowing nothing about it whatever) and that was that the American public would accept much greater hardships and sacrifices if the Government were to impose them. I wonder?

Monday, March 26. Quite a disturbed night. Several rockets, and one warning woke me, and we had only been saying this evening that perhaps we had seen the last of the rockets. One fell in Charlotte Street, near Tottenham Court Road, another in Shadwell, and yet another somewhere in the Southwark Park area. The bridgehead is 30 miles long and 7 miles deep in places and still the news is good. Several pontoons have now been thrown across the Rhine. At the Club tonight we had a full house, but they weren't terribly thirsty, so I had a good bit of time to talk to Eileen. She is very pleased with herself because Dan is now on his way home, so her plans look like coming through. A new supervisor at the Club, a Scottish lady, who has been a supervisor in National Service Canteens in Scotland, which are apparently canteens for Bevin Boys. She told me a lot about these boys and said that she had come into contact with a good many hundreds of them, and that a fair number were boys from good homes, some university boys and public school boys, and nearly all of them absolutely unused to the kind of life they have to lead now. Odd that almost everyone you speak to sympathises with the Bevin boys, and feels that they have a raw deal. She said that the general feeling up in the Scottish mining districts is that the job would be more efficiently done if the few thousand trained miners were released from the forces, because they could work much faster than untrained boys from other parts of the country and from different lives [see page 98]. The only snag as I see it is that probably the miners in the forces have no intention of being recalled to the mines, and would far rather stay above ground now that they have the chance. Heard from Philip. They are getting no leave at Easter, but will probably get the following weekend off. [Former Prime Minister David] Lloyd George has died this evening. I am very sorry. I wish he had lasted through the war. I wonder if he knew anything about the advance across the Rhine or whether he was too ill to be told? In my opinion the last great deed he did was his speech in the Commons when he told [Neville] Chamberlain to go, surely the last fiery deed of this great Welshman.

Tuesday, March 27. ... Reports this evening say that the Yanks are in the suburbs of Frankfurt, but no official news of the fall of the city is through yet. With the Russians now only 40 miles from the Austrian frontier, the Germans must be grinding their teeth with rage. It seems extraordinary that they are continuing the fight, but I suppose the Nazis will make them fight till the bitter end, and then on afterwards. I can't imagine the real Nazis ever admitting that they are beaten. I feel full of gloom sometimes at the prospect of ever really beating the Nazis. They are so clever with their underground hideouts and factories, etc., and we would need millions of men to see that no intrigue goes on, and with so many thousands of prisoners being taken, they are all alive to fight another day sometime. I know I am pessimistic, but I often think that we are the losers sometimes, because we just can't keep ourselves up to the pitch of hate for Germany and distrust for her motives. We slip back very easily and become complacent.

[Intervening entry omitted]

Thursday, March 29. The Russians have captured Gdynia [coastal city north of Danzig, later Gdansk] and are advancing quite quickly along the Polish Corridor. Air reports say that the German army is retreating on most of the Western front, and even the most pessimistic souls (like myself) are beginning to think that the end is in sight. Newspapers are full of detailed arrangements for Victory night, and boroughs seem to have made plans for celebrations on that day. This morning the buses were full of people armed with cases and parcels, presumably off for the Easter holiday, which in many cases is the longest of the year. I should imagine that it will be pretty chaotic at most coast towns, and I expect food will be the greatest problem. I hope the weather holds though. I am sure most of those going away deserve a holiday. We are going to spring-clean this holiday as we did last, and have written to Philip to tell him what he is missing. We should have the place looking clean and shining by the time he comes home next week. At the canteen this evening.

Friday, March 30 [Good Friday]. Started fairly early with our work and soon the things began to shine, although there is so much to clean in a house, and the paint must all be done if once one starts on a little of it. Began dyeing the curtains, but the weather is not good for drying them. The news, although rather scanty as yet, continues good, and with no papers the wireless comes into its own with a vengeance. We had it on all day in the hope of catching anything urgent. The Russians now are drawing near Vienna, which will be a real prize when they get it. I should imagine even the Austrians are tired of the Nazis by this time, and certainly the Czechs in their turn will be pleased to see the Russians. This evening's part of *The Man Born to be King* was most movingly performed.[42] Surely no one could really take exception to this play.

---

42. This play about the life of Jesus, specially written for broadcasting by Dorothy L. Sayers, was presented in five parts (this was the fourth episode). It retold the gospel story in modern language.

It upset me, I must admit, making me feel very mean and inferior. Rene's mother thinks it irreverent, I know, and doesn't care for the modern colloquialisms, which to my mind make the thing live. Good Friday programmes are very different now compared with pre-war days, when it was by far the most miserable day of the year. Surely we have gone from one bad extreme to another.

For the next fortnight Kathleen's diary is dominated by political news and military reports from the continent and overseas, most of them encouraging. She listened to the radio and read newspapers, which told of the Allies' impressive progress. On April 5 she wrote of how 'the French have captured Karlsruhe. British and Canadians are drawing around Arnhem, and are now almost certain to over-run the rocket sites in Holland fairly soon. We are getting none now, and hope to get no more.' In fact, there had been no rocket attacks since March 27. Consequently, London was much safer, though not always particularly quiet. On April 4 Kathleen wrote that she 'Couldn't get to sleep last night. The planes were droning around and the searchlights playing on our windows into the early hours. I was still awake at 1.40 a.m. and went to the window to watch. It seems to have been an immense practice. I am surprised really. I sleep through everything almost, yet a few of our planes flying around keep me awake for hours. Lots of people during the day said that they too had been unable to sleep, so perhaps I am not unique as I imagined.' As for the soon-to-be-defeated Germans, Kathleen had little sympathy for whatever suffering they were now going through. 'The Germans ought to be made to suffer just as occupied countries have had to endure,' she wrote on April 4, 'particularly the women of Germany.' She disapproved strongly of marriages between British servicemen and German women: 'I should have thought the troops themselves would by now [April 4] have seen enough of the horrors perpetrated by the master race to make them think twice about bringing them into our race. After all there are enough single girls here – and widows – to go round!!'

Some of Kathleen's diary writing continued to touch upon the everyday life of London's civilians during the last weeks of the War. While the Tipper sisters worked hard, both for pay and as volunteers, they still found time for recreation. On April 2, Easter Monday, Kathleen and Joyce went to the West End to get tickets to see Lesley Storm's Great Day *that afternoon 'and spent an hour or so walking around Oxford Street, Regent Street and the various parks, a practice which interests Joyce because she does it so rarely. Had some tea with no difficulty. Eat ice cream, also with no trouble, and then wandered to the theatre. London was less full than on many weekdays recently, so we got about easily. The longest queues were for "Ladies' Conveniences", of which there are insufficient in London.' Entertainment on the radio was, as usual, a major source of pleasure and solace. On Thursday, April 5 Kathleen was working in the evening at the YMCA canteen on Lee Green and 'was most amused to see how quietly the assembled multitude listened to a programme called, I think,* Mr. & Mrs. Brown *[by Peter Watts], which was the simple story of an ordinary London couple during this war. Not even Mr. Churchill has caused the soldier customers of our canteen to sit so quietly and attentively. I didn't care for the* sounds of the sirens and falling bombs, but thought the programme terribly good, although too short.' [43] *One of the changes that Kathleen reported was the return from the provinces of some of her neighbours to a now much more tranquil metropolis. On Friday, April 6 'Mr. L. called this evening for the key and told us that Mrs. L. and Pauline are coming back on Thursday – the first of the evacuees near us to return – and I expect the rest will be back with a rush just as soon as they think they will be safe.'*

The most shocking event of mid April was the sudden death of President Roosevelt on the 12th. Kathleen was a great admirer of the American President. On February 13, at the end of the meeting of the Big Three leaders at Yalta, she had noted that 'President Roosevelt looked ill at the Conference, judging by the issued photographs. What a terrible strain it must be for him to do all this travelling, and so wearing to his health. I think he is a wonderful man, apart from his political brilliance, and I wonder if he will manage to get right through his fourth term of office.' She was, of course, right to wonder; and she again wrote about him with feeling on the day after his death.

Friday, April 13. I couldn't believe the dreadful news of President Roosevelt's death when I heard it this morning. It just seems impossible. What a tragedy when the end of Germany seems so near. Yet what a wonderful way to die. It seems rather a pity to me that Mr. Wallace is not Vice President [he had been VP during FDR's preceding presidential term], because President Roosevelt I am sure had a man with his own ideals in Mr. Wallace, whereas no one here, at least, knows much about Mr. Truman. I think everyone here, whatever their opinion of Mr. Roosevelt's politics, will feel that the world has lost one of its really great men with his death. He was so courageous to go on with his great and difficult job, suffering as he did from such bad health. I imagine his journeys to take part in the various Big Three meetings have strained him particularly. For him a journey was so much more of an ordeal than to the other two. Mr. Churchill and Stalin must feel his loss keenly, because whatever their opinion of his politics and the politics of his country, they can't have failed to recognise his greatness. I wonder if Americans can quite realise how strong a hold President Roosevelt had on the affections of ordinary folk here. I have been most struck by the observations today from all sorts of people, people to whom the death of a great figure or king means nothing usually. I think we all felt that he was a real friend of Britain when Britain had few friends, and when we could sift the real from the false.

Saturday, April 14. A glorious day, really very hot by this afternoon. Vienna is echoing to the strains of Strauss waltzes, according to Russian reports. They are being played on Russian loud-speakers, for the joyful citizens. The city has been spared total destruction, although one imagines that many buildings have been destroyed or damaged by the fighting that has gone on these past few weeks. Our house begins to look like a bower of flowers, as several of Joyce's

43. No script of this programme survives in the BBC Written Archives Centre.

friends have given her flowers for her [24ᵗʰ] birthday tomorrow, and we have them everywhere, mostly in jam pots I am afraid. As I type this [apparently on a subsequent weekday] the bell has rung at the office and a tiny old man has delivered a cable. I wonder what will happen to all these old men after the war. I suppose they will be chucked out just as soon as employers can find younger men? It does seem a shame, because obviously a poor old man like this one would have been able to get no work in peacetime because no one would employ him. Some people always say when this subject crops up 'Well, they have been lucky to work all through the war – that is money they didn't expect to earn', but this seems rather hard.

Sunday, April 15. A brilliant day again, and the sky was filled almost the whole day with fleets of great four-engined bombers, flying just above roof level. Sometimes everyone seemed to run into the garden when one of these monsters came particularly low, so we all thought it was going to land in the garden. Thank heavens we are not at the receiving end of these planes. This is one time when I am thankful I am not German. [Vyacheslav] Molotov [Soviet Commissar of Foreign Affairs] is going to San Francisco [for the meeting to establish the United Nations]. It hasn't taken Stalin long to come to this decision, and it is obviously a smart one. Now it looks as if it will be Britain vs. Russia with a vengeance, unless goodwill triumphs in memory of President Roosevelt. This evening Edward Murrow gave an account of his visit to Buchenwald concentration camp last Thursday. He is a man of great integrity, and for whom I have a great admiration, and I think his words will carry great weight. What he told filled me with horror and a feeling of weakness. How can we hope to deal with Germany, whose citizens allow this sort of thing to happen; whose citizens do these dreadful things and take part in these mass executions, etc.? One is inclined to disbelieve some of the atrocity stories we hear, but Edward Murrow's words are good enough for me, and every word was said with such feeling and truth that it should convince all but the stony-hearted or pro-German. I wish everyone could hear it.[44] It made me think of Dean Inge's article this week calling for fraternization with the Germans as soon as the war is won. I wonder if the inmates of Buchenwald would agree

---

44. In this broadcast, the highly regarded Murrow spoke of his visit to the Buchenwald concentration camp. 'There surged around me an evil-smelling horde. Men and boys reached out to touch me; they were in rags and the remnants of uniform. Death had already marked many of them, but they were smiling with their eyes. I looked over the mass of men to the green fields beyond where well-fed Germans were ploughing.'

Later he toured one of the barracks, where some 242 men had died during the previous month. 'As I walked down to the end of the barracks, there was applause from the men too weak to get out of bed. It sounded like the hand clapping of babies; they were so weak.... As we walked out into the courtyard, a man fell dead. Two others – they must have been over sixty – were crawling toward the latrine. I saw it but will not describe it.' Later he inspected piles of hundreds of corpses. It was a ghastly scene, and 'For most of it', Murrow admitted, 'I have no words'. 'If I've offended you by this rather mild account of Buchenwald, I'm not in the least sorry.' Here, clearly, was powerful proof to Kathleen and others in Britain and the United States and around the world that the Allies had fought for a good cause against a vile enemy. (Edward Bliss, Jr., ed., *In Search of Light: The Broadcasts of Edward R. Murrow 1938–1961* [New York: Knopf, 1967], pp. 90–95.)

with his Christian views?[45] The Germans are making a stand, their last according to correspondents, and the Americans have had to withdraw from one of their bridgeheads over the Elbe. In fact everywhere the Germans are slowing down our advance, but tonight they say that the Russians are on the move again.

Monday, April 16. The *Evening Standard* prints this evening more or less the whole of Edward Murrow's broadcast, with, I notice, one or two slight omissions.[46] It is really peculiar that, whereas in the past people have been inclined to discredit stories of atrocities and concentration camp horrors, especially if they came from the Russians, now most people believe the reports of released prisoners and Allied troops and reporters. Someone told me today that a friend of theirs had occasion to visit a hotel up here on Friday and all around were weeping Americans. This man, it seems, asked what was the matter with these great fellows who seem so tough and was told that they were weeping because the President was dead. This evening had a very interesting talk with two New Zealand Army Captains, home (in England) from the New Zealand division in Italy, who are going out to Germany in search of New Zealand prisoners of war. There will be such chaos in Germany that theirs will be a very great task, but they were such a good type, so intelligent and interested in people, that I am sure they will succeed. We talked a lot about the war and about the reactions of civilians to wars taking place well away from them, and they said the people of New Zealand have very little idea of what war means, and can't be blamed for that. I said I didn't think any country that hadn't been occupied by Germans could really understand the horror of the Germans, and they both said 'Oh England has suffered enough – we wouldn't have wanted England to have to take any more'. Quite a generous tribute I thought. Not one younger and less thoughtful fighting men from the Dominions usually make.

---

45. William Ralph Inge (b.1860), who had been Dean of St. Paul's, was a prolific author and regular contributor to the *Evening Standard*. In 'Why not fraternise after V-Day?' (10 April 1945, p.6), he proposed that, 'now that our fear of the Germans is vanishing, we are ready, I hope, to admit that they have put up a magnificent fight.' He thought that 'it is difficult not to like the Germans when one meets them in private life' and asserted that 'I do not think that the mass of the German people wanted this war, though they did welcome the war of 1914'. These views, clearly, were not endorsed by Kathleen.

     British attitudes toward the soon-to-be-defeated Germans had undoubtedly hardened during 1944–45. Mollie Panter-Downes of the *New Yorker* twice remarked on these changes, notably in connection with the renewed bombing of (mainly) south-east England. On 9 July 1944 she wrote that, 'bad haters though Britons are, the flying bomb seems certain to harden British hearts on the question of the postwar treatment of Germany.' She revisited this proposition on 18 February 1945. 'There is no tendency at the moment, with V-bombs thudding down, to think kindly of the Germans.... The English of this generation will never forget the years of bombing, but they are afraid of forgiving too easily or too soon.' (*London War Notes 1939–1945*, ed. William Shawn [New York: Farrar, Straus and Giroux, 1971], pp. 334 and 360.)

46. 'It is here set down as a document [declared the editor] – lest the British people ever forget this greatest Nazi crime against humanity.' (*Evening Standard*, 16 April 1945, p. 3.) These revelations of Nazi barbarity made a big impact on Londoners and others.

Tuesday, April 17. Planes last night kept people awake I understand, but I didn't hear them until about 6 o'clock this morning when they came zooming down. The memorial service to President Roosevelt at St. Paul's took place today, and Miss Hendry, whom I met for lunch, had been up there, and had seen all the notables. She was very indignant about the presence there of Sarah Churchill so soon after her divorce (Miss H. has very strong ideas on the subject of morals and divorce etc., as have many Scottish people) but thought Princess Elizabeth looked charming, although most of my acquaintances think she looks very plain in this uniform. This evening after the news an account was given of the various relief that has been given immediately to the pathetic rescued [prisoners] in Buchenwald. I should think everyone who heard or read Edward Murrow has been wondering about this, and it does seem that as much as is possible is being done at once. Many of the prisoners it seems are so near death's door that only amelioration of their last days can be given them.

[Intervening entry omitted]

Thursday, April 19. British troops are only 17 miles from Hamburg, which will now soon be in our hands. But the Germans are not going to lose it easily – it is too big a prize. *The Times* today quotes a former member of its staff just released from a prison-camp, who says that many famous prisoners have been moved to special hiding-places by the Germans, including Lord Lascelles, Lord Haig, Captain Alexander, Mr. John Winant, and several others. Presumably the Germans are really going to use them as hostages. One can only sympathise with the relatives of these men, because after the horrors we have been hearing during the past few days, nothing the Germans might do seems at all far-fetched. More stories are coming from the Belsen concentration camp, where Allied doctors took straight over from the Germans without any fighting, and where typhoid, typhus and other plagues are raging. The stories of suffering and cruelty in this camp are indescribable, and it is said that cannibalism went on there – and who here could judge these poor people, and find them guilty of any great crime for doing it? News from Italy continues good. As my New Zealand friends said on Monday night, people here are apt to forget that our troops in Italy are holding as many Germans as are fighting against us on the Western front, so surely they must be beaten in Italy before V-Day really means anything.

Friday, April 20. A party of MPs including Tom Driberg and Mrs. [Mavis] Tate are off today at the invitation of General Eisenhower to see for themselves the concentration camps and prison camps we are overrunning. I feel this is a splendid idea because, although few people here are now disbelieving, first-hand accounts by MPs will certainly carry weight.[47] The atrocity stories of the last war sound rather like fairy stories compared with our present civilized revelations. Bought [a] Utility bag for Joyce's birthday present from Pop and

47. This all-party delegation comprised eight Members of the House of Commons, including critics of the Government, and two peers.

had to pay 31s 6d for it – worth in peacetime about 7s 11d, I suppose. Mrs. Law called me this evening to say that she had secured a 'Mrs. Mop' for us, who will come in on Friday afternoon and clean around for us. I am pleased, as it will make such a difference for us.[48] Mrs. L. has certainly justified her return to London by this good deed. It seems that Mrs. T. has worked for another woman in the road for about nine years, and has suddenly been sacked for no reason, so we are very lucky to have got her.

[Intervening entries omitted]

Monday, April 23. St. George's Day opened for me with patriotic music by [Edward] Elgar, but even so we seem to make less fuss of our national day than we do over every other country's national day. The Russians are in the suburbs of Berlin, the defence of which is said to be directed personally by Hitler. I wonder? The weather here is bitterly cold and although heating has been instituted again, we didn't get a glimmer through our radiators at work. It will take about a week for them to warm up, by which time the weather may have changed again. We were really busy at the Club this evening. Lots of fellows are on their way home and a good many are repatriates. Eileen is off to New Zealand House tomorrow to make first enquiries about 'emigration', under which heading her trip comes. This rather amuses me, but she doesn't mind what it is called as long as she gets there.

Tuesday, April 24. Another wintry day, with no heating at the office, although by this evening the radiators were just warming up. In the streets everyone was walking around with hunched shoulders, which seemed incredible after last week. Marshal Pétain has got to Switzerland and has given himself up to the French authorities in order to face trial. Pop's reaction to this item of news was 'Poor old boy, surely they won't shoot him, after all he won't live long anyway', which is typical I think of what will happen after the war, when as each criminal is tried some excuse for not executing them will be found. In my opinion Marshal Pétain was a traitor to France, and certainly he did everything in his power to do England harm. Several visitors interrupted the *Brains Trust* this evening when we were most interested in Lord Vansittart's opinions [a guest on that evening's programme], which are now becoming rather popular. He has been a hero of mine for some years, and is now being proved right in his views.[49] In Italy the river Po has been crossed by British troops, and

---

48. 'Mrs. Mopp' (with two 'p's), a Cockney charlady, was a famous character in the persistently popular radio programme *It's That Man Again*, commonly known as *ITMA*, starring Tommy Handley. Her most famous line was 'Can I do you now, Sir?' The role was played by Dorothy Summers, whose photograph appears in Francis Worsley, *ITMA 1939–1948* (London: Vox Mundi, 1948), p. 101. 'Mrs. Mop' quickly became familiar slang for a charlady or cleaning-woman.

49. Baron Vansittart of Denham (b.1881), a former diplomat and senior civil servant and member of the House of Lords since 1941, advocated a tough-minded treatment of Germany after her defeat. His book *Bones of Contention* (n.d.), published towards the end of the war, summarised some of his hard-line views (especially chapter 6, 'Peace Terms for Germany'). See also Norman Rose, *Vansittart: Study of a Diplomat* (London: Heinemann, 1978), chap. 12.

listening to this news made me smile as I thought of the savage delight we used to get as children in making a pathetic geography mistress of ours pronounce the name of this river – how she used to blush, poor thing. But I suppose compared with present-day youth, our 'pleasures' were innocent enough.

Wednesday, April 25. The flags flying today were, I suppose, in memory of ANZAC Day? Feeling is becoming rather inflamed in this country (London at least) about the question of Germany after the war. People are saying that in Europe, owing to German cruelty and cleverness, the youth of those countries (except Germany) are dead, dying or sickly, yet Germany's children (judging by what one's friends tell us on their return) are strong, numerous and healthy. If all these German prisoners go back to Germany well fed and healthy, still ardent Nazis, all they will do will be to breed millions of children who will also be strong and healthy, whereas when the men folk of Europe get back to their homes, if ever, they will not stand any sort of chance in the population race. Various people would have these German prisoners kept away from Germany forcibly, in the same way that the Germans kept the millions of Frenchmen away from their homes, or R. would have them all sterilised so that Germany would in time become a minor nation. She says they would have done it here if they had had the chance, and I think she is right. Anyway the Government would be wise to listen to some of the things people are saying. I feel that many people here at last realise how vile the Nazis are and want to make sure that in twenty years there are at least not as many of them as there were this time. Major Lewis Hastings gave a *War Commentary* from Germany tonight and as usual talked with force – also touching on the question of concentration camps. He too said that the worst things they saw they couldn't put into words. There seemed no more lights than usual tonight. I had my nightly look out of the window before retiring, and there were no more lights than there have been all winter. Miss Hendry said that having lived for a short while in Golders Green and Beckenham, she thought there were far more lights in North London. She presumes that Southern Londoners had had such a bad time that they were still careful.

[Intervening entries omitted]

Saturday, April 28. A statement from Downing Street today (3 p.m.) said that the Germans had offered unconditional surrender to America and Britain, and that they had replied that they would have to surrender to all the Allies [including the Soviet Union]. This offer is said to have been made in the name of Himmler, who has said that Hitler is dying, and may not last for long. Odd things are obviously happening in Germany, but I hope the country is really battered before they give in. I almost feel now that I agree with people who have said that after the armistice is signed we should go on bombing for a fortnight. Barbaric perhaps, but they are a barbaric race, and understand such actions. The Russians and Americans have linked near Torgau on the Elbe and today we have heard eye-witness accounts of this historic meeting, which will certainly go down into history. [U.S.] General [George] Patton's army are now

173

in Austria and once more the map is looking very gloomy for Germany. The report by the MPs who visited Buchenwald is issued this morning and although it is written in a restrained manner, it is a shocking document, and will be on record for future generations. The weather has been terrible, and this morning around lunchtime and again this afternoon we had snow-blizzards when it simply tore down. What a summer. Rather a disappointment after a week ago. Pop has gone off to Colchester to see Grandma, who is ill. Win is down there and says she has had a slight stroke.

Sunday, April 29. British observers have seen the body of Mussolini and say that it is him. His body is being displayed in the town square in Milan where people are kicking and firing shots into the body. I think it is a good thing that the Italians themselves shot the dictator, because I doubt whether he would ever have been punished if we had taken him. ... Went to see the Buchenwald film this evening, and although it was terrible, it was not as bad as I had imagined it would be. Somehow to me the living were more pitiful than the dead, of whom at least one thought they were out of their misery, but some of the poor women who tottered about the camp were nothing but bones covered with rags, with dreadful faces. Obviously their treatment had caused them to lose their minds. The camera showed thousands of dead bodies, and hundreds of people who were almost dead, and at times the audience in the cinema gasped with horror. The commentary was good and the voice said several times as a particular horror was revealed 'Never forget that but for the "Battle of Britain" this might have been you', a fact which we should never forget. Certainly anyone who sees this film will never forget it. I feel that to my dying day I shall see some of the faces, and the general feeling now I am sure is that someone must pay for all this horror, and the Germans who perpetrated them must be the ones to suffer most of all.

Monday, April 30. There has been a little snow in the night and it was laying when I went out this morning. This morning's papers contain grim pictures of Mussolini's end – horrible, but people seem to get satisfaction out of this sight. Met Win at Paddington at lunchtime. She was telling me about the German patients they have in their hospital. The other week when our papers first published the pictures from the concentration camps the Marines who guard the Germans collected every paper together and showed them to these prisoners, who whimpered and said it was nothing to do with them. The mentality of the German, male or female, seems to be the same. They seem to think they are not at all responsible for anything carried on by their government in their territory. Well they must learn I suppose.

This evening at the Club we were very busy, partly because we had quite a few repatriated prisoners in. I talked with most of them. One particular man told me a lot about his life in Germany during the past 4½ years, during which time he has been in more than a dozen camps. He had a grim humour, and spoke highly of the morale in the camps. He said that his camp, at Magdeburg, was deserted by the guards before the Americans got there, but every man waited there perfectly disciplined until the NCOs in charge decided they could all make for our lines. When the RAF raided Magdeburg the Germans forced the prisoners to go and clear up the debris, which my friend said was 'lovely work', and his description of the way they worked, all the while admiring the most bombed or burned buildings, was tragically funny. The prisoners all agreed that near them the Belgian and French workers were as bad as the Germans, [and] would never share any food or cigarettes with the British, who nevertheless always gave these workers a share of whatever they got themselves. However when our prisoners left Magdeburg they said the foreign workers were indulging in an orgy of throat-cutting and looting. The New Zealanders in the camp were captured in Libya by the Germans early in 1941, then handed over to the Italians, who used to ask them every day 'Who captured you?', and when they received the reply 'the Germans', proceeded to punish our men. Our informant said he had never met a prisoner who had been really captured by the Italians. When the days of liberation were drawing near, the Belgian workers in the camp hoisted a Belgian flag, much to the disgust of the Britons, who said to them 'We notice that it is British and American soldiers who are coming to free us – no Belgians' and they then tore down the Belgian flag. The general opinion in the Club of prisoner and soldier alike is that there is no one like an 'old Briton', and later I wondered why people can't understand the difficulties at San Francisco when there are such different outlooks on just ordinary things in life. I was pleased when all the prisoners said that everything was being done to make them feel at home and welcome – this despite some rather nasty remarks by the boys on the staff of the Club, who imagine their year or so on the staff in Italy or Egypt has been a major part of the war effort.

Tuesday, May 1. ... The Americans have captured Munich and apparently the town is severely damaged – never to be repaired I hope. We are given official instructions how to celebrate 'V-night' and with great enthusiasm the announcers revealed that we may light a bonfire. This is all so childish. Those who are in the habit of celebrating every night will most certainly celebrate in style on V-night, but I shouldn't imagine many ordinary people will have anything to celebrate with – perhaps a glass of orange squash. Joyce has warned us to keep plenty of bread in the house, a warning I probably will ignore as I prefer no bread to stale bread. I was amused last night to see a Canadian in the Club with eleven iron crosses on a chain. He wouldn't part with one, but I have a feeling he might have done with a little persuasion. But he was a little too tough for me to risk persuasion.

Wednesday, May 2. Hitler is dead. Words we longed to hear five years ago are almost unimportant now and people don't seem really interested. Admiral [Karl] Doenitz has become führer in his place, and has said that Hitler died at his headquarters defending Berlin against the Russians, but that is probably merely a tale. Opinion here seems to think (a) that he has been murdered, and (b) that he has gone into hiding and will appear again at a later date. I am inclined to think the latter is true. British troops have landed south of Rangoon and will probably link up with those troops coming down the river to the city. British troops in Germany are pushing on towards Kiel, and newspapers have them across the Kiel Canal already and on towards Denmark, which country is

175

expecting to be freed at any time now. Wonderful news from Italy. Over a million German troops have surrendered unconditionally to the Allies there. In fact the surrender took place on Sunday. To think that the war in Italy is over is almost too much for us to take in. Never before have so vast an army surrendered to one man, and what could be more fitting than that man should be General Alexander. Trams, trolley buses and many buses are on strike, and it took me ages to get to work, and Joyce had to walk all the way. This is a dreadful time for these men and women to come out on strike – so near the end of the war – and they will lose much sympathy for themselves. Anyway it falls on the same people who have had to put up with so much inconvenience during the war, but I suppose they don't care.[50]

Thursday, May 3. The Russians have captured Berlin – surely the most thrilling news of this wonderful week. At one time this city seemed impossible to take, but somehow our troops and the Russians got there in giant strides. The Germans this time must really know that they are beaten, especially when the Red flag is flying over the Reichstag. The lunchtime papers say that Monty has linked up with [Marshal Konstantin] Rokossosky's army and also that the British are in Hamburg, which has surrendered without a fight. Australian troops have made a landing in Borneo, supported by Australian naval forces and Australian planes. Mr. [Eamon] de Valera [Prime Minister of Eire] is calling forth much bitterness from the British people, who have tried to forget some of his actions, by visiting the German legation and offering them condolences on Hitler's death. It seems to me that this country, after playing an important part in destroying the German Reich, could do the rather less arduous job of getting rid of this bitter Catholic, who is as much an enemy of Britain as is Goering or Laval. The strike continues and today I got soaked to the skin walking to a station, and wetter still on my way home, when with thousands of workers from Kidbrooke and other factories I tried to dodge the columns of water set up by a passing convoy. Got wetter too this evening walking to the canteen, and coming home when the rain simply fell down. A good thing the war is nearly over, or we might get a little short-tempered!! Well no news of V-Day so far, so Dorothy looks like being wrong [she had predicted that Germany would surrender this day], but there is time yet.

Friday, May 4. … The strike is still on, and causing a great deal of inconvenience to people in our part of the world who depend almost entirely on trams, buses and trolleys to get to work. This evening we heard the great news that the German armies facing the British in Germany had surrendered unconditionally

---

50. According to the *Evening Standard*, 2 May 1945, p. 5, 'Thousands of City workers scrambled to work today as best they could – walking, hitch-hiking or by taxi – as they once did in the blitz, when tram, trolley bus and a few petrol bus workers struck in protest against London Transport's summer schedule, begun today after a week's suspension.' The *Kentish Mercury* of 4 May 1945 (p.1) claimed that 'Many who arrived late for their work at factories will have money stopped for time lost, but some factories arranged to take their workers home by lorry on Tuesday night.' The strike, which was unofficial and not supported by the Transport and General Workers Union, had a major impact on south-east London, which lacked underground service. This industrial action was ended almost everywhere by the end of the week.

to General Montgomery, and at 10.15 we heard a broadcast of the signing of the surrender, and heard Monty reading the terms to the German representatives. His voice sounded triumphant, as well it might, as this surrender involved well over a million men in Germany, Holland, Denmark and all islands off those territories, and is to come into operation at 8 o'clock tomorrow morning. For two of our generals to have accepted the surrender of a million men within a week is most wonderful news, and leads us to know that the end is nearly upon us.

Saturday, May 5. All sorts of congratulations are flying about today – General Eisenhower to Alexander etc. etc. – and of course this is in order. We never have had such news before. … France has been invited to join the Big Four, which will then be known as the Big Five presumably. I am still amazed at the audacity of the French who seem to imagine that they are able now to rank with the great powers of the world. Let us hope that these past five years have purged France of the rottenness which overwhelmed the whole country between the two great wars. Joyce and I left London to go down to Leigh-on-Sea to spend the weekend with D.R., who is now living with an Aunt there. We arrived about 5.30, and this wretched old woman, who is mean, rude, ignorant, dirty, etc., greeted us as we entered with 'If you two girls take sugar, you will have to have saccharine', before we had got into the house. She is one of the worst people I have ever met, serving only enough food to go 'one to each person', yet indulging herself thoroughly. She treats D. like a servant, and doesn't seem to understand that she gave up a good job in London, with fine prospects, to go down there to live with the old harridan. I don't know if I will be able to stay in the house till tomorrow, and I really think D. ought to leave her. We went into Southend to the pictures this evening as it was pouring with rain and saw *A Song to Remember* [on the life of Frederic Chopin], which I enjoyed again. The old lady sulked because we went out – happy holiday.

Sunday, May 6. We didn't hear the news this morning because the Aunt won't have the wireless on as it wastes electricity. Nor could we have toast, because that is extravagant with gas. We took our meat with us because D. said her Aunt wouldn't be able to manage if we didn't, and then the old woman said 'I don't know what I shall do with all this meat'. Surely a good idea would be to knock her over the head, and drop her into the river or something. We went out by the sea this morning and again this afternoon, and I bought a paper to see that the war was still going on. We travelled back in fair comfort and got in around 9.30, and it is turning rather hot. It has been announced that Mr. Churchill will broadcast on the 10th but will probably have announced V-E Day before that time, so we still don't know when the war will end.

Monday, May 7. Back to work, although everyone is certain the war will be over today, and we didn't do much work, nor did anyone else in the buildings around us. The Air Ministry windows opposite were full of people all afternoon, and when the news of the surrender of all U-boats was announced we really thought it over. First people said Mr. Churchill was speaking at 11 a.m., then 2 o'clock, then 3 o'clock, then 4, then 6 o'clock. We have made no plans at the office. They will not face up to the fact that staff must be given instructions. Our boss this afternoon said 'If Mr. Churchill says it is a holiday I suppose you must take it, but I shall be in as usual', so on that vague note we left the office. At the Club we were frantically busy and sold out soon after 7, after I and the Sergeant had practically served it all ourselves. Everyone is in good spirits, and at 6 p.m. the BBC said there was no announcement yet. At 9 o'clock we heard the news 'Mr. Churchill will speak at 3 o'clock tomorrow and announce V-E Day, and the following day will be a holiday'. I think this whole thing has been badly managed, and all the spontaneity has gone from us. A few of us wandered around Trafalgar Square on the way home, and certainly the flags and bunting are coming out in a big way now. Flags do look attractive, especially the lovely things they hang on some of the more important buildings. We are still undecided as to what to do tomorrow, but I think I will ring D. in the morning around 8 a.m. How strange to think that the war will soon be over. It will need a lot of getting used to I think. As we went to bed, many bonfires had been lit all around – a little early celebrating. The roads all around look colourful, and no doubt by tomorrow it will all be gay.

Tuesday, May 8. So this is V-Day. I got up in my pyjamas and went into Mrs. L.'s to phone Dorothy. She is going to the office, but we are not, so that is good news. Mrs. L. and I sat talking about peace. The only solemn note is the action of Russia, who haven't yet announced the end to the war. I hope and pray that our troubles with Russia will soon be overcome. It seems so dreadful that after all we have gone through together, clever propaganda on the part of the Germans and enemies of democracy is splitting us. Surely a little give and take on both sides will help these troubles. We have only to think of the feelings we all shared a year or so ago to know that disaster will follow any break in our friendship. The Polish question is difficult, but surely men who have planned this war, [and] have made such wonderful inventions and discoveries to defeat the Germans, can find some way out of this deadlock. I suppose it is inevitable to think back on a day like this, and to think of all those who are not here to celebrate this victory. I like to think that they all know that we have won, although when some of them died things didn't look very hopeful. Listened to Churchill's broadcast this afternoon, and found it most difficult to take in what he was saying, but no doubt it will sink in later on. This evening Pop, Joyce and I went up to town about 8 o'clock, arriving at Charing Cross just before 9, where we heard the King's speech, [and] watched the seething, pushing crowds in Trafalgar Square, with Pop saying the whole time 'My this is nothing like the crowd on Armistice night 1918', the while trying to get through the vast mob of people. Then we went on down to Woolwich, where on the parade ground the Royal Artillery band gave a concert, and the barracks and academy were floodlit and we had a searchlight display which was quite thrilling, in a peacetime way. The band played until 11.45 and the vast crowd sang last-war songs and hymns and danced. Then the soldiers from the garrison put on a firework display which was reminiscent of the Blitz, with hand grenades and Very [flare] lights going off and various other noisy fireworks adding to the din. Several children around were frightened, thinking no doubt that it was a raid, but the men loved it. We walked home around midnight and watched the wonderful searchlight display. At one point there seemed hundreds of these lights all concentrated on one spot. On our way home wirelesses were playing through open doors and windows and people were sitting in gardens. In fact it was a grand night. The lack of salute by guns disappointed many people I think. I went to bed about 1.30 with searchlights still popping and bonfires going, and I was exhausted![51]

Wednesday, May 9. Up pretty late this morning and listened to various martial music programmes on the wireless. Today the papers show wonderful pictures of the crowds in London celebrating yesterday. Many thousands were stranded in London, I read. This afternoon went with Joyce to see *The Keys of the Kingdom*, which I enjoyed quite well, although I have not read the book [by A.J. Cronin]. The programme contained various patriotic shorts designed to celebrate the end of the war, and suffered I think because they tried to show so much in a short space of time. The newsreel too was the same. Not much of the war can be shown in ten minutes. I feel a longer film comprising newsreel shots of the past 5½ years would be of great interest to the people of this country. I left Joyce in the cinema and went off to town to meet Eileen and Linda, but we found that [the much-praised 1944 film] *Henry V* [starring and directed by Laurence Olivier] was not showing today, all cinemas being shut, so we consoled ourselves by walking around and looking at the crowds. We wandered down to the Palace and shortly after we arrived the King, Queen and two Princesses came out on the balcony and were afforded a grand reception. Later we were in Whitehall when Mr. Churchill came down in summer grey suit and sitting on top of a car. As I am tallish I had a grand view. The others didn't see quite as well. It was moving to hear the way people cheered, and I didn't begrudge him his reception, although I wondered if he was thinking 'How long will they think of me in this way?' Mr. Churchill knows better than anyone how fickle is public favour. I felt quite exhausted by the time I got home, and listened to Joyce telling me what I had missed of the film, and also describing this evening's victory variety programme and the Churchill programme, etc. These two days have been grand. People seem to have celebrated in their own way, and there seemed to me to be little riotous merry-making, except for a few sailors on Tuesday in Trafalgar Square.

Thursday, May 10. Back to work – and as I looked around in the tram I realised that we all looked as grim as ever. I suppose I had imagined that the sort of triumphant expression most people wore on Tuesday would last, but I suppose that was too much of a sacrifice to ask of the British people. Crowds still in town. I suppose many folk are making a week of it. Everyone seems to have had a little trouble with the holiday. At Joyce's office many of them had come

---

51. Flags, bunting, and emblems were widely on display, and in Woolwich, according to the *Kentish Mercury*, 11 May 1945, p. 8, 'by the morning of V-E Day the shopping thorough-fares, and the side streets too, presented a gay appearance. In fact it was noticeable that the little streets had generally speaking a brighter show of colour than the shopping centres. There seemed to have been a keen rivalry as to who could produce the best show.'

in over the entire holiday, and rather crowed over those who had taken official instructions to heart. The same at ours. Most of them were in on Tuesday – all except Rene and I in fact. This doesn't depress us as it would have done a few years ago. At the canteen this evening we were very busy indeed. The place has been packed more or less continuously since Tuesday morning, and we have done great business. This evening most of the fellows were thinking about getting out of the Army and Air Forces, and no wonder – some of them have had more than five years of it, and that is a great slice out of a young life. Joyce was telling me this evening that John W. was in Hamburg at the weekend – he is a pilot who is flying people about on missions now that bombing is over – and the CO of the aerodrome at which he landed warned him before he started off on a sightseeing tour to beware of all young boys from the age of about seven, as they are all in the habit of carrying revolvers and are likely to try and shoot our men. This is a most grim side of our enemy. It will be difficult to educate young children who have been brought up in this way. Mr. Churchill's broadcast was postponed till Sunday, a better day for listening I think.

Friday, May 11. The King and Queen and Princesses were seen by almost all of our neighbours yesterday, and on the way to work Pauline told me how her entire school was marched out and they stood by the roadside and got a good view. She described the King and Queen rather oddly – the Queen looked pretty and the King wore his sailor's suit. She can't tell one princess from another, but I suppose all small children are the same.[52] The Germans are still resisting the Russians in Czechoslovakia and yesterday bombed a concentration camp near Prague. London is still packed with people and the floodlighting is to continue, although apart from that there is just nothing to see up there.

Saturday, May 12. A lovely day for the party in our road, and in every other road in London it seems. The citizens of our part of the world are doing a great deal of organisation. Mrs. M., hiding her personal grief [she had recently been widowed] in an attempt to give the children a good time, is leading it, and Mrs. L. is helping her. The party finished up this evening after 12 with dancing and singing in which hundreds of grown-ups participated quite happily.[53] *The*

52. This royal visit was directed to bomb-damaged south-east London, including the site where a flying bomb fell and exploded in the High Street in Lewisham on 28 July 1944 and destroyed many lives. 'Crowds of people perched themselves on every available ruin around Lewisham market to greet the royal party', according to the *Kentish Mercury*, 11 May 1945. 'They sat on the girders of ruined buildings and on the roofs of others, as well as on the top of air-raid shelters and wardens' posts.' The *Lewisham Borough News*, 15 May 1945, reported that 'A group of excited flag-waving children standing on top of one of the public air-raid shelters began to sing the National Anthem as the Royal Family chatted with some of Lewisham's worst bombed residents who were grouped on the right side of the market site.' The King and Queen spent time commiserating with some of these victims.
53. This was one of dozens of street parties in south-east London held to celebrate the victorious ending of war, and many of them were reported in the local press. Some 70 children from Strathaven Road and three nearby streets sat down to a festive tea, which was followed by games, races, singing, dancing, a visit by the Mayor of Woolwich (Councillor E.T. Lamerton), and a display of fireworks. (*Kentish Independent*, 18 May 1945, p. 6.)

Times today prints a letter from Mrs. [Mavis] Tate, MP, following up much discussion recently about conditions in prisons everywhere, and she suggests that the matter be discussed at San Francisco – a fine idea I think. Certainly there should be some sort of an organization that would be able to enter prisons of every kind, military and civil, in every country, and whose business it would be to see that the unfortunate residents of these places are not ill-treated. We are not all satisfied in this country that conditions in our prisons are as honourable as some of the self-righteous nonsense spouted by various statesmen would imply.

Sunday, May 13. Services of Thanksgiving held all over the country, led by a great service in St. Paul's at which the King and Queen, etc. were present, as were everyone who is anyone in the country, as well as '50 typical housewives' – I would love to have seen them!! Joyce and I attended a United Service on the Common, at which all the Woolwich ministers attended and each took a separate part of the service. The Royal Artillery Band played. It started to rain half-way through and became very cold. We who were attired only in thin summer dresses felt the cold. Spent the evening waiting for visitors who didn't show up. Very annoying.

Kathleen spent most of the following week feeling sick – sometimes very sick – with a gastro-intestinal complaint. Her next door neighbour tried to ease her discomfort, and visited on several days, and on Wednesday, May 16 they talked about sex and the Americans. 'She agrees with me after a year near a big 8th Army Air Force station that the morals of the Americans are as low as they could possibly be. She thinks Yanks are sex-mad, and that I fear is my opinion. What can it be like in their own country, and what sort of a country will America be in 20 years time if these are the accepted standards of life?' As usual, Kathleen often commented on military and political news. On Saturday, May 19 there were clear signs that the Churchill government would soon split up. 'This weekend looks like deciding whether the Coalition stays or goes, and by now I think it will be a good thing for it to break up. Feeling is getting rather high in the country and all is obviously not well in the cabinet itself, as we can see by odd speeches.' This was Whitsun weekend, and though the weather was wet and windy on Sunday, there was sunshine on the Bank Holiday Monday, May 21st, so Kathleen and Joyce were able, as planned, to go to Lord's. 'The ground was absolutely crowded [in fact, the gates had to be closed], and was seething with Australians, who had reason to crow by the time the day was out. England will have to search diligently for some bowlers or the position will be very similar to that existing after the last war when Australia dominated this sporting world. I was amused sitting at Lord's, though, to hear the men talking just as if the war had never occurred. Their world is the cricket world and everything else is unimportant.' These Victory Tests, pitting England against the Dominions, marked the revival of first-class cricket and attracted large crowds. Cricket was not the only pleasure for the Tipper family that holiday. 'Pop went to the White City and enjoyed his day too. He loves athletic meetings.' The following day, Tuesday the 22nd, she was 'Back at work, and I didn't like it. The election seems to be more or less definite for July, and in the mean-time a "caretaker" government will govern the country.'

Unsurprisingly, the aftermath of the war in Europe, both at home and abroad, continued to be a major concern.

Wednesday, May 23. German prisoners are at work in Charlton and Lewisham, and about time too. I can't imagine why the press devote so much space to this fact. Joyce came home hopping mad after hearing some of the silly women at her work saying they felt lumps come into their throats when they looked at these poor fellows ('great hulking toughs' was a soldier's description of the same men) at work, and another woman thought they should have been given a month's holiday at home before starting working. I can't imagine the mentality of such people. I expect there will be hundreds of girls watching them, and no doubt there will be fraternisation. I should like to take some repatriated prisoners I have talked to to see them – I am sure they would weep at the sight. Monty is to command the British Army in Germany, a decision which will please everyone I think – but what a difficult job. Judging by correspondents, the most difficult job now is to prevent fraternisation. Mr. Churchill has resigned and is now in process of forming a new Government to look after affairs until July. I expect we shall see the reappearance of many old familiar names – Anderson, Simon, Hoare, etc. – all men associated with the rise and support of the Nazis and Chamberlain, but now they seem to have acquired an aura of patriotism.

Thursday, May 24. My birthday today [her 26th]. I didn't stumble over the pile of letters and presents this morning. Those remembering get fewer each year fortunately. As one gets older one doesn't care for too many reminders of one's age!! Correspondence in *The Times* about the Tito regime [in Yugoslavia] has become interesting. An American war correspondent denies charges made by 'a soldier' yesterday of mass shootings, kidnapping etc., and I expect there will be many words more on this subject, but I am afraid most people are biased before they start thinking about the subject. Doenitz and his gang have been arrested at last, and Admiral [Hans von] Friedeburg has committed suicide. I am always pleased to note this. Obviously those who do this are not so familiar with British methods. They will all be quite safe in our hands I imagine, especially now that there are political differences here. My boss's son, an officer in the Army, has been visiting some old friends in Germany, and has come to the conclusion that there are good and bad Germans, but most of them are good. He also should talk to men who have been prisoners in German hands. I feel he might learn a thing or two.

EPILOGUE

The end of war (initially in Europe, by August in the Far East) certainly did not mean a return to prewar conditions. To be sure, people could enjoy a little more light, both because of celebratory illuminations to mark the Allied victories and the complete ending of blackout restrictions. 'From my bedroom we can see roads going in all directions,' Kathleen wrote on 15 July 1945 after coming home at night, 'and all of them very well lit. It will be good for morale I am sure, even if it uses a good bit of fuel.' For most people, there was less acute worry and a bit more fun. To Kathleen this sometimes meant outings to Lord's or the Oval for cricket or, occasionally, to Charlton's football ground. Indeed, cricket was something of a passion for Kathleen. In the four months of June through September 1945 she attended at least a dozen matches and mentioned the sport in her diary on nine other occasions, and she reported no less than seven visits to the Oval or Lord's during May of 1946.

There was, however, much drabness and privation in postwar London. Many people were worn out, and frustrated at the slowness of the return to normal life. There was a continued austerity that made most people's everyday existence remarkably pinched. Rationing, widely supported in a spirit of fair sharing during the war, became irksome once danger was past. Similarly, ongoing shortages of a wide range of goods were now harder to put up with in the comradely spirit of common hardship that had sustained home front morale during the darkest days of war. When she was shopping on Saturday, 26 May 1945, Kathleen 'noticed a continued shortage of bread, which shopkeepers assert is a result of evacuees returning in large numbers, but I think people are buying a great deal more, and judging from the amount in pig-bins, throwing a great away a great deal more too. I had to join an immense queue for soapflakes and washing soap too. It was practically as long as the ice cream queue.' Perpetual queueing was a major irritant, and social inequities rubbed salt in the wound. One Friday, 15 June 1945, Kathleen and Joyce journeyed to affluent Kensington in West London, where 'Barker's [an upscale Department store] food counters truly amazed me. There was so much stuff there, and once again we realised that those people with money can live very well indeed still. There was poultry, fish etc., all very expensive, but there in plenty.' (Luxury foods such as shellfish, caviar, and game were never rationed and could be obtained throughout the war by those with deep pockets.) The following day, Saturday, 16 June, en route to a cricket game at Lord's, Kathleen noticed the very different realities that confronted less favoured Londoners. 'As we went through Deptford, Greenwich and Bermondsey this morning the queues were longer than I have ever seen them before. People were queueing up for everything – greengrocery, bread, fish, meat. I felt that the Minister of Food should have to deal in these districts. Then he might feel compelled to do something about this terrible situation. After looking at Barker's yesterday we both doubted that their customers ever had to queue for anything.'

Woven throughout the rest of Kathleen's diary – she wrote until 1 February 1947 – are tales of the routine frustrations of coping with daily life in postwar London. Kathleen decided to forego the tempting luxury of ice-cream or cherries on a warm summer's day because the queues were just too daunting (21 June 1945). Necessities like shoes and a winter coat could be obtained, if at all, only after much searching, and they were often of poor quality. 'No one I know possesses a pair of wartime-bought shoes that are really waterproof,' Kathleen complained on 19 June 1946, 'yet we have all spent a great deal of money on the pairs we have – money wasted as far as I am concerned.' A shopping trip on 25 April 1946 to find a lightweight coat involved going to 'about 30 shops in Oxford Street and Regent Street' where she was 'rarely shown anything at all, and at the most only one or two. All the coats on sale seem to be the same weight for winter or summer. The Utility makers seem to forget that we occasionally have very hot or very cold weather, and I have yet to try on the Utility coat which feels really heavy and warm. Shopping is depressing and we got so hot as we whizzed in and out of this large number of shops.' Maintaining a basic wardrobe was clearly a challenge. 'The weather continues very hot and has us all wishing we had more summer clothes', Kathleen noted on 24 July 1946. 'However they really are not worth buying for the very short period of heat we get as a rule in this country. But when I feel warm I long for one really good summer dress, smart and attractive. I can't imagine ever being able to pay the price demanded in London for a smart and attractive summer dress for a few days wear though.'

Dogged persistence, as veteran queuers knew, could sometimes yield results. With this hope in mind, on 1 August 1946 Kathleen 'Got up at 5.30 this morning in order to queue up at Bata's for some sandals and white slippers. We were near the front of the queue, but at 8.20 the manager came up to say there would be no sandals on sale today. The women nearly lynched him, and I felt most sorry for him.' Towards the end of the month (23 August 1946) she was similarly disappointed when she encountered 'Tremendous queues at all the shops today trying to buy dried milk, or tinned milk of some kind. At the stores when I arrived there wasn't a tin of any kind left.' Reading material was also hard to get, and the Tippers liked to send magazines to family and friends abroad. 'When papers and books are plentiful again the war will really seem to be over,' Kathleen remarked on 13 September 1945. 'I find it irksome to have to appease street vendors in order to get a copy of a 3d magazine to send overseas, but it has to be done, and anyway my little man is pretty good and quite nice'.

Feeding the family was an ongoing struggle. On 16 August 1945 Kathleen 'Had to spend a few more hours in a fish queue this morning, much to my horror, but we must eat, and with four people at home and nothing at all in the cupboard there was no other alternative.' On this occasion she met with success and 'came out with herrings for lunch, shrimps for tea and kippers for breakfast.' (She also had 'a pleasant chat with a very nice woman in the queue', which led her to observe that 'I know now why so many women really enjoy queuing'.) Fish and fresh fruit, highly perishable foodstuffs, were not rationed, but their uneven availability was an ongoing source of complaint. The food that was available was often unpalatable – or at least unappealing – and when one item was in the shops, its usual mate might not be. 'To use up my points' on 10 November 1945 after failing to find bread, 'I got some porridge oats, but wondered afterwards whether I shall ever get enough milk to use them. We get a pint a day (more than we are entitled to with three [in the family] even so) and we find it difficult to manage.' Weary people stood in endless queues and swapped gloomy rumours. 'The bread is to be much darker and there is talk of further cuts in fat', Kathleen heard on 3 May 1946. 'If this is so I think the housewives will really start a revolution or something.' A sense that the British were enduring a disproportionate share of postwar hardship fuelled some of the conversations among discontented queuers. 'This morning everyone starts talking about food, and several people who formerly never mentioned the subject made comments like "Looks as if we shall be starving before long" today. The trouble is there are such conflicting stories from these starving countries. People back in high places tell us that we must give up our food for them, yet soldiers and civilians (ordinary people like myself) come back saying that there is more food about in Europe than there is at home. There is a feeling too I think that the food saved by cuts here doesn't really get to those who need it. Anyway I think European countries should do something about their black markets before we are asked to make further reductions.' (3 May 1946) Pessimism among Londoners was understandable. Bread was rationed in July 1946 for the first time, a significant departure from the wartime policy which had left bread and potatoes uncontrolled. Diets were limited further as the Government struggled to repay the country's huge Lend-Lease debt to the United States, limit the import of costly foreign foodstuffs, and provide food aid to starving Europeans.

People's charitable impulses were sometimes tempered by their own hardships, and by memories of their own country's wartime sufferings. On 9 August 1945 Kathleen reported having a discussion 'in a little restaurant in Alfriston' with a German refugee about the extraordinary fact of the atom bomb. The refugee 'began talking a great deal about the wickedness of the Allies in using the atom, and we let her know our views on this subject very firmly. I said that my only regret was that we didn't use them on the Germans; then we would have had no German problem (not my real opinion, but these well-dressed German refugees make me sick, and this one was wearing a pair of shoes I have been trying to buy for years!).' Americans came in for much criticism as well, particularly with the abrupt ending of Lend-Lease. American sacrifices were thought to be modest indeed. 'The behaviour of the Americans during and since the war, and their reluctance to sacrifice any of their own pleasures and indulgences, has made most people despise them quite a bit, and at the same time, we have very good reason to be grateful to the Dominions who are still rationing themselves with food of various kinds, in order that our own meagre rations may be kept going. Personally I hope the feeling that is demanding less films and tobacco and more food from America will cause the Government to take action. I suspect something drastic would happen if

Britain started reducing the amount of films she imported. The moguls in Hollywood would probably wish to start a new war.' (7 February 1946)

It was understandable that war-fatigued Londoners would air their frustra-tions from time to time, but it seems that for the most part they coped with restrictions and constraints with aplomb and resourcefulness. All three Tippers were employed but the family budget was still very tight. A car would have delighted Kathleen, especially since she had learned to drive as part of her volunteer work with the YMCA mobile canteen, but this was clearly impos-sible. However, the sisters did manage to buy bicycles for themselves in 1946. 'It is lovely to own a vehicle for the first time!' Kathleen exclaimed after she and Joyce took their cycles out for a first run (6 May 1946). The 'make do and mend' slogan was a very real one for Kathleen and Joyce. Everyday life was an ongoing round of stretching limited resources – just as they had been doing for years. Mending and sewing were constant chores. On 8 July 1945 'Grandma called this afternoon' and 'earned her tea by helping me to darn about 30 socks full of holes'. ('A good idea for the future,' she added. 'Give a party but insist on one's guests doing some of the household tasks before they get their food.') On 8 October 1946 Kathleen rose at 5.30 a.m. to join a queue for tickets to *King Lear* and by the time her brother came to relieve her at 9 a.m. she 'had darned about 11 pairs of socks'. Philip was in the Navy and needed to be fitted out for his posting overseas. Since the amount he would be reimbursed for his kit did not come close covering the real cost, Kathleen 'decided to try to make Phil's boiler suits'. She borrowed a sewing machine and struggled with the heavy material, and wondered 'whether I have taken on too much' (20 July 1945). By the next day she had conscripted her sister and brother to cut out the material while she sewed. 'The material is so hard, and the garment is so large, that we were soon all swearing about our respective tasks. How simple is life', she pondered, 'for those with sufficient money to buy anything they want. I wonder they are ever worried or old-looking. But I suppose if one didn't have to worry about making boiler suits, to save the cost of buying them, we would find something else to worry about.' (21 July 1945) These boiler suits were not finally completed until Kathleen sought help from Rene at the office who was a more expert seamstress. She later made overalls for Kathleen and her other office mates from old blackout curtains, and deco-rated them with 'green buttons made of dyed fish skin' procured from one of the factories owned by their employer, Alfred Booth & Company (8 April 1946). On 30 May 1946 Kathleen 'Spent the entire day mending and patching my old rags and those of the rest of the family. I sat by our wardrobes and took one garment off at a time and turned up hems, sewed on buttons, etc., and but for the fact that I was at it all day, I wouldn't have believed that such trivial jobs would have taken such a time.' All this making-do sometimes depressed Kathleen. 'I am undoing some bed-socks in order to knit them into something more useful, but I am thoroughly sick of this system of renovating and would just love to collect all my old rags together and burn them in a bonfire.' (7 October 1945)

The privations endured made small treats all the more welcome. At Christmas in 1945 'Joyce and I called on Auntie Lila [and Uncle Arthur] and gave them their presents, a half a bottle of our port, some fat, tea, three cups and saucers, and various oddments. Then we called on Grandma and gave her hers, a calendar made with ferns and leaves, a Christmas pudding, some tea and fat, and we sat drinking tea with her and finishing our knitting.' (21 December 1945) Occasionally a benefactor appeared unexpectedly. On 16 September 1946 a clearly delighted Kathleen reported that 'I am now the possessor of a real pair of nylons – marked with that wonderful name too. The head of our American branch arrived in London and brought each of we four girls a pair, also a huge box of delicious chocolates for the office generally, and a lovely bar of soap for we four as well. Indeed, it was quite a day for us. We don't get such a lovely present often in a lifetime now.' Another memorable gift arrived a few weeks later, on 4 November 1946. 'Had a wonderful present given us today at the office – two white doeskins, the size of the whole animal....Often we have had skins in the office, but never before have any been given away to the dogsbodies....We are now going to try to find some shoemaker who will make them up for us. I shall have enough to share with Joyce.' Two days later, on 6 November, she reported that 'Pop thinks we should get four pairs of shoes and two pairs of sandals out of one skin – his father was a bootmaker and Pop still has some of his patterns for cutting out shoes'. This fine gift became a major project as it was difficult to find a shoe-maker who would make up the footgear at a reasonable price. One quote was a shocking twelve pounds (13 November 1946), but the work did get done and the first two pairs of shoes, one for each sister, were finally produced by early December (9 December 1946). This good news was followed the next week by a misfortune: 'Our Christmas dinner was stolen last night. The cockerel being fattened by one of Pop's colleagues was, like most of the chickens in the same road, stolen during the fog last night. We are all disappointed, but Joyce says we can always open a tin of stewed steak for Christmas dinner.' (12 December 1946)

On the whole, the Christmas season of 1946 disclosed signs of bounty and well-being. On 20 December 1946 Kathleen noted that 'My boss [is] back on the *Queen Elizabeth* and brought a pair of nylons for we three, and are we thrilled. I often think they can't realise how thrilled we are with these gifts, because even if plentiful here, more than likely these goods are out of the range of my pocket, even with my rise, which is really good.' Three days later another member of the firm added two more pairs of nylons as a Christmas gift (23 December 1946). This Christmas, in fact, permitted something of a splurge. On Christmas Eve the Tippers 'Opened the ham which Philip brought back from Australia and it looks lovely. We haven't a tin or anything big enough to hold it, so it goes on a plate in the front room with the Christmas cake.' For dinner on Christmas Day Mr. Tipper had bought a chicken from a friend to replace the stolen cockerel and, for once, shortages and monotonous fare were forgotten. 'Our sideboard groaned under the weight of unaccustomed fruit, we had three pounds of apples, two pounds of pears, some oranges, a few walnuts, some chestnuts and, wonder of wonders, some bananas which Joyce got in the market last night. We ate too much and drank quite nicely, enjoying particularly the Cherry Brandy which Joyce got for us.' (25 December 1946)

The Tipper sisters were very fond of their young brother and did any number of tasks for him, from preparing, cleaning, labelling, and packing his naval gear through to cooking his breakfast, doing his typing, and otherwise providing fond sisterly care. Philip returned the favours. He scoured foreign ports for things that were hard to come by in postwar England. For instance, on 9 April 1946 he returned from a tour of duty with – and Kathleen saw fit to record every detail – 'some marvellous treasures – tins of fat, several tins of jam, some tinned fruit, tinned meat, a Christmas pudding, some tomato juice, condensed milk, soap, starch, boiled sweets, Turkish delight, six tennis balls, two hot water bottles, and eight ounces of wool each for Joyce and I. Also a tinned picnic ham weighing 9 pounds 7 ounces was amongst the treasure – we will have a party to use that. He also brought six jellies, mixed fruit, honey and lemon butter – and the sight of it all on the dining-room table made one's eyes almost pop out.' One wonders how he carried it all. A couple of weeks later, after eating one of the jellies he had brought, Kathleen reflected that 'until one tastes these good things again, we don't remember really what we are going without' (22 April 1946). Young relatives invited for tea on 25 November 1945 'could hardly remember peaches and pears, so they did full justice to those Philip brought'.

In stringent times gifts from those who travelled were warmly welcomed – as was less exotic home-generated produce. On 20 June 1946 Philip surprised his sisters by bringing them each a watch: 'they are lovely things, Swiss watches and are most delicate, small and attractive. I never imagined I would possess anything quite so good.' That evening he opened his luggage and gave them more. 'He has bought us a set of underclothes each, which just about saves our bacon, as we both only possess one slip fit to be seen in, and now will be able to manage for two weeks on holiday. He has also bought some stockings for us, but since they are rather small, Joyce may benefit entirely there. Some Morny soap is much appreciated, and he has brought a few tins of fruit, etc., and a coconut for me. He is a jolly good lad, and we certainly appreciate what he does for us.' The other Tipper male, their father, made his own contribution to the family's welfare through his extensive gardening skills. Many a family meal consisted largely of produce from his garden. Some fruits and vegetables were bottled and preserved, yet there was still ample to share with friends and neighbours (2 June 1946). Gardening to Kathleen's father seems to have been a pleasure and calling, and not just a chore. 'If he had a small piece of land I am sure he could make himself a nice little living, doing work he likes and can do well, whereas continuing his present job [for a public works contractor], he will slave himself until he is too old to be useful to his firm, and then will be on the scrap-heap.' (17 October 1945) A particularly telling bit of work in the garden took place on 24 February 1946 when Mr. Tipper toiled 'like a slave' to remove the family's air-raid shelter, and while he did so, according to Kathleen, 'People keep calling over the fence, "I should leave that in if I were you, you'll be needing it before long" – not that I imagine any small shelter will be of any use whatsoever in the next war.'

The military presence in and near London remained prominent for months; so did talk about victory, war, and its aftermath. Soldiers still clogged many trains, thus forcing civilians to stand, and this inconvenience was not always endured silently. Travelling home from Colchester on 13 June 1945, Kathleen reported that 'The train was crowded and we had to stand the whole way, every seat being taken by a soldier. Now I didn't mind standing, but there were lots of elderly ladies and men standing in the corridors, but not one of these soldiers offered up a seat, and I felt that the remark of one lady, "Well, the war is over

– what are they doing now?", was justified, although I couldn't have said it myself.' Reminders of war were everywhere. Almost a year and a half after victory in Europe, on 6 October 1946, Kathleen and Philip were riding on their bicycles and 'passed our old school sports ground – a gun-site during the war, then an Italian POW camp, and now it holds Germans'. From May of 1945 the clientele at the New Zealand Club and the YMCA canteen included former prisoners of war who sometimes had harrowing tales to tell. Some of them also told of the intimacies that were already occurring between some victors and former enemies. On 9 July 1945 one ex-POW 'said he had seen cellars in Germany full up with English soldiers and German girls, and says that the moment the non-fraternisation order is lifted thousands of British troops will marry Germans. He admits the charms of these girls, particularly the Austrian girls, but the rest of the Europeans he finds too hot-blooded for him.' While Kathleen heartily approved of this prohibition on fraternisation, 'I realise how difficult it is to administer, especially as men are so weak-minded.'

These stresses had not, of course, yet reached the Far East, where hostilities continued, but victory over Japan seemed assured. On 13 August it was 'Quite busy this evening at the Club, and it was quite a pleasant one. The atmosphere seemed so happy. Possibly the imminent end of the Far Eastern War is cheering them up, because many of these fellows would have had to go out there. We received several rather early victory kisses, but with these fellows it is difficult to get annoyed.' Two days later, with the final defeat of Japan, Kathleen and others 'Talked a good deal of rubbish about peace on earth today, but when we smiled at the absurdity of the of the idea, I thought of all those wives and mothers with boys in Jap prison camps and wondered just how they were feeling. Somehow I never expected to see the day when their return seemed even possible.' (15 August) A few hours later – it was VJ Day – she went with Eileen to the Lyric Theatre and observed that 'The crowds were immense, perhaps not so dense as on VE night, but they seemed to stretch further afield than they did before. I also thought them less jolly. The people seemed much more noisy than they were before. In fact I didn't like the crowds tonight, but I did like the floodlighting, which was beautiful. St. Paul's looked lovely with two searchlights on the cross, and the lighting on Thames side was most attractive.'

Soldiers could now expect to be spared death in battle, and those whom Kathleen was meeting were primarily concerned with their futures. On 16 August 1945 'The fellows [at the canteen] don't seem very thrilled about the end of the war. All they are concerned with is getting out of the Army, which most of them have served in [in] England for three or four years.' A week later at the canteen (23 August) the men 'were as usual talking about demobilisation, and several admitted that they would like to do some sort of a job whilst waiting for that happy state. Some said they would like to help with the harvest. Others would like to help in shops and factories, yet are forced to waste week after week doing absolutely nothing.' Kathleen was impressed with New Zealand's programmes for demobilising its troops. The demobbed soldiers, she thought, were treated sensitively as 'responsible human beings' and given every opportunity to make the transition to a decent position in civilian life. The men administering these programmes gained her respect. 'I have met quite a few of the New Zealanders now connected with rehabilitation and repatriation, etc., and they are certainly some of the finest men I have ever met.' (11 July 1945) Whatever aid might be offered, though, some New Zealanders were bound to have reason to wonder how they might be received back home. On 3 September 1945 Kathleen spoke of some 'new boys' at the Club 'who are ex-POWs and who have married Czechs and Austrians, and as a result do nothing but abuse English girls. I suppose they are expecting criticism and abuse and are thus very truculent. Personally I wonder what the parents back in New Zealand are going to think when they meet these Europeans.' The men who faced the most daunting challenges of reintegration into civilian society were those maimed by war. A Flight Lieutenant whom Kathleen knew at the Club gave her cause to ponder these men's futures. 'A couple of years ago he was in a terrible state, burned all over, but each time we have seen him he has improved, and today, although still terribly disfigured, he was better, and he seemed so much more cheerful in himself. Perhaps he notices the difference. His hands too I noticed were more flexible. These boys carry a dreadful burden, I think, and it seems so unfair that they must walk around all their lives watching people either look sorry for them, or look away. I don't know which is worse.' (22 October 1945)

Uncertain futures were also connected to less traumatic realities, and Kathleen mentioned several men who were concerned about, or troubled by, their return to the mundane circumstances of living in peacetime. She thought that one New Zealander she knew 'is a little afraid of going home. He wonders if he will be able to pick up his work and married life after five years away. This is a common enough problem, but it makes me miserable because G. is such a nice fellow, who has really led an exemplary life here, and obviously his wife is the same sort, yet he is frightened to go home.' (20 August 1945) Settling back into civilian life might well be challenging. Moreover, men released from service sometimes returned to a daily life very different from the one they had left. One soldier at the canteen shared his economic worries with Kathleen. He had run a building firm in Suffolk until 'he was called up. It is closed down now and he can't get out to start it up. Yet a rival young man has kept out of the Army and is grabbing all the contracts in that part of the world.' (4 April 1946) Some men who had exercised authority during the war probably missed their lack of authority when they returned to civilian duties – Kathleen complained of a former officer who came back to his job in her firm and tried to order people around: 'anyway, he is not in the Army now, and we are certainly not his batwomen' (16 November 1945). Intimate relations might have to be reconstructed after a serviceman returned to his spouse – and not always for predictable reasons. On 23 September 1945 Kathleen met a couple who had recently been reunited; the husband was 'just home from Italy after four years, with an acquired taste for opera (which they all seem to get) which doesn't please [his] wife who prefers boogie-woogie'. (In order to help former POWs understand developments during their incarceration, a cinema in Woolwich, Kathleen noticed on 19 December 1945, 'has programmes at intervals on Sunday mornings in which are shown newsreels of everything important that has happened since they were taken prisoner'.)

Recollections of and reflections upon the war persisted in Kathleen's postwar diary. 'Today is the fifth anniversary of the Battle of Britain,' she wrote on 15 September 1945, 'and a fly past of Fighter Command took place.

I did all my jobs near the back door when 12.30 came round as I was listening for planes. We saw some in the distance. Then I saw the formations going towards Woolwich. Then they wheeled and came right overhead (it seemed like that anyway). It was most splendid and moving, and the sight brought back many memories, some of them humorous, but mostly otherwise. I think most people approved of this display and would like something similar to mark the occasion each year. It will be something to remind Londoners and South Englanders of what happened during the war.' Two days later (17 September) she watched a military procession from the City to Trafalgar Square and wondered aloud, 'are people like myself worth all the sacrifices these men have made? And the answer is usually in the negative.' A celebratory highlight for Londoners was 'Victory Weekend' in June 1946. On Saturday, 8 June, Kathleen 'Got up early and left home around 4.30 [a.m.], catching the 4.55 train. I was astonished at the number of people in the train and on the platform, all expecting to be the only folk travelling.' She headed for Northumberland Avenue, where she took up a viewing position at the bottom of the street. Kathleen was an enthusiast for military processions – over the years she had seen quite a few of them – and this 'parade was of course the finest I have ever seen, and as usual I thought the Guards got pride of place for their marching and bearing.... Some of the troops from overseas were remarkably smart, and we were amused because they all seemed so tall. I suppose each country had picked their tallest men. The Americans were unusually smart, but got only a faint cheer.' During a halt in the procession contingents of West African and Maltese troops stopped nearby 'and the crowd fed them with apples, sweets, sandwiches, cake, sausage rolls, etc., as well as supplying them with cigarettes. They had a good time and then were besieged by people asking them to autograph programmes.' Kathleen returned to Woolwich for a 'fete' later in the day, which concluded with gin, other drinks, and conversation. 'Some of the ladies,' she observed, 'whom we are given to understand live a very gay and daring life, show little ability to drink more than one or two drinks. We must have seemed like regular soakers to them I fear.'

With peace, Kathleen had fewer duties to perform and more time for herself. On 30 November 1945 the New Zealand Club, where she had volunteered for so many Monday evenings, closed its doors. The occasion was marked by a farewell social and dance, which Kathleen attended with Eileen and another woman. They ate 'a fine supper, sandwiches, cream cakes, real sausage rolls, pears and cream and thickly iced New Zealand cake', and she and other long service volunteers were presented with 'a powder compact with a fernleaf on the lid, very attractive'. While 'the evening was quite pleasant' (see photograph p. 192), she was aware that she was meeting 'many old friends for the last time'. With more time on her hands, Kathleen signed up for a millinery course and later a cookery class. She continued to serve men at the YMCA canteen for much of 1946 but in September, with the start of a new session of evening millinery and cookery classes, she decided to sever her ties with it. 'I have been there over six years', she wrote, 'and feel we have done our share of work. Anyway custom this week has fallen off we hear. The local camp [on Kidbrooke Park Road] has been taken over by squatters and there are not going to be replacements of troops there in the future, so Mr. W., the manager, expects the canteen to close anyhow. I didn't like leaving before

Kathleeen, front, at the closing of The New Zealand Club in November 1945.

the end, but as it is so close, probably we haven't deserted the ship too soon.' (19 September 1946) (The canteen in fact closed in early November.) Peace, predictably, permitted more time for recreation. Over the Easter holiday that year, which was blessed with splendid weather, the Tippers revived their interest in tennis. 'We are keen again to play, and are inspired to make the effort to try and completely re-kit ourselves. Anyway Philip says I can use his racquet. So we have that, and six new balls – quite a start. I never thought I would play tennis again when we were bombed and our things went [in January 1943], but this nice weather makes me keen.' (19 April 1946)

On 5 July 1945 Kathleen voted in the general election – the first one for a decade. 'I cast my first vote, and felt very good afterwards. Somehow there is something pleasant about the fact that I can help to choose my government.' When the results were announced on July 26th (the votes from soldiers posted around the globe had taken three weeks to count), Kathleen was delighted. 'One of the most astonishing days of my life', she wrote. The news was of Tory losses and Labour gains. 'We have never had a Labour member in our constituency, not even in 1929, and East Lewisham has always been Tory. By this afternoon we realised that the Labour Party was winning hands down, and Joyce telephoned me several times to give me odd snippets of news. Another piece of good news, that Randolph Churchill had been beaten – how catty we are?' At the canteen that evening 'the fellows were pretty jubilant, but our manager Mr. W. was strangely quiet, and kept out of the way most of the evening'. Some people she knew were deeply shocked, others were surprised, including (probably) 'Our boss', who 'took the fact that his entire typing staff voted Labour in good part' (27 July).[1] Six decades later Kathleen recalled how her political consciousness was enlarged when, shortly after the election, her boss, the well-connected George Booth, dictated a letter to the leading Labour minister, Sir Stafford Cripps, in the same familiar style – 'My Dear Stafford …' – that he had employed when addressing Conservative leaders.

Kathleen was interested in public issues and current affairs, some close to home, some far away. She commented on the dropping of the atomic bombs, concentration camp atrocities, war crimes trials, a dock strike, the independence movement in India, and tensions in Egypt. Clearly, Britain's position in the world was changing, and on 19 May 1946 she noted that 'My birthday falls on Friday, on Empire Day, and during the evening we wondered whether there would be any Empire left by then.' While she continued to read the press, references to the radio became rare after May 1945, and on one occasion she highlighted the contrast between wartime and postwar subject matter. 'This evening after the 9 o'clock news some old gentleman talked about wild flower collecting and, intentionally or not, succeeded in sending us all into fits of laughter. What a change from *War Commentary*!' (1 July 1945) Local issues sometimes attracted her attention. Like many London commuters, she occasionally railed against the transportation system. In November 1945 she was particularly miffed by officious bus and tram conductors and conductresses who were limiting the number of standing passengers, thereby exacerbating the all-too-common delays (5 November). She found a way to retaliate. 'I am conducting my own private war against these pocket Hitlers. I always offer a large silver coin for my fare, however short the journey – and are the conductresses mad!! I am passing on this system to my friends, in the hope that they will follow me until we get some civility and consideration from London Transport employees.' (6 November 1945) Later she took a more positive step by (seemingly) joining the London Passenger Association (20 January 1946) and attending its inaugural meeting in Caxton Hall; '[I] was one of about ten people from South-East London much to my disgust'. The

1. Kathleen later altered her political views, and in 2005 wrote that, 'Having voted Churchill out in 1945, we couldn't wait to vote him in charge again as soon as we could. My love affair with the Labour Party was somewhat short-lived.'

evening was, apparently, lively, and Kathleen noted wryly that an announce-ment by London Transport of improved services coincided with holding of the meeting (21 February 1946). A few days later she wrote a letter about 'trans-port difficulties' to 'our local paper' (25 February 1946).[2] Towards the end of that year new buses were being promised to replace the antiquated trams (16 November 1946).

Kathleen's diary ends suddenly on 1 February 1947 – she was ill with pleu-risy, spent time in hospital, and was off work until August. 'Booth's sent me to Switzerland to recuperate (Joyce too),' she recalled in 2004, 'and I shall never forget arriving at the Swiss frontier where we had breakfast in the station restaurant. We couldn't believe our eyes at the feast of butter, rolls, and black cherry jam and real coffee compared with what we were putting up with at home.' Kathleen continued to work for Alfred Booth & Company for another decade, until 1957, when her boss, George Booth, retired. She enjoyed working with this traditional family firm. As a young woman from a modest background, her job with Booth's allowed her to expand her contacts and her sense of the world. Booth's trade was international; its subsidiaries and commercial connections spread across the Empire and to North America. Working for Booth's fostered an outward-looking attitude. From 1957 Kath-leen went on to work for three other companies, Skyways, Lobitos Oil, and Meter Manufacturers Association, in both secretarial and marketing roles, retiring in 1980. Her retirement years have been active and varied. She continued to enjoy the theatre and follow cricket. She has been a member of the Royal Horticultural Society and paid annual visits to the Chelsea Flower Show. She has belonged to the Friends of the Imperial War Museum and Friends of the Gurkhas, volunteered with the Red Cross, and travelled frequently to the European continent (often with Holt's Battlefield Tours: she and Joyce went on nearly 20 of these tours), to visit and tend war graves from both World Wars and to attend significant memorial events.

War defined Kathleen Tipper. It touched her very directly – and persistently – as a young woman. She and her family were almost destroyed by a German bomb in January 1943. Many friends and relatives were injured or killed during the war, and she had almost daily contact with men and women in the services during the first half of the 1940s. Kathleen grew up in Woolwich, a community with a strong consciousness of military facts and traditions. The Arsenal and the Royal Naval College at Greenwich were part of her broader community. Her parents had met through their work in the Arsenal and married at the end of the Great War. Alice, her mother, had worked filling armaments with high explosives, a job that her family believed led to her early death in 1943 from cancer. Bugles from Woolwich Garrison were readily heard in the Tipper home. Kathleen was proud of the military culture of her

2. This letter, which was published in the *Kentish Independent*, Friday, 1 March 1946, p. 6, was prompted by the serious overcrowding on trains, trams, and buses in south-east London. Kathleen commended the London Passenger Association as a lobby group that was likely to be listened to, and advised commuters in her part of London to attend its next meeting: 'if any reader is interested and would care to send me his or her name and address, I will gladly inform them of time, place and date, in order that South-East London may be able to put forth grievances and suggestions for improved public services at that meeting'.

neighbourhood. She 'helped the boys' during the war and remembered them with fondness and respect in her later life. From serving 'millions of beans on toast' during the war, she moved on to be active in organisations that celebrated and encouraged the remembrance of Britain's wartime past, such as the *Lancastria* Association, which preserves the memory of the terrible loss of life from the sinking of the troopship *Lancastria* on 17 June 1940 (her uncle Wilfred, her father's youngest brother, was one of at least 3,500 men who lost their lives in this disaster).

Kathleen and Joyce continued to live in the neighbourhood of their youth, initially on Weigall Road, subsequently on Courtlands Avenue, both SE12, just down the road from where they volunteered during the war at the YMCA canteen. In 2005 there were celebrations to mark the sixtieth anniversary of the war's end, and on 10 July, as part of the official commemorative events, Kathleen and Joyce attended a luncheon at Buckingham Palace along with some 2,000 other invited veterans of both the armed forces and the home front. (Unexpectedly, their gathering also honoured the victims of the terror bombings of the capital's public transport system just three days before.) Kathleen's identity had always been local and military. She continued in 2005 to hold to this focused sense of her life in the London – both her 'village' and the metropolis – whose wartime trials and moods and human relations she recounted so well.

INDEX

This index focuses on events and activities of which Kathleen Tipper had direct experience, or at least had information got directly from personal connections, and on issues on which she or people known to her expressed opinions, fears, and expectations. It ignores some references to news items heard on the radio or read in the press, especially news from battlefronts or other places abroad. We have not indexed the names of private individuals, including family members.

LONDON RECORD SOCIETY

President: The Rt. Hon. the Lord Mayor of London

Chairman: Professor Caroline M. Barron, MA, PhD, FRHistS
Hon. Secretary: Dr Helen Bradley
Hon. Treasurer: Mr Geoff Pick
Hon. General Editors: Dr Vanessa Harding, Dr Stephen O'Connor,
                    Dr Hannes Kleineke

The London Record Society was founded in December 1964 to publish transcripts, abstracts and lists of the primary sources for the history of London, and generally to stimulate interest in archives relating to London. Membership is open to any individual or institution; the annual subscription is £12 (US $22) for individuals and £18 (US $35) for institutions. Prospective members should apply to the Hon. Secretary, Dr Helen Bradley, c/o Institute of Historical Research, Senate House, London WC1E 7HU (email londonrecord.society@ntlworld.com).

The following volumes have already been published:

Most volumes are still in print; apply to the Hon. Secretary, who will forward requests to the distributor. Price to individual members £12 ($22) each, to non-members £20 ($38) each.